from
Jack.

S. Denny.

THE BIGLOW PAPERS, BY JAMES
RUSSELL LOWELL: WITH A
PREFATORY NOTE BY ERNEST
RHYS.

London: Walter Scott, Ltd.,
24 Warwick Lane, Paternoster Row.

CONTENTS.

THE BIGLOW PAPERS (*Second Series*)—

PREFATORY NOTE.

THE author of the *Biglow Papers* was a liberal influence for too long among us, to soon lose his contemporary effect; but death changes many things, and we do well, perhaps, to recount his achievements while we still feel him to be, by his life and writings, one of us. Fifty years hence, and who shall say what the estimate of his contributions to nineteenth century literature will be? Possibly the new criticism then, with the easy aid of the twentieth century, will calmly point out that he was not a great poet, as most American and some English critics would have us now believe; that he was not an essayist of the first rank, the rank of Montaigne and Charles Lamb, as the *Times* told us in its obituary; and that, even as a humorist, in the *Biglow Papers*, he was more American than immortal. All this is conceivable; but we are at any rate safe in maintaining that his total effect, as far as we of to-day are concerned, is remarkable. He was fortunate in his opportunities, and adroit and manly in his use of them, as the *Biglow Papers* alone serve to show. He wrote well and vigorously, spoke eloquently, and worked hard in the cause that poets and men have at heart. He was, with his own weapons, a good soldier in the War of Liberation of Humanity, and of the Slaves. By reason, indeed, of his double relationship to this country and to America, and his double influence as man of letters and man of affairs, he counted to us with an international importance beyond other, and perhaps greater, men of letters, his contemporaries; and we feel so much the poorer because he is gone.

When we have lost a great contemporary, we recall our meetings with him with a new interest. The unveiling, by Mr. Lowell, of the memorial bust of Coleridge in Westminster Abbey, when Robert Browning and other English poets were of the company, and when Lord Coleridge paid a characteristic tribute to his great relative, was the occasion of my first seeing the former American minister. Only a few days before I had returned from a pilgrimage to Nether Stowey and the Quantocks, where Coleridge spent perhaps the happiest days of his youth—the days when his first great poetical ambitions were still potential; and this adventure served to give to the ceremony at Westminster an added impressiveness, and to the words of the eloquent American an added weight, when he spoke of his greater predecessor and the long line of English poets whose names are written in Poets' Corner. Already then it struck those of his hearers who knew him best, that he showed signs of decaying strength: an impression enhanced by the shadow of some late bereavement that lay upon him at the time. Very different was the effect of meeting him a year or two later in his native New England; at Cambridge, close to which lies the old homestead of the Lowells, Elmwood, where he was born, and died; or at Boston, hospitable, admirable Boston, where they discuss Browning's poetry *à pleine voix* in the street cars, and street urchins whistle bits from Wagner on the way from school. At Boston one evening I heard him speak again after a dinner of the evergreen Lotus Club, the club which has associations with Hawthorne and Emerson, Longfellow and

Dr. Oliver Wendell Holmes, and which has a delightful motto,

> " I'd rather live in Bohemia,
> Than in any other land !"

And then, among those Bohemians, the veteran seemed as young as any of the younger rhymesters and prose-writers of America who sat round him. He told us that evening, with much characteristic humour, of the fortunate ill-fortune that happened to his own boyish first book of poems. It had been published, he said, for some little time, and the whole edition still lay, so little was the demand for it, almost untouched on the publisher's shelves, when a lucky fire broke out on the premises, and burnt up every volume. As the stock of books was fully insured, the young author made as much by this covetable disaster as if every copy had been eagerly bought up. "Thus encouraged," added Mr. Lowell, "in that reckless career of poetry, I grew hardened in iniquity, and wrote on more irrepressibly than ever !" The results of that verse-writing we know, and can review, in the five hundred closely-printed pages to which the young rhymester's first book grew at length : a volume which, including, as it does, the *Biglow Papers*, has been more popular in England than that of any other American poet, save Longfellow.

Other occasions of pleasant memory, more informal, served to show how delightful in talk Mr. Lowell could be. London did not fail to discover this, but he was to be found at his best in some of the hospitable, old-fashioned homesteads that surround his favourite Cambridge oversea, whose praises he has recited in one of his liveliest essays, which opens his characteristic but little-known volume of *Fireside Travels.* Such a house was his own Elmwood, one of the typical wooden New England houses, surrounded by park-like English elms and ash trees, and standing close to Mount Auburn Cemetery, where he now lies buried. Such a house, too, is Shady Hill, the residence of Professor Charles Eliot Norton, his old friend and *collaborateur;* which again brings recollections of one winter's after-noon spent in listening to various stories of New England character recounted by the creator of Hosea Biglow. Some one had complained that Americans were fond of declaring Englishmen to be wanting in wit, and cited the average Cockney to the contrary. But this set Mr. Lowell going inimitably for once in the particular vein of Biglow, as he expatiated on the difference between Yankee and Cockney wit. On his lips, the suggested mispronunciations, the idioms, the drawl, of the New England dialect had an unction which you shall hardly find as effective in the written humours of the poet of Jaalam. Indeed, in the *Biglow Papers* English readers are apt to find the wit of misrendering the language a little tedious, when it arrives at such cheap eccentricities as "candid 8's" for "candidates." But, recited in a voice full of telling inflections, as good for purposes of humour as of eloquence, a story told by Mr. Lowell never failed of its effect.

Up to the last, it is said, Mr. Lowell kept that vigour of speech and mental energy which made it hard to realise how long a career lay behind him when he exchanged New, for Old England, for the last time. Born in 1819, he died on August 16th of this year of 1891. The first of the *Biglow Papers* was begun in the forties, almost half a century ago, when Mr. Lowell, who lived to be over seventy, was still a young man under thirty. He was born, I have said, at Elmwood. "His father, and his father's father," says Mr. E.

C. Stedman,[1] "were clergymen, well read, bearing honoured names; his mother, a gifted woman, mistress of various languages, and loving the old English songs and ballads,— no wonder that three of her children came to be authors, and this one, the youngest, a famous citizen and poet. It is not hard to fill in these outlines with something of the circumstance that foreordains the training of genius." In all this early circumstance Lowell was exceptionally favoured, under the influence of local and family traditions, the home-culture, the method of his father, and the taste of the mother, from whom he inherited his bent towards letters and song.

In the essay on "Cambridge Fifty Years Ago," and in some of his other essays, recalling the still remoter past of New England, one may glean many descriptive touches to fill up the outline of Lowell's early history. "Passing through some Massachusetts village, perhaps at a distance from any house, it may be in the midst of a piece of woods where four roads meet, one may sometimes even yet see a small square one-storey building, whose use would not be long doubtful. It is summer, and the flickering shadows of forest-leaves dapple the roof of the little porch, whose door stands wide, and shows, hanging on either hand, rows of straw hats and bonnets, that look as if they had done good service. As you pass the open windows, you hear whole platoons of high-pitched voices discharging words of two or three syllables with wonderful precision and unanimity.

"If you had the good fortune," he continues, "to be born and bred in the Bay State, your mind is thronged with half-sad, half-humorous recollections. The *a-b abs* of little voices long since hushed in the mould, or ringing now in the pulpit, at the bar, or in the Senate-chamber, come back to the ear of

[1] *The Poets of America.*

memory. You remember the high stool on which culprits
used to be elevated with the tall paper fool's cap on their
heads, blushing to the ears; and you think with wonder
how you have seen them since as men climbing the world's
penance-stools of ambition without a blush, and gladly
giving everything for life's caps and bells. And you have
pleasanter memories of going after pond-lilies, of angling for
horn-pouts—that queer bat among the fishes,—of nutting, of
walking over the creaking snow-crust in winter, when the
warm breath of every household was curling up silently in
the keen blue air."

At sixteen he went to Harvard, and his college life there
fills up another, and very formative, period of his history.
Those who have visited the American Cambridge, and felt
its architectural and other difference from its English namesake, will read a great deal into some of his references in
verse or prose to this part of his life there, and understand how its associations haunted him afterwards.

> "There in red brick, which softening time defies,
> Stand stiff and square the Muses' factories."

> .   .   .   .   .   .

> " Yes, dearer far thy dust than all that e'er,
> Beneath the awarded crown of victory,
>   Gilded the blown Olympic charioteer ;
> Though lightly prized the ribboned parchments three,
>   Yet, *collegisse juvat*, I am glad,
>   That here what colleging was mine I had—
> It linked another tie, dear native town, with thee !"

"It seems," says Mr. Stedman, "that the light-hearted
Cambridge student was eager for all books, except those
of the curriculum, and troubled himself little as to
mathematics and other prosaic branches. This was quite
in accordance with precedent, *teste* Landor or Shelley; yet I

doubt not that he was more than once sorry for it in after years." At Harvard, Lowell wrote the class poem, which abounded, as has been pointed out, in satire of the reformers whom the poet was afterwards to join in the *Biglow Papers.* He printed this poem; but as prize and class poems hardly count, we may consider his first book really that published in 1841, when he had left Harvard, and was an incipient lawyer in Boston : the volume whose curious fate has been told. It was entitled *A Year's Life,* and contains several of the pieces now included in his complete poems, with other *juvenilia* not reprinted, making up a thin, pretty volume, now, for the reasons given, one of the scarcest first books of verse published during the century. This led him on to new schemes, one of which bore fruit in an obscure magazine, *The Pioneer,* which he edited with a friend, but which did not live long. A second volume of poems followed in 1844; and the same year saw him married to the "Una" of his first book. "A Legend of Brittany," included in this volume, gave its author more reputation than he had hitherto made by his verse. Edgar Poe praised it as "the noblest poem yet written by an American!" to which we may rejoin now that Poe himself had already written far nobler.

Already, in this volume of 1844, the young poet had begun to show signs in his work of the pressure of actuality and the reform movement, which presently led him to the point where he found his happier inspiration in the *Biglow Papers.* He is described at this time as "a young idealist," whose "broad collar and flowing hair set off a handsome, eager face, with the look of Keats and the resolve of a Brook-Farmer." If he was ever inclined to pose as the typical young poet of a sentimental type, however, he soon found a humoristic deliverance. It was in 1846 that the first of the *Biglow Papers* began to appear in a local weekly paper, the *Boston Courier*, which you may still buy for five cents every Friday in that famous city. Begun so unpretentiously, under cover of journalism, rather than of literature pure and simple, they made an almost immediate effect. The historical events that called forth the first, and much the best, of the two series are now almost forgotten in England; for the invasion of Mexico in the forties, though very potential, had not the effect, naturally enough, of the great Civil War of North and South that inspired the second series of the Papers in the sixties. But Mexico was only the accident which served to fire a long-smouldering mine in young Lowell's imagination; and it is New England, and not any more foreign cause, that was the essential impulse to this highly original writing. Mr. Bret Harte told us recently that, in these strange chronicles in verse and prose from the village of Jaalam, "their author had for the first time discovered the real Yankee — that wonderful evolution of the English Puritan who had shaken off the forms and superstitions, the bigotry and intolerance, of religion, but never the deep consciousness of God, . . . not only an all-wise God, but one singularly perspicacious of wily humanity, and one that you had to get up early to take in!" Elsewhere Mr. Bret Harte refers to a book which was a forerunner in some ways of the *Biglow Papers:* Dr. Judd's *Margaret*, which was "a New England classic when Hosea Biglow was born, . . . a dialect romance, so provincial as to be almost unintelligible to even the average American reader; but while painted with a coarse Flemish fidelity, its melodrama was conventional and imported." That Lowell had been much impressed by the book is evident. In his essay, "A Good Word for Winter," he brings the book and its author fairly into context with Homer, with delightful New Englander's audacity:— "There is admirable snow scenery in Judd's *Margaret,* but some one has confiscated my copy of that admirable book, and perhaps Homer's picture of a snow-storm is the best yet in its large simplicity." By searching the files of old Massachusetts country papers and magazines, you may come upon other hints of what was perfected finally out of the mouth of Hosea Biglow. A New Hampshire bucolic rhymester, Fessenden, had, we are told, too, given Lowell the immediate suggestion of "The Courtin'," in his *Country Lovers,* similar to that, but less perfect in subject and method. Similarly, the queer prose notes, and prefaces, and appendices, by no means the least successful part of the whole work, are clearly inspired, in the first instance, by Carlyle and his Scoto-Teutonic Teufelsdröckh. The Rev. Homer Wilbur is indeed a *Sartor Resartus* of a type not contemplated by Carlyle in his humorous masterpiece; and yet not an unworthy reappearance in this grotesque New England garb. But the creator of the Rev. Homer Wilbur, and his *protégé* at Jaalam, only borrowed so far as all originators may, without detriment to their good fame. Thus, before he was thirty, we find Lowell securely placed among his own countrymen, although he had to wait longer, until the second series of the *Biglow Papers* appeared in the time of the Civil War, for the full international recognition afterwards gained by him.

The last of the first series appeared in 1848; in the same year he published *A Fable for Critics,* which, in its entirely different vein of satire, proved quite as popular. In his serious verse Lowell had always inclined to be imitative, as his earlier volumes prove, in which we find traces in turn of Keats, Shelley, Tennyson, Leigh Hunt, and Hood. In *A Fable for Critics* he imitated Pope— that Pope of whom he said afterwards : "There was a time when I could not read Pope, but disliked him on principle." After one's salad days, however, one revises many old, off-hand prejudices, and before he was thirty Lowell had studied the author of the *Dunciad* to some purpose. *A Fable for Critics* has nothing of the unpleasantness that Lowell complained of in the *Dunciad,* and something less than the art and wit that he fully admired. "This New England Pope," said one critic, "is a very immature Pope." But his *Fable* is the best thing of the kind yet produced by America, and will long be turned to for its witty account of many figures on what has been as wittily called "the Parnassus of the Rev. Mr. Griswold," of immortal ignominy. As an example of the *Fable* at its best, take these references to Emerson, which form one of the most familiar parts of the satire—

"There comes Emerson first, whose rich words, every one,
Are like gold nails in temples to hang trophies on,
Whose prose is grand verse, while his verse, the Lord knows,
Is some of it pr—— No ! 'tis not even prose.

In the worst of his poems are mines of rich matter,
But thrown in a heap with a crush, and a clatter ;
Now it is not one thing nor another alone
Makes a poem, but rather the general tone,
The something pervading, uniting the whole,
The before unconceived, unconceivable soul.

But, to come back to Emerson (whom, by the way,
I believe we left waiting), his is, we may say,
A Greek head on right Yankee shoulders, whose range
Has Olympus for one pole, for t'other the Exchange.

All admire, and yet scarcely six converts he's got,
To I don't (nor they either) exactly know what ;
For though he builds glorious temples, 'tis odd
He leaves never a doorway to get in a god.
'Tis refreshing to old-fashioned people like me
To meet such a primitive Pagan as he,
In whose mind all creation is duly respected,
As parts of himself—just a little projected ;
And who's willing to worship the stars and the sun,
A convert to—nothing but Emerson."

It has been the main purpose of this introductory note
to outline those periods of our author's life, and those
conditions of life and literature in New England, which
went to the making of the *Biglow Papers*, here reprinted.
Before the second series of the *Papers* appeared there
had been many new chapters in Lowell's history. His
professorship at Harvard, his co-editorship of the *Atlantic
Monthly* with Professor C. E. Norton, and various
European adventures, left their mark on the later Lowell
of *My Study Windows ;* but they did not affect the later
Biglow Papers in their revived, readjusted application to
the anti-slavery movement and the fatal war that followed.
With this second series of the Papers, which appeared first
in the *Atlantic Monthly* from 1862 onwards, we may end
our tale for the time being.

On a last reconsideration, we may well find it difficult to
pronounce critically upon this curious book of the *Biglow
Papers*, so unlike some books of admitted perfection that
New England has given us through such writers as
Hawthorne and Emerson. The humour, the originality,
the idiomatic raciness of the book, we must all admit,
without feeling quite convinced, perhaps, with their author's
fellow-countrymen, that they are of the literary stuff of all
time, instead of only their own time. For one thing, their

dialect is, in point of poetry, against them ; no amount of genius could render that quite poetical. Their author was as unfortunate in this as he was fortunate in the great opportunity that the Slavery struggle in America brought him, which floated so many poets of a more local and temporary faculty than his into the high seas of fame for a time. It was a similar stimulus that some earlier English poets, Wordsworth, Coleridge, Shelley, Byron, and others, found in the ferment of the French Revolution ; but with what different result.

If we turn for light from the *Biglow Papers* to Lowell's mature work in poetry of a quite different order, we are similarly unconvinced, I think. Possibly, it is our defect, and not his. However this may be, there is no doubt that such strong and inspiriting writing, as we find in his famous stanzas in honour of Lloyd-Garrison, rank him high, as a man speaking with authority, and not as the scribes, to the men of his own time :—

> ' O Truth ! O Freedom ! how are ye still born,
>   In the rude stable, in the manger nursed !
> What humble hands unbar those gates of morn,
>   Through which the splendours of the New Day burst !
>
> Men of a thousand shifts and wiles, look here !
>   See one straightforward conscience put in pawn
> To win a world ; see the obedient sphere
>   By bravery's simple gravitation drawn.
>
> Shall we not heed the lesson taught of old,
>   And by the Present's lips repeated still,
> In our own single manhood to be bold,
>   Fortressed in conscience and impregnable will ? "

There is the heroic ring in these lines, and others, like them, that Mr. Lowell wrote : the ring of a manly voice that did not fail to make itself eloquently heard on the council of our literary senate. The voice, indeed, of a strong man, a true and masterful contemporary; who beside his literary effect, let us remember, used all his diplomatic influence, while he was American Minister, to aid the federation of the great nations for which he was the first to discover the harmonious common title of the "English-speaking" people of the world; and more than this, to aid that wider federation still, which is of all mankind.

EDITOR.

THE BIGLOW PAPERS.

THE BIGLOW PAPERS.

NOTICES OF AN INDEPENDENT PRESS.

[I HAVE observed, reader (bene- or male-volent, as it may happen),
that it is customary to append to the second editions of books, and to
the second works of authors, short sentences commendatory of the first,
under the title of *Notices of the Press*. These, I have been given to
understand, are procurable at certain established rates, payment being
made either in money or advertising patronage by the publisher,
or by an adequate outlay of servility on the part of the author. Con-
sidering these things with myself, and also that such notices are neither
intended, nor generally believed, to convey any real opinions, being a
purely ceremonial accompaniment of literature, and resembling certifi-
cates to the virtues of various morbiferal panaceas, I conceived that it
would be not only more economical to prepare a sufficient number of
such myself, but also more immediately subservient to the end in view,
to prefix them to this our primary edition rather than await the contin-
gency of a second, when they would seem to be of small utility. To
delay attaching the *bobs* until the second attempt at flying the kite
would indicate but a slender experience in that useful art. Neither
has it escaped my notice, nor failed to afford me matter of reflection,
that, when a circus or a caravan is about to visit Jaalam, the initial step
is to send forward large and highly ornamented bills of performance to
be hung in the bar-room and the post-office. These having been sufficiently gazed at, and beginning to lose their attractiveness except for the
flies, and, truly, the boys also (in whom I find it impossible to repress,
even during school hours, certain oral and telegraphic communications
concerning the expected show), upon some fine morning the band enters

in a gaily-painted waggon, or triumphal chariot, and with noisy advertisement, by means of brass, wood, and sheepskin, makes the circuit of
our startled village streets. Then, as the exciting sounds draw nearer
and nearer, do I desiderate those eyes of Aristarchus, "whose looks were
as a breeching to a boy." Then do I perceive, with vain regret of
wasted opportunities, the advantage of a pancratic or pantechnic education, since he is most reverenced by my little subjects who can throw the
cleanest summerset or walk most securely upon the revolving cask.
The story of the Pied Piper becomes for the first time credible to me
(albeit confirmed by the Hameliners dating their legal instruments from
the period of his exit), as I behold how those strains, without pretence
of magical potency, bewitch the pupillary legs, nor leave to the
pedagogic an entire self-control. For these reasons, lest my kingly
prerogative should suffer diminution, I prorogue my restless commons,
whom I also follow into the street, chiefly lest some mischief may chance
befall them. After the manner of such a band, I send forward the
following notices of domestic manufacture, to make brazen proclamation, not unconscious of the advantage which will accrue, if our little
craft, *cymbula sutilis*, shall seem to leave port with a clipping breeze,
and to carry, in nautical phrase, a bone in her mouth. Nevertheless, I
have chosen, as being more equitable, to prepare some also sufficiently
objurgatory, that readers of every taste may find a dish to their palate.
I have modelled them upon actually existing specimens, preserved in
my own cabinet of natural curiosities. One, in particular, I had copied
with tolerable exactness from a notice of one of my own discourses,
which, from its superior tone and appearance of vast experience, I concluded to have been written by a man at least three hundred years of age,
though I recollected no existing instance of such antediluvian longevity.
Nevertheless, I afterwards discovered the author to be a young gentleman preparing for the ministry under the direction of one of my brethren
in a neighbouring town, and whom I had once instinctively corrected in
a Latin quantity. But this I have been forced to omit, from its too
great length.—H. W.]

From the Universal Littery Universe.

Full of passages which rivet the attention of the reader. . . . Under
a rustic garb, sentiments are conveyed which should be committed to the
memory and engraven on the heart of every moral and social being.

. . . We consider this a *unique* performance. . . . We hope to see it soon introduced into our common schools. . . . Mr. Wilbur has performed his duties as editor with excellent taste and judgment. . . . This is a vein which we hope to see successfully prosecuted. . . . We hail the appearance of this work as a long stride toward the formation of a purely aboriginal, indigenous, native, and American literature. We rejoice to meet with an author national enough to break away from the slavish deference, too common among us, to English grammar and orthography. . . . Where all is so good, we are at a loss how to make extracts. . . . On the whole, we may call it a volume which no library, pretending to entire completeness, should fail to place upon its shelves.

From the Higginbottomopolis Snapping-turtle.

A collection of the merest balderdash and doggerel that it was ever our bad fortune to lay eyes on. The author is a vulgar buffoon, and the editor a talkative, tedious old fool. We use strong language, but should any of our readers peruse the book (from which calamity Heaven preserve them !), they will find reasons for it thick as the leaves of Vallumbrozer, or, to use a still more expressive comparison, as the combined heads of author and editor. The work is wretchedly got up. . . . We should like to know how much *British gold* was pocketed by this libeller of our country and her purest patriots.

From the Oldfogrumville Mentor.

We have not had time to do more than glance through this handsomely printed volume, but the name of its respectable editor, the Rev. Mr. Wilbur, of Jaalam, will afford a sufficient guaranty for the worth of its contents. . . . The paper is white, the type clear, and the volume of a convenient and attractive size. . . . In reading this elegantly-executed work, it has seemed to us that a passage or two might have been retrenched with advantage, and that the general style of diction was susceptible of a higher polish. . . . On the whole, we may safely leave the ungrateful task of criticism to the reader. We will barely suggest, that in volumes intended, as this is, for the illustration of a provincial dialect and turns of expression, a dash of humour or satire might be thrown in with advantage. . . . The work is admirably got up. . . .

This work will form an appropriate ornament to the centre-table. It is beautifully printed, on paper of an excellent quality.

From the Dekay Bulwark.

We should be wanting in our duty as the conductor of that tremendous engine, a public press, as an American, and as a man, did we allow such an opportunity as is presented to us by "The Biglow Papers" to pass by without entering our earnest protest against such attempts (now, alas! too common) at demoralising the public sentiment. Under a wretched mask of stupid drollery, slavery, war, the social glass, and, in short, all the valuable and time-honoured institutions justly dear to our common humanity, and especially to republicans, are made the butt of coarse and senseless ribaldry by this low-minded scribbler. It is time that the respectable and religious portion of our community should be aroused to the alarming inroads of foreign Jacobinism, sansculottism, and infidelity. It is a fearful proof of the wide-spread nature of this contagion, that these secret stabs at religion and virtue are given from under the cloak (*credite, posteri!*) of a clergyman. It is a mournful spectacle indeed to the patriot and Christian to see liberality and new ideas (falsely so called,—they are as old as Eden) invading the sacred precincts of the pulpit. . . . On the whole, we consider this volume as one of the first shocking results which we predicted would spring out of the late French "Revolution" (!).

From the Bungtown Copper and Comprehensive Tocsin (a *tryweakly family journal*).

Altogether an admirable work. . . . Full of humour, boisterous, but delicate,—of wit withering and scorching, yet combined with a pathos cool as morning dew,—of satire ponderous as the mace of Richard, yet keen as the scymitar of Saladin. . . . A work full of "mountain-mirth," mischievous as Puck and lightsome as Ariel. . . . We know not whether to admire most the genial, fresh, and discursive concinnity of the author, or his playful fancy, weird imagination, and compass of style, at once both objective and subjective. . . . We might indulge in some criticisms, but were the author other than he is, he would be a different being. As it is, he has a wonderful *pose*, which flits from flower to flower, and bears the reader irresistibly along on its eagle pinions (like Ganymede) to the "highest heaven of invention." . . . We love a book so purely objective. . . . Many of his pictures of natural scenery have an extraordinary subjective clearness and fidelity. . . . In fine, we consider this as one of the most extraordinary volumes of this or any age. We know of no English author who could have written it. It is a work to which the proud genius of our country, standing with one foot on the Aroostook and the other on the Rio Grande, and holding up the star-spangled banner amid the wreck of matter and the crush of worlds, may point with bewildering scorn of the punier efforts of enslaved Europe. . . . We hope soon to encounter our author among those higher walks of literature in which he is evidently capable of achieving enduring fame. Already we should be inclined to assign him a high position in the bright galaxy of our American bards.

From the Saltriver Pilot and Flag of Freedom.

A volume in bad grammar and worse taste. . . . While the pieces here collected were confined to their appropriate sphere in the corners of obscure newspapers, we considered them wholly beneath contempt, but as the author has chosen to come forward in this public manner he must expect the lash he so richly merits. . . . Contemptible slanders. . . . Vilest Billingsgate. . . . Has raked all the gutters of our language. . . . The most pure, upright, and consistent politicians not safe from his malignant venom. . . . General Cushing comes in for a share of his vile calumnies. . . . The *Reverend* Homer Wilbur is a disgrace to his cloth. . . .

From the World-Harmonic-Æolian-Attachment.

Speech is silver ; silence is golden. No utterance more Orphic than this. While, therefore, as highest author, we reverence him whose works continue heroically unwritten, we have also our hopeful word for those who with pen (from wing of goose loud-cackling, or seraph God-commissioned) record the thing that is revealed. . . . Under mask of quaintest irony, we detect here the deep, storm-tost (nigh shipwracked) soul, thunder-scarred, semi-articulate, but ever climbing hopefully toward the peaceful summits of an Infinite Sorrow. . . . Yes, thou poor, forlorn

Hosea, with Hebrew fire-flaming soul in thee, for thee also this life of ours has not been without its aspects of heavenliest pity and laughingest mirth. Conceivable enough! Through coarse Thersites-cloak, we have revelation of the heart, wild-glowing, world-clasping, that is in him. Bravely he grapples with the life-problem as it presents itself to him, uncombed, shaggy, careless of the "nicer proprieties," inexpert of "elegant diction," yet with voice audible enough to whoso hath ears, up there on the gravelly side-hills, or down on the splashy, Indiarubber-like salt-marshes of native Jaalam. To this soul also the *Necessity of Creating* somewhat has unveiled its awful front. If not Œdipuses and Electras and Alcestises, then in God's name Birdofredum Sawins! These also shall get born into the world, and filch (if so need) a Zingali subsistence therein, these lank, omnivorous Yankees of his. He shall paint the Seen, since the Unseen will not sit to him. Yet in him also are Nibelungen-lays, and Iliads, and Ulysses-wanderings, and Divine Comedies,—if only once he could come at them! Therein lies much, nay all; for what truly is this which we name *All*, but that which we do *not* possess? . . . Glimpses also are given us of an old father Ezekiel, not without paternal pride, as is the wont of such. A brown, parchment-hided old man of the geoponic or bucolic species, grey-eyed, we fancy, *queued* perhaps, with much weather-cunning and plentiful September-gale memories, bidding fair in good time to become the Oldest Inhabitant. After such hasty apparition, he vanishes and is seen no more. . . . Of " Rev. Homer Wilbur, A.M., Pastor of the First Church in Jaalam," we have small care to speak here. Spare touch in him of his Mele-sigenes namesake, save, haply, the—blindness! A tolerably caliginose, nephelegeretous elderly gentleman, with infinite faculty of sermonising, muscularised by long practice, and excellent digestive apparatus, and, for the rest, well-meaning enough, and with small private illuminations (somewhat tallowy, it is to be feared) of his own. To him, there, " Pastor of the First Church in Jaalam," our Hosea presents himself as a quite inexplicable Sphinx-riddle. A rich poverty of Latin and Greek,—so far is clear enough, even to eyes peering myopic through horn-lensed editorial spectacles,—but naught farther? O purblind, well-meaning, altogether fuscous Melesigenes-Wilbur, there are things in him incommunicable by stroke of birch! Did it ever enter that old bewildered head of thine that there was the *Possibility of the Infinite* in him? To thee, quite wingless (and even featherless) biped, has not so much even as a dream of wings ever come? " Talented young parishioner?" Among the Arts whereof thou art *Magister*, does that of *seeing* happen to be one? Unhappy *Artium Magister!* Somehow a Nemean lion, fulvous, torrid-eyed, dry-nursed in broad-howling sand-wildernesses of a sufficiently rare spirit-Libya (it may be supposed) has got whelped among the sheep. Already he stands wild-glaring, with feet clutching the ground as with oak-roots, gathering for a Remus-spring over the walls of thy little fold. In Heaven's name, go not near him with that flybite crook of thine! In good time, thou painful preacher, thou wilt go to the appointed place of departed Artillery-Election Sermons, Right-Hands of Fellowship, and Results of Councils, gathered to thy spiritual fathers with much Latin of the Epitaphial sort; thou, too, shalt have thy reward; but on him the Eumenides have looked, not Xantippes of the pit, snake-tressed, finger-threatening, but radiantly calm as on antique gems; for him paws impatient the winged courser of the gods, champing unwelcome bit; him the starry deeps, the empyrean glooms, and far-flashing splendours await.

From the Onion Grove Phœnix.

A talented young townsman of ours, recently returned from a Continental tour, and who is already favourably known to our readers by his sprightly letters from abroad which have graced our columns, called at our office yesterday. We learn from him, that, having enjoyed the distinguished privilege, while in Germany, of an introduction to the celebrated Von Humbug, he took the opportunity to present that eminent man with a copy of the *Biglow Papers.* The next morning he received the following note, which he has kindly furnished us for publication. We prefer to print it *verbatim*, knowing that our readers will readily forgive the few errors into which the illustrious writer has fallen, through ignorance of our language.

"HIGH-WORTHY MISTER!

"I shall also now especially happy starve, because I have more or less a work of one those aboriginal Red-Men seen in which have I so deaf an interest ever taken fullworthy on the self shelf with our Gottsched to be upset.

"Pardon my in the English-speech unpractice!

"VON HUMBUG."

He also sent with the above note a copy of his famous work on *Cosmetics*, to be presented to Mr. Biglow; but this was taken from our friend by the English custom-house officers, probably through a petty national spite. No doubt it has by this time found its way into the British Museum. We trust this outrage will be exposed in all our American papers. We shall do our best to bring it to the notice of the State Department. Our numerous readers will share in the pleasure we experience at seeing our young and vigorous national literature thus encouragingly patted on the head by this venerable and world-renowned German. We love to see these reciprocations of good-feeling between the different branches of the great Anglo-Saxon race.

[The following genuine "notice" having met my eye, I gladly insert a portion of it here, the more especially as it contains one of Mr. Biglow's poems not elsewhere printed.—H. W.]

———

From the Jaalam Independent Blunderbuss.

. . . But while we lament to see our young townsman thus mingling in the heated contests of party politics, we think we detect in him the presence of talents which, if properly directed, might give an innocent pleasure to many. As a proof that he is competent to the production of other kinds of poetry, we copy for our readers a short fragment of a pastoral by him, the manuscript of which was loaned us by a friend. The title of it is "The Courtin'."

> ZEKLE crep' up, quite unbeknown,
>   An' peeked in thru the winder,
> An' there sot Huldy all alone,
>   'ith no one nigh to hender.
>
> Agin' the chimbly crooknecks hung,
>   An' in amongst 'em rusted
> The ole Queen's arm thet gran'ther Young
>   Fetched back frum Concord busted.
>
> The wannut logs shot sparkles out
>   Towards the pootiest, bless her!
> An' leetle fires danced all about
>   The chiny on the dresser.
>
> The very room, coz she wus in,
>   Looked warm frum floor to ceilin',
> An' she looked full ez rosy agin
>   Ez th' apples she wuz peelin'.

She heerd a foot an' knowed it, tu,
    Araspin' on the scraper,—
All ways to once her feelins flew
    Like sparks in burnt-up paper.

He kin' o' l'itered on the mat,
    Some doubtfle o' the seekle;
His heart kep' goin' pitypat,
    But hern went pity Zekle.

An' yet she gin her cheer a jerk
    Ez though she wished him furder,
An' on her apples kep' to work
    Ez ef a wager spurred her.

"You want to see my Pa, I spose?"
    "Wall, no; I come designin'——"
"To see my Ma? She's sprinklin' clo'es
    Agin to-morrow's i'nin'."

He stood a spell on one foot fust,
    Then stood a spell on tother,
An' on which one he felt the wust
    He couldn't ha' told ye, nuther.

Sez he, "I'd better call agin;"
    Sez she, "Think likely, *Mister;*"
The last word pricked him like a pin,
    An'—wal, he up and kist her.

When Ma bimeby upon 'em slips,
    Huldy sot pale ez ashes,
All kind o' smily round the lips
    An' teary round the lashes.

Her blood riz quick, though, like the tide
    Down to the Bay o' Fundy,
An' all I know is they wuz cried
    In meetin', come nex Sunday.

SATIS multis sese emptores futuros libri professis, Georgius Nichols, Cantabrigiensis, opus emittet de parte gravi sed adhuc neglecta historiæ naturalis cum titulo sequenti, videlicet :

Conatus ad Delineationem naturalem nonnihil perfectiorem Scarabæi Bombilatoris, vulgo dicti HUMBUG, ab HOMERO WILBUR, Artium

Magistro, Societatis historico-naturalis Jaalamensis Præside (Secretario, Socioque (eheu !) singulo), multarumque aliarúm Societatum eruditarum (sive ineruditarum) tam domesticarum quam transmarinarum Socio— forsitan futuro.

PROEMIUM.

LECTORI BENEVOLO S.

Toga scholastica nondum deposita, quum systemata varia entomologica, a viris ejus scientiæ cultoribus studiosissimis summa diligentia ædificata, penitus indagâssem, non fuit quin luctuose omnibus in iis, quamvis aliter laude dignissimis, hiatum magni momenti perciperem. Tunc, nescio quo motu superiore impulsus, aut qua captus dulcedine operis, ad eum implendum (Curtius alter) me solemniter devovi. Nec ab isto labore, δαιμονίως imposito, abstinui antequam tractatulum sufficienter inconcinnum lingua vernacula perfeceram. Inde, juveniliter tumefactus, et barathro ineptiæ τῶν βιβλιοπωλῶν (necnon "Publici Legentis") nusquam explorato, me composuisse quod quasi placentas præfervidas (ut sic dicam) homines ingurgitarent credidi. Sed, quum huic et alio bibliopolæ MSS. mea submisissem et nihil solidius responsione valde negativa in Musæum meum retulissem, horror ingens atque misericordia, ob crassitudinem Lambertianam in cerebris homunculorum istius muneris cœlesti quadam ira infixam, me invasere. Extemplo mei solius impensis librum edere decrevi, nihil omnino dubitans quin "Mundus Scientificus" (ut aiunt) crumenam meam ampliter repleret. Nullam, attamen, ex agro illo meo parvulo segetem demessui, præter gaudium vacuum bene de Republica merendi. Iste panis meus pretiosus super aquas literarias fæculentas præfidenter jactus, quasi Harpyiarum quarundam (scilicet bibliopolarum istorum facinorosorum supradictorum) tactu rancidus, intra perpaucòs dies mihi domum rediit. Et, quum ipse tali victu ali non tolerarem, primum in mentem venit pistori (typographo nempe) nihilominus solvendum esse. Animum non idcirco demisi, imo æque ac pueri naviculas suas penes se lino retinent (eo ut e recto cursu delapsas ad ripam retrahant), sic ego Argô meam chartaceam fluctibus laborantem a quæsitu velleris aurei, ipse potius tonsus pelleque exutus, mente solida revocavi. Metaphoram ut mutem, *boomarangam* meam a scopo aberrantem retraxi, dum majore vi, occasione ministrante, adversus Fortunam intorquerem. Ast mihi, talia volventi, et, sicut Saturnus ille παιδοβόρος, liberos intellectus mei depascere fidenti, casus miserandus, nec antea inauditus, supervenit. Nam, ut ferunt Scythas pietatis causa et parsimoniæ, parentes suos mortuos devorâsse, sic filius hic meus primogenitus, Scythis ipsis minus mansuetus, patrem vivum totum et calcitrantem exsorbere enixus est. Nec tamen hac de causa sobolem meam esurientem exheredavi. Sed famem istam pro valido testimonio virilitatis roborisque potius habui, cibumque ad eam satiandam, salva paterna mea carne, petii. Et quia bilem illam scaturientem ad æs etiam concoquendum idoneam esse estimabam, unde æs alienum, ut minoris pretii, haberem circumspexi. Rebus ita se habentibus, ab avunculo meo Johanne Doolittle, Armigero, impetravi ut pecunias necessarias suppeditaret, ne opus esset mihi universitatem relinquendi antequam ad gradum primum in artibus pervenissem. Tunc ego, salvum facere patronum meum munificum maxime cupiens, omnes libros primæ editionis operis mei non venditos una cum privilegio in omne ævum ejusdem imprimendi et edendi avunculo meo dicto pigneravi. Ex illo die, atro lapide notando, curæ vociferantes familiæ singulis annis crescentis eo usque insultabant ut nunquam tam carum pignus e vinculis istis aheneis solvere possem.

Avunculo vero nuper mortuo, quum inter alios consanguineos testamenti ejus lectionem audiendi causa advenissem, erectis auribus verba talia sequentia accepi :—" Quoniam persuasum habeo meum dilectum nepotem Homerum, longa et intima rerum angustarum domi experientia, aptissimum esse qui divitias tueatur, beneficenterque ac prudenter iis divinis creditis utatur,—ergo, motus hisce cogitationibus, exque amore meo in illum magno, do legoque nepoti caro meo supranominato omnes singularesque istas possessiones nec ponderabiles nec computabiles meas quæ sequuntur, scilicet : quingentos libros quos mihi pigneravit dictus Homerus, anno lucis 1792, cum privilegio edendi et repetendi opus istud ' scientificum ' (quod dicunt) suum, si sic elegerit. Tamen D. O. M. precor oculos Homeri nepotis mei ita aperiat eumque moveat, ut libros istos in bibliotheca unius e plurimis castellis suis Hispaniensibus tuto abscondat."

His verbis (vix credibilibus) auditis, cor meum in pectore exsultavit. Deinde, quoniam tractatus Anglice scriptus spem auctoris fefellerat, quippe quum studium Historiæ Naturalis in Republica nostra inter factionis strepitum languescat, Latine versum edere statui, et eo potius quia nescio quomodo disciplina academica et duo diplomata proficiant, nisi quod peritos linguarum omnino mortuarum (et damnandarum, ut dicebat iste πανοῦργος Gulielmus Cobbett) nos faciant.

Et mihi adhuc superstes est tota illa editio prima, quam quasi crepitaculum per quod dentes canines, entibam retineo.

OPERIS SPECIMEN.

(Ad exemplum Johannis Physiophili speciminis Monachologiæ.)

12. S. B. *Militaris*, WILBUR. *Carnifex*, JABLONSK. *Profanus*, DESFONT.

[Male hancce speciem *Cyclopem* Fabricius vocat, ut qui singulo oculo ad quod sui interest distinguitur. Melius vero Isaacus Outis nullum inter S. milit. S.que Belzebul (Fabric. 152) discrimen esse defendit.]

Habitat civitat. Americ. austral.

Aureis lineis splendidus ; plerumque tamen sordidus, utpote lanienas valde frequentans, fœtore sanguinis allectus. Amat quoque insuper septa apricari, neque inde, nisi maxima conatione, detruditur. *Candidatus* ergo populariter vocatus. Caput cristam quasi pennarum ostendit. Pro cibo vaccam publicam callide mulget ; abdomen enorme ; facultas suctus haud facile estimanda. Otiosus, fatuus ; ferox nihilominus, semperque dimicare paratus. Tortuose repit.

Capite sæpe maxima cum cura dissecto, ne illud rudimentum etiam cerebri commune omnibus prope insectis detegere poteram.

Unam de hoc S. milit. rem singularem notavi ; nam S. Guineens. (Fabric. 143) servos facit, et idcirco a multis summa in reverentia habitus, quasi scintillas rationis pæne humanæ demonstrans.

24. S. B. *Criticus*, WILBUR. *Zolius*, FABRIC. *Pygmæus*, CARLSEN.

[Stultissime Johannes Stryx cum S. punctato (Fabric. 64–109) confundit. Specimina quamplurima scrutationi microscopicæ subjeci, nunquam tamen unum ulla indicia puncti cujusvis prorsus ostendentem inveni.]

Præcipue formidolosus, insectatusque, in proxima rima anonyma sese abscondit, *we, we*, creberrime stridens. Ineptus, segnipes.

Habitat ubique gentium ; in sicco ; nidum suum terebratione indefessa ædificans. Cibus : Libros depascit ; siccos præcipue seligens, et forte succidum.

MELIBŒUS-HIPPONAX.

THE

BIGLOW PAPERS,

EDITED,

WITH AN INTRODUCTION, NOTES, GLOSSARY,
AND COPIOUS INDEX,

BY

HOMER WILBUR, A.M.,

PASTOR OF THE FIRST CHURCH IN JAALAM AND (PROSPECTIVE)
MEMBER OF MANY LITERARY, LEARNED, AND
SCIENTIFIC SOCIETIES.

(*For which see page* 19.)

"The ploughman's whistle, or the trivial flute,
Finds more respect than great Apollo's lute."
Quarles's Emblems, B. ii. E. 8.

"Margaritas, munde vorcine, calcâsti: en, siliquas accipe."
Jac. Car. Fil. ad Pub. Leg. § 1.

NOTE TO TITLE-PAGE.

IT will not have escaped the attentive eye that I have, on the title-page, omitted those honorary appendages to the editorial name which not only add greatly to the value of every book, but whet and exacerbate the appetite of the reader. For not only does he surmise that an honorary membership of literary and scientific societies implies a certain amount of necessary distinction on the part of the recipient of such decorations, but he is willing to trust himself more entirely to an author who writes under the fearful responsibility of involving the reputation of such bodies as the *S. Archæol. Dahom.*, or the *Acad. Lit. et Scient. Kamtschat.* I cannot but think that the early editions of Shakespeare and Milton would have met with more rapid and general acceptance, but for the barrenness of their respective title-pages; and I believe that, even now, a publisher of the works of either of those justly distinguished men would find his account in procuring their admission to the membership of learned bodies on the Continent,—a proceeding no whit more incongruous than the reversal of the judgment against Socrates, when he was already more than twenty centuries beyond the reach of antidotes, and when his memory had acquired a deserved respectability. I conceive that it was a feeling of the importance of this precaution which induced Mr. Locke to style himself "Gent." on the title-page of his Essay, as who should say to his readers that they could receive his metaphysics on the honour of a gentleman.

Nevertheless, finding that, without descending to a smaller size of type than would have been compatible with the dignity of the several societies to be named, I could not compress my intended list within the limits of a single page, and thinking, moreover, that the act would carry with it an air of decorous modesty, I have chosen to take the reader aside, as it were, into my private closet, and there not only exhibit to him the diplomas which I already possess, but also to furnish him with a prophetic vision of those which I may, without undue

2

presumption, hope for, as not beyond the reach of human ambition and attainment.   And I am the rather induced to this from the fact, that my name has been unaccountably dropped from the last triennial catalogue of our beloved *Alma Mater.*   Whether this is to be attributed to the difficulty of Latinising any of those honorary adjuncts (with a complete list of which I took care to furnish the proper persons nearly a year beforehand), or whether it had its origin in any more culpable motives, I forbear to consider in this place, the matter being in course of painful investigation.   But, however this may be, I felt the omission the more keenly, as I had, in expectation of the new catalogue, enriched the library of the Jaalam Athenæum with the old one then in my possession, by which means it has come about that my children will be deprived of a never wearying winter evening's amusement in looking out the name of their parent in that distinguished roll.   Those harmless innocents had at least committed no—— but I forbear, having intrusted my reflections and animadversions on this painful topic to the safe keeping of my private diary, intended for posthumous publication.   I state this fact here, in order that certain nameless individuals, who are, perhaps, overmuch congratulating themselves upon my silence, may know that a rod is in pickle which the vigorous hand of a justly-incensed posterity will apply to their memories.

The careful reader will note that, in the list which I have prepared, I have included the names of several Cisatlantic societies to which a place is not commonly assigned in processions of this nature.   I have ventured to do this, not only to encourage native ambition and genius, but also because I have never been able to perceive in what way distance (unless we suppose them at the end of a lever) could increase the weight of learned bodies.   As far as I have been able to extend my researches among such stuffed specimens as occasionally reach America, I have discovered no generic difference between the antipodal *Fogrum Japonicum* and the *F. Americanum* sufficiently common in our own immediate neighbourhood.   Yet, with a becoming deference to the popular belief that distinctions of this sort are enhanced in value by every additional mile they travel, I have intermixed the names of some tolerably distant literary and other associations with the rest.

I add here, also, an advertisement, which, that it may be the more readily understood by those persons especially interested therein, I have written in that curtailed and otherwise maltreated canine Latin, to the writing and reading of which they are accustomed.

OMNIB. PER TOT. ORB. TERRAR. CATALOG. ACADEM. EDD.

Minim. gent. diplom. ab inclytiss. acad. vest. orans, vir. honorand. operosiss., at sol. ut sciat. quant. glor. nom. meum (dipl. fort. concess.) catal. vest. temp. futur. affer., ill. subjec., addit. omnib. titul. honorar. qu. adh. non tant. opt. quam probab. put.

*_** Litt. Uncial. distinx. ut Præs. S. Hist. Nat. Jaal.

HOMERUS WILBUR, Mr., Episc. Jaalam, S. T. D. 1850, et Yal. 1849, et Neo-Cæs. et Brun. et Gulielm. 1852, et Gul. et Mar. et Bowd. et Georgiop. et Viridimont. et Columb. Nov. Ebor. 1853, et Amherst. et Watervill. et S. Jarlath. Hib. et S. Mar. et S. Joseph. et S. And. Scot. 1854, et Nashvill. et Dart. et Dickins. et Concord. et Wash. et Columbian. et Charlest. et Jeff. et Dubl. et Oxon. et Cantab. et cæt. 1855, P.U.N.C.H. et J.U.D. Gott. et Osnab. et Heidelb. 1860, et Acad. BORE US. Berolin. Soc., et SS. RR. Lugd. Bat. et Patav. et Lond. et Edinb. et Ins. Feejee. et Null. Terr. et Pekin. Soc. Hon. et S. H. S. et S. P. A. et A. A. S. et S. Humb. Univ. et S. Omn. Rer. Quarund. q. Aliar. Promov. Passamaquod. et H. P. C. et I. O. H. et A. Δ. Φ. et II. K. P. et Φ. B. K. et Peucin. et Erosoph. et Philadelph. et Frat. in Unit. et Σ. T. et S. Archæolog. Athen. et Acad. Scient. et Lit. Panorm. et SS. R. H. Matrit. et Beeloochist. et Caffrar. et Caribb. et M. S. Reg. Paris. et S. Am. Antiserv. Soc. Hon. et P. D. Gott. et LL. D. 1852, et D. C. L. et Mus. Doc. Oxon. 1860, et M. M. S. S. et M. D. 1854, et Med. Fac. Univ. Harv. Soc. et S. pro Convers. Pollywog. Soc. Hon. et Higgl. Piggl. et LL. B. 1853, et S. pro Christianiz. Moschet. Soc., et SS. Ante-Diluv. ubiq. Gent. Soc. Hon. et Civit. Cleric. Jaalam. et S. pro Diffus General. Tenebr. Secret. Corr.

INTRODUCTION.

When, more than three years ago, my talented young parishioner, Mr. Biglow, came to me and submitted to my animadversions the first of his poems which he intended to commit to the more hazardous trial of a city newspaper, it never so much as entered my imagination to conceive that his productions would ever be gathered into a fair volume, and ushered into the august presence of the reading public by myself. So little are we short-sighted mortals able to predict the event! I confess that there is to me a quite new satisfaction in being associated (though only as sleeping partner) in a book which can stand by itself in an independent unity on the shelves of libraries. For there is always this drawback from the pleasure of printing a sermon, that, whereas the queasy stomach of this generation will not bear a discourse long enough to make a separate volume, those religious and godly-minded children (those Samuels, if I may call them so) of the brain must at first lie buried in an undistinguished heap, and then get such resurrection as is vouchsafed to them, mummy-wrapt with a score of others in a cheap binding, with no other mark of distinction than the word "*Miscellaneous*" printed upon the back. Far be it from me to claim any credit for the quite unexpected popularity which I am pleased to find these bucolic strains have attained unto. If I know myself, I am measurably free from the itch of vanity; yet I may be allowed to say that I was not backward to recognise in them a certain wild, puckery, acidulous (sometimes even verging toward that point which, in our rustic phrase, is termed *shut-eye*) flavour, not wholly unpleasing, nor un-wholesome, to palates cloyed with the sugariness of tamed and cultivated fruit. It may be, also, that some touches of my own, here and there, may have led to their wider acceptance, albeit solely from my larger experience of literature and authorship.[1]

I was, at first, inclined to discourage Mr. Biglow's attempts, as knowing that the desire to poetise is one of the diseases naturally incident to adolescence, which, if the fitting remedies be not at once and with a bold hand applied, may become chronic, and render one, who might else have become in due time an ornament of the social circle, a painful object even to nearest friends and relatives. But thinking, on a further experience, that there was a germ of promise in him which required only culture and the pulling up of weeds from around it, I thought it best to set before him the acknowledged examples of English com-positions in verse, and leave the rest to natural emulation. With this view, I accordingly lent him some volumes of Pope and Goldsmith, to the assiduous study of which he promised to devote his evenings. Not long afterward, he brought me some verses written upon that model, a speci-men of which I subjoin, having changed some phrases of less elegancy, and a few rhymes objectionable to the cul-tivated ear. The poem consisted of childish reminiscences, and the sketches which follow will not seem destitute of

---

[1] The reader curious in such matters may refer (if he can find them) to "A Sermon preached on the Anniversary of the Dark Day," "An Artillery Election Sermon," "A Discourse on the Late Eclipse," "Dorcas, a Funeral Sermon on the Death of Madam Submit Tidd, Relict of the late Experience Tidd, Esq.," etc., etc.

truth to those whose fortunate education began in a country village. And, first, let us hang up his charcoal portrait of the school-dame.

" Propt on the marsh, a dwelling now, I see
　The humble school-house of my A, B, C,
　Where well-drilled urchins, each behind his tire,
　Waited in ranks the wished command to fire,
　Then all together, when the signal came,
　Discharged their *a-b abs* against the dame.
　Daughter of Danaus, who could daily pour
　In treacherous pipkins her Pierian store,
　She, 'mid the volleyed learning firm and calm,
　Patted the furloughed ferule on her palm,
　And, to our wonder, could divine at once
　Who flashed the pan, and who was downright dunce.

　There young Devotion learned to climb with ease
　The gnarly limbs of Scripture family-trees,
　And he was most commended and admired
　Who soonest to the topmost twig perspired ;
　Each name was called as many various ways
　As pleased the reader's ear on different days,
　So that the weather, or the ferule's stings,
　Colds in the head, or fifty other things,
　Transformed the helpless Hebrew thrice a week
　To guttural Pequot or resounding Greek,
　The vibrant accent skipping here and there,
　Just as it pleased invention or despair ;
　No controversial Hebraist was the Dame ;
　With or without the points pleased her the same ;
　If any tyro found a name too tough,
　And looked at her, pride furnished skill enough ;
　She nerved her larynx for the desperate thing,
　And cleared the five-barred syllables at a spring.

　Ah, dear old times ! there once it was my hap,
　Perched on a stool, to wear the long-eared cap ;
　From books degraded, there I sat at ease,
　A drone, the envy of compulsory bees ;

Rewards of merit, too, full many a time,
Each with its woodcut and its moral rhyme,
And pierced half-dollars hung on ribbons gay
About my neck—to be restored next day,
I carried home, rewards as shining then
As those which deck the lifelong pains of men,
More solid than the redemanded praise
With which the world beribbons later days.
Ah, dear old times ! how brightly ye return !
How, rubbed afresh, your phosphor traces burn !
The ramble schoolward through dew-sparkling meads ;
The willow-wands turned Cinderella steeds ;
The impromptu pinbent hook, the deep remorse
O'er the chance captured minnow's inchlong corse ;
The pockets, plethoric with marbles round,
That still a space for ball and pegtop found,
Nor satiate yet could manage to confine
Horse-chestnuts, flagroot, and the kite's wound twine,
And, like the prophet's carpet could take in,
Enlarging still, the popgun's magazine ;
The dinner carried in the small tin pail,
Shared with the dog, whose most beseeching tail
And dripping tongue and eager ears belied
The assumed indifference of canine pride ;
The caper homeward, shortened if the cart
Of neighbour Pomeroy, trundling from the mart,
O'ertook me,—then, translated to the seat,
I praised the steed, how staunch he was and fleet,
While the bluff farmer, with superior grin,
Explained where horses should be thick, where thin,
And warned me (joke he always had in store)
To shun a beast that four white stockings wore.
What a fine natural courtesy was his !
His nod was pleasure, and his full bow bliss ;
How did his well-thumbed hat, with ardour rapt,
Its decorous curve to every rank adapt !
How did it graduate with a courtly ease
The whole long scale of social differences,
Yet so gave each his measure running o'er,
None thought his own was less, his neighbour's more ;

The squire was flattered, and the pauper knew
Old times acknowledged 'neath the threadbare blue !
Dropped at the corner of the embowered lane,
Whistling I wade the knee-deep leaves again,
While eager Argus, who has missed all day
The sharer of his condescending play,
Comes leaping onward with a bark elate
And boisterous tail to greet me at the gate ;
That I was true in absence to our love
Let the thick dog's-ears in my primer prove."

I add only one further extract, which will possess a melancholy interest to all such as have endeavoured to glean the materials of revolutionary history from the lips of aged persons, who took a part in the actual making of it, and, finding the manufacture profitable, continued the supply in an adequate proportion to the demand.

" Old Joe is gone, who saw hot Percy goad
His slow artillery up the Concord road,
A tale which grew in wonder, year by year,
As, every time he told it, Joe drew near
To the main fight, till, faded and grown grey,
The original scene to bolder tints gave way ;
Then Joe had heard the foe's scared double-quick
Beat on stove drum with one uncaptured stick,
And, ere Death came the lengthening tale to lop,
Himself had fired, and seen a red-coat drop ;
Had Joe lived long enough, that scrambling fight
Had squared more nearly with his sense of right,
And vanquish'd Percy, to complete the tale,
Had hammer'd stone for life in Concord gaol."

I do not know that the foregoing extracts ought not to be called my own rather than Mr. Biglow's, as, indeed, he maintained stoutly that my file had left nothing of his in them. I should not, perhaps, have felt entitled to take so great liberties with them, had I not more than suspected an hereditary vein of poetry in myself, a very near ancestor having written a Latin poem in the Harvard *Gratulatio* on the accession of George the Third. Suffice it to say, that, whether not satisfied with such limited approbation as I could conscientiously bestow, or from a sense of natural inaptitude, certain it is that my young friend could never be induced to any further essays in this kind. He affirmed that it was to him like writing in a foreign tongue,—that Mr. Pope's versification was like the regular ticking of one of Willard's clocks, in which one could fancy, after long listening, a certain kind of rhythm or tune, but which yet was only a poverty-stricken *tick, tick,* after all,—and that he had never seen a sweet-water on a trellis growing so fairly, or in forms so pleasing to his eye, as a fox-grape over a scrub-oak in a swamp. He added I know not what, to the effect that the sweet-water would only be the more disfigured by having its leaves starched and ironed out, and that Pegāsus (so he called him) hardly looked right with his mane and tail in curl-papers. These and other such opinions I did not long strive to eradicate, attributing them rather to a defective education and senses untuned by too long familiarity with purely natural objects, than to a perverted moral sense. I was the more inclined to this leniency since sufficient evidence was not to seek, that his verses, as wanting as they certainly were in classic polish and point, had somehow taken hold of the public ear in a surprising manner. So, only setting him right as to the quantity of the proper name Pegasus, I left him to follow the bent of his natural genius.

Yet could I not surrender him wholly to the tutelage of the pagan (which, literally interpreted, signifies village) muse without yet a further effort for his conversion, and to this end I resolved that whatever of poetic fire yet burned in myself, aided by the assiduous bellows of correct models, should be put in requisition. Accordingly, when my ingenious young parishioner brought to my study a copy of verses which he had written touching the acquisition of territory resulting from the Mexican war, and the folly of leaving the question of slavery or freedom to the adjudication of chance, I did myself indite a short fable or apologue after the manner of Gay and Prior, to the end that he might see how easily even such subjects as he treated of were capable of a more refined style and more elegant expression. Mr. Biglow's production was as follows :—

THE TWO GUNNERS.

A FABLE.

Two fellers, Isrel named and Joe,
One Sundy mornin' 'greed to go
Agunnin' soon's the bells wuz done
And meetin' finally begun,
So'st no one wouldn't be about
Ther Sabbath-breakin' to spy out.

Joe didn't want to go a mite;
He felt ez though 'twarnt skeercely right,
But, when his doubts he went to speak on,
Isrel he up and called him Deacon,
An' kep' apokin' fun like sin,
An' then arubbin' on it in,
Till Joe, less skeered o' doin' wrong
Than bein' laughed at, went along.

Past noontime they went trampin' round
An' nary thing to pop at found,
Till, fairly tired o' their spree,
They leaned their guns agin a tree,
An' jest ez they wuz settin' down
To take their noonin', Joe looked roun'

And see (across lots in a pond
That warn't more'n twenty rod beyond)
A goose that on the water sot
Ez ef awaitin' to be shot.

Isrel he ups and grabs his gun;
Sez he, "By ginger, here's some fun!"
"Don't fire," sez Joe, "it aint no use,
That's Deacon Peleg's tame wild-goose;"
Sez Isrel, "I don't care a cent,
I've sighted an' I'll let her went;"
Bang! went queen's-arm, ole gander flopped
His wings a spell, an' quorked, an' dropped.

Sez Joe, "I wouldn't ha' been hired
At that poor critter to ha' fired,
But, sence it's clean gin up the ghost,
We'll hev the tallest kind o' roast;
I guess our waistbands 'll be tight
'Fore it comes ten o'clock ternight."

"I won't agree to no such bender,"
Sez Isrel; "keep it till it's tender;
'Taint wuth a snap afore it's ripe."
Sez Joe, "I'd jest ez lives eat tripe;
You *air* a buster ter suppose
I'd eat what makes me hole my nose!"

So they disputed to an' fro
Till cunnin' Isrel sez to Joe,
"Don't less stay here an' play the fool,
Less wait till both on us git cool;
Jest for a day or two less hide it,
An' then toss up and so decide it."
"Agreed!" sez Joe, an' so they di.l,
An' the ole goose wuz safely hid.

Now 'twuz the hottest kind o' weather,
An' when at last they come together,
It didn't signify which won,
Fer all the mischief hed ben done:

The goose wuz there, but, fer his soul,
Joe wouldn't ha' tetched it with a pole;
But Isrel kind o' liked the smell on't,
An' made *his* dinner very well on't.

My own humble attempt was in manner and form following, and I print it here, I sincerely trust, out of no vainglory, but solely with the hope of doing good.

LEAVING THE MATTER OPEN.

A TALE.

By Homer Wilbur, A.M.

Two brothers once, an ill-matched pair,
Together dwelt (no matter where),
To whom an Uncle Sam, or some one,
Had left a house and farm in common:
The two in principles and habits
Were different as rats from rabbits;
Stout Farmer North, with frugal care,
Laid up provision for his heir,
Not scorning with hard sun-browned hands
To scrape acquaintance with his lands;
Whatever thing he had to do
He did, and made it pay him, too;
He sold his waste stone by the pound,
His drains made water-wheels spin round,
His ice in summer time he sold,
His wood brought profit when 'twas cold,
He dug and delved from morn till night,
Strove to make profit square with right,
Lived on his means, cut no great dash,
And paid his debts in honest cash.

On tother hand, his brother South
Lived very much from hand to mouth,
Played gentleman, nursed dainty hands,
Borrowed North's money on his lands,

And culled his morals and his graces
From cock-pits, bar-rooms, fights, and races.
His sole work in the farming line
Was keeping droves of long-legged swine,
Which brought great bothers and expenses
To North, in looking after fences;
And, when they happened to break through,
Cost him both time and temper too;
For South insisted it was plain
He ought to drive them home again,
And North consented to the work
Because he loved to buy cheap pork.

Meanwhile, South's swine increasing fast,
His farm became too small at last,
So, having thought the matter over,
And feeling bound to live in clover,
And never pay the clover's worth,
He said one day to brother North:—

" Our families are both increasing,
And, though we labour without ceasing,
Our produce soon will be too scant
To keep our children out of want;
They who wish fortune to be lasting
Must be both prudent and forecasting;
We soon shall need more land; a lot
I know, that cheaply can be bo't;
You lend the cash, I'll buy the acres,
And we'll be equally partakers."

Poor North, whose Anglo-Saxon blood
Gave him a hankering after mud,
Wavered a moment, then consented,
And, when the cash was paid, repented;
To make the new land worth a pin,
Thought he, it must be all fenced in,
For, if South's swine once get the run on't
No kind of farming can be done on't;
If that don't suit the other side,
'Tis best we instantly divide,

But somehow South could ne'er incline
This way or that to run the line,
And always found some new pretence
'Gainst setting the division fence;
At last he said :—

       " For peace's sake,
Liberal concessions I will make ;
Though I believe, upon my soul,
I've a just title to the whole.
I'll make an offer which I call
Gen'rous,—we'll have no fence at all ;
Then both of us, whene'er we choose,
Can take what part we want to use ;
If you should chance to need it first,
Pick you the best, I'll take the worst."

"Agreed !" cried North ; thought he, this fall
With wheat and rye I'll sow it all,
In that way I shall get the start,
And South may whistle for his part ;
So thought, so done ; the field was sown,
And, winter having come and gone,
Sly North walked blithely forth to spy
The progress of his wheat and rye ;
Heavens, what a sight ! his brother's swine
Had asked themselves all out to dine ;
Such grunting, munching, rooting, shoving,
The soil seemed all alive and moving,
As for his grain, such work they made on't,
He couldn't spy a single blade on't.

Off in a rage he rushed to South,
" My wheat and rye "—grief choked his mouth ;
" Pray don't mind me," said South ; "but plant
All of the new land that you want ;"
" Yes, but your hogs," cried North.

               " The grain
Won't hurt them," answered South again ;
" But they destroy my grain ;"

　　　　　　　　　　　"No doubt;
'Tis fortunate you've found it out;
Misfortunes teach, and only they,
You must not sow it in their way;"
"Nay, you," says North, "must keep them out:"
"Did I create them with a snout?"
Asked South demurely; "as agreed,
The land is open to your seed,
And would you fain prevent my pigs
From running there their harmless rigs?
God knows I view this compromise
With not the most approving eyes;
I gave up my unquestioned rights
For sake of quiet days and nights,
I offered then, you know 'tis true,
To cut the piece of land in two."
"Then cut it now," growls North.

　　　　　　　　　　　"Abate
Your heat," says South, "'tis now too late;
I offered you the rocky corner,
But you, of your own good the scorner,
Refused to take it; I am sorry;
No doubt you might have found a quarry,
Perhaps a gold-mine, for aught I know,
Containing heaps of native rhino;
You can't expect me to resign
My right——"

　　　　　　　"But where," quoth North, "are mine?"
"*Your* rights," says tother, "well, that's funny,
I bought the land——"

　　　　　　　　　　"*I* paid the money;"
"That," answered South, "is from the point,
The ownership, you'll grant, is joint.
I'm sure my only hope and trust is
Not law so much as abstract justice,
Though, you remember, 'twas agreed
That so and so—consult the deed;

Objections now are out of date,
They might have answered once, but Fate
Quashes them at the point we've got to ;
Obsta principiis, that's my motto."
So saying, South began to whistle
And looked as obstinate as gristle,
While North went homeward, each brown paw
Clenched like a knot of natural law,
And all the while, in either ear,
Heard something clicking wondrous clear.

To turn now to other matters, there are two things upon which it would seem fitting to dilate somewhat more largely in this place,—the Yankee character and the Yankee dialect. And, first, of the Yankee character, which has wanted neither open maligners, nor even more dangerous enemies in the persons of those unskilful painters who have given to it that hardness, angularity, and want of proper perspective, which, in truth, belonged, not to their subject, but to their own niggard and unskilful pencil.

New England was not so much the colony of a mother country as a Hagar driven forth into the wilderness. The little self-exiled band which came hither in 1620 came, not to seek gold, but to found a democracy. They came that they might have the privilege to work and pray, to sit upon hard benches and listen to painful preachers as long as they would, yea, even unto thirty-seventhly, if the spirit so willed it. And surely if the Greek might boast his Thermopylæ, where three hundred men fell in resisting the Persian, we may well be proud of our Plymouth Rock, where a handful of men, women, and children not merely faced but vanquished winter, famine, the wilderness, and the yet more invincible *storge* that drew them back to the green island far away. These found no lotus growing upon the surly shore, the taste of which could make them forget their

3

little native Ithaca; nor were they so wanting to themselves in faith as to burn their ship, but could see the fair west wind belly the homeward sail, and then turn unrepining to grapple with the terrible Unknown.

As Want was the prime foe these hardy exodists had to fortress themselves against, so it is little wonder if that traditional feud is long in wearing out of the stock. The wounds of the old warfare were long ahealing, and an east wind of hard times puts a new ache in every one of them. Thrift was the first lesson in their horn-book, pointed out, letter after letter, by the lean finger of the hard school-master, Necessity. Neither were those plump, rosy-gilled Englishmen that came hither, but a hard-faced, atrabilious, earnest-eyed race, stiff from long wrestling with the Lord in prayer, and who had taught Satan to dread the new Puritan hug. Add two hundred years' influence of soil, climate, and exposure, with its necessary result of idiosyncrasies, and we have the present Yankee, full of expedients, half-master of all trades, inventive in all but the beautiful, full of shifts, not yet capable of comfort, armed at all points against the old enemy Hunger, longanimous, good at patching, not so careful for what is best as for what will *do*, with a clasp to his purse and a button to his pocket, not skilled to build against Time, as in old countries, but against sore-pressing Need, accustomed to move the world with no ποῦ στῶ but his own two feet, and no lever but his own long forecast. A strange hybrid, indeed, did circumstance beget, here in the New World, upon the old Puritan stock, and the earth never before saw such mystic-practicalism, such niggard-geniality, such calculating-fanaticism, such cast-iron-enthusiasm, such sour-faced-humour, such close-fisted-generosity. This new *Græculus esuriens* will make a living out of anything. He will invent new trades as well as tools. His brain is his capital, and he will get education at all risks. Put him on Juan Fernandez, and he would make a spelling-book first, and a salt-pan afterward. *In cœlum jusseris, ibit,*—or the other way either,—it is all one, so anything is to be got by it. Yet, after all, thin, speculative Jonathan is more like the Englishman of two centuries ago than John Bull himself is. He has lost somewhat in solidity, has become fluent and adaptable, but more of the original groundwork of character remains. He feels more at home with Fulke Greville, Herbert of Cherbury, Quarles, George Herbert, and Browne, than with his modern English cousins. He is nearer than John, by at least a hundred years, to Naseby, Marston Moor, Worcester, and the time when, if ever, there were true Englishmen. John Bull has suffered the idea of the Invisible to be very much fattened out of him. Jonathan is conscious still that he lives in the world of the Unseen as well as of the Seen. To move John you must make your fulcrum of solid beef and pudding; an abstract idea will do for Jonathan.

⁎ TO THE INDULGENT READER.

My friend, the Reverend Mr. Wilbur, having been seized with a dangerous fit of illness before this introduction had passed through the press, and being incapacitated for all literary exertion, sent to me his notes, memoranda, etc., and requested me to fashion them into some shape more fitting for the general eye. This, owing to the fragmentary and disjointed state of his manuscripts, I have felt wholly unable to do; yet being unwilling that the reader should be deprived of such parts of his lucubrations as seemed more finished, and not well discerning how to segregate these from the rest, I have concluded to send them all to the press precisely as they are.

COLUMBUS NYE,
Pastor of a Church in Bungtown Corner.

It remains to speak of the Yankee dialect. And, first, it may be premised, in a general way, that any one much read in the writings of the early colonists need not be told that the far greater share of the words and phrases now esteemed peculiar to New England, and local there, were brought from the mother country. A person familiar with the dialect of certain portions of Massachusetts will not fail to recognise, in ordinary discourse, many words now noted in English vocabularies as archaic, the greater part of which were in common use about the time of the King James translation of the Bible. Shakespeare stands less in need of a glossary to most New Englanders than to many a native of the Old Country. The peculiarities of our speech, however, are rapidly wearing out. As there is no country where reading is so universal and newspapers are so multitudinous, so no phrase remains long local, but is transplanted in the mail-bags to every remotest corner of the land. Consequently our dialect approaches nearer to uniformity than that of any other nation.

The English have complained of us for coining new words. Many of those so stigmatised were old ones by them forgotten, and all make now an unquestioned part of the currency, wherever English is spoken. Undoubtedly we have a right to make new words, as they are needed by the fresh aspects under which life presents itself here in the New World; and, indeed, wherever a language is alive it grows. It might be questioned whether we could not establish a stronger title to the ownership of the English tongue than the mother-islanders themselves. Here, past all question, is to be its great home and centre. And not only is it already spoken here by greater numbers, but with a far higher popular average of correctness than in Britain. The great writers of it, too, we might claim as ours, were ownership to be settled by the number of readers and lovers.

As regards the provincialisms to be met with in this volume, I may say that the reader will not find one which is not (as I believe) either native or imported with the early settlers, nor one which I have not, with my own ears, heard in familiar use. In the metrical portion of the book I have endeavoured to adapt the spelling as nearly as possible to the ordinary mode of pronunciation. Let the reader who deems me over-particular remember this caution of Martial:—

> " *Quem recitas, meus est, O Fidentine, libellus ;*
> *Sed male cum recitas, incipit esse tuus,*"

A few further explanatory remarks will not be impertinent. I shall barely lay down a few general rules for the reader's guidance.

1. The genuine Yankee never gives the rough sound to the *r* when he can help it, and often displays considerable ingenuity in avoiding it even before a vowel.

2. He seldom sounds the final *g*, a piece of self-denial, if we consider his partiality for nasals. The same of the final *d*, as *han'* and *stan'* for *hand* and *stand*.

3. The *h* in such words as *while, when, where*, he omits altogether.

4. In regard to *a*, he shows some inconsistency, sometimes giving a close and obscure sound, as *hev* for *have*, *hendy* for *handy*, *ez* for *as*, *thet* for *that*, and again giving it the broad sound it has in *father*, as *hânsome* for *handsome*.

5. To the sound *ou* he prefixes an *e* (hard to exemplify otherwise than orally).

The following passage in Shakespeare he would recite thus :—

" Neow is the winta uv eour discontent
Med glorious summa by this sun o' Yock,
An' all the cleouds thet leowered upun eour heouse
In the deep buzzum o' the oshin buried;
Neow air eour breows beound 'ith victorious wreaths;
Eour breused arms hung up fer monimunce;
Eour starn alarums changed to merry meetins,
Eour dreffle marches to delightful measures.
Grim-visaged war heth smeuthed his wrinkled front,
An' neow, instid o' mountin' barebid steeds
To fright the souls o' ferfle edverseries,
He capers nimly in a lady's chamber,
To the lascivious pleasin' uv a loot."

6. *Au*, in such words as *daughter* and *slaughter*, he pro-
nounces *ah*.

7. To the dish thus seasoned add a drawl *ad libitum.*

[Mr. Wilbur's notes here become entirely fragmentary.—C. N.]

a. Unable to procure a likeness of Mr. Biglow, I thought
the curious reader might be gratified with a sight of the
editorial effigies. And here a choice between two was
offered—the one a profile (entirely black) cut by Doyle, the
other a portrait painted by a native artist of much promise.
The first of these seemed wanting in expression, and in
the second a slight obliquity of the visual organs has been
heightened (perhaps from an over-desire of force on the
part of the artist) into too close an approach to actual
strabismus. This slight divergence in my optical apparatus
from the ordinary model—however I may have been taught
to regard it in the light of a mercy rather than a cross,
since it enabled me to give as much of directness and
personal application to my discourses as met the wants of
my congregation, without risk of offending any by being
supposed to have him or her in my eye (as the saying is)—

seemed yet to Mrs. Wilbur a sufficient objection to the engraving of the aforesaid painting. We read of many who either absolutely refused to allow the copying of their features, as especially did Plotinus and Agesilaus among the ancients, not to mention the more modern instances of Scioppius, Palæottus, Pinellus, Velserus, Gataker, and others, or were indifferent thereto, as Cromwell.

β. Yet was Cæsar desirous of concealing his baldness. *Per contra*, my Lord Protector's carefulness in the matter of his wart might be cited. Men generally more desirous of being *improved* in their portraits than characters. Shall probably find very unflattered likenesses of ourselves in Recording Angel's gallery.

γ. Whether any of our national peculiarities may be traced to our use of stoves, as a certain closeness of the lips in pronunciation, and a smothered smoulderingness of disposition, seldom roused to open flame? An unrestrained intercourse with fire probably conducive to generosity and hospitality of soul. Ancient Mexicans used stoves, as the friar Augustin Ruiz reports, Hakluyt, III., 468,—but Popish priests not always reliable authority.

To-day picked my Isabella grapes. Crop injured by attacks of rose-bug in the spring. Whether Noah was justifiable in preserving this class of insects?

δ. Concerning Mr. Biglow's pedigree. Tolerably certain that there was never a poet among his ancestors. An ordination hymn attributed to a maternal uncle, but perhaps a sort of production not demanding the creative faculty.

His grandfather a painter of the grandiose or Michael Angelo school. Seldom painted objects smaller than houses or barns, and these with uncommon expression.

———

є. Of the Wilburs no complete pedigree. The crest said to be a *wild boar*, whence, perhaps, the name (?). A connection with the Earls of Wilbraham (*quasi* wild boar ham) might be made out. This suggestion worth following up. In 1677, John W. m. Expect ——, had issue, 1. John, 2. Haggai, 3. Expect, 4. Ruhamah, 5. Desire.

> " Hear lyes yᵉ bodye of Mrs. Expect Wilber,
>   Yᵉ crewell salvages they kil'd her
>   Together wᵗʰ other Christian soles eleaven,
>   October yᵉ ix daye, 1707.
>
> Yᵉ stream of Jordan sh' as crost ore
> And now expeacts me on yᵉ other shore:
> I live in hope her soon to join;
> Her earthlye yeeres were forty and nine."
>   —*From Gravestone in Pekussett, North parish.*

This is unquestionably the same John who afterward (1711) married Tabitha Hagg or Ragg.

But if this were the case, she seems to have died early; for only three years after, namely, 1714, we have evidence that he married Winifred, daughter of Lieutenant Tipping.

He seems to have been a man of substance, for we find him in 1696 conveying "one undivided eightieth part of a salt-meadow" in Yabbok, and he commanded a sloop in 1702.

Those who doubt the importance of genealogical studies *fuste potius quam argumento erudiendi.*

I trace him as far as 1723, and there lose him. In that year he was chosen selectman.

No gravestone. Perhaps overthrown when new hearse-house was built, 1802.

He was probably the son of John, who came from Bilham Comit. Salop. *circa* 1642.

This first John was a man of considerable importance, being twice mentioned with the honourable prefix of *Mr.* in the town records. Name spelt with two *l*-s.

> " Hear lyeth yᵉ bod [*stone unhappily broken.*]
> Mr. Ihon Willber [Esq.] [*I inclose this in brackets as doubtful.*
> *To me it seems clear.*]
> Ob't die [*illegible; looks like xviii.*]......iii [*prob.* 1693.]
> .   .   .   .   .   paynt
> .   .   .   .   deseased seinte :
> A friend and [fath]er untoe all yᵉ opreast,
> Hee gave yᵉ wicked familists noe reast,
> When Sat[an bl]ewe his Antinomian blaste,
> Wee clong to [Willber as a steadf]ast maste.
> [A]gaynst yᵉ horrid Qua[kers]   .   .   .   . "

It is greatly to be lamented that this curious epitaph is mutilated. It is said that the sacrilegious British soldiers made a target of this stone during the war of Independence. How odious an animosity which pauses not at the grave ! How brutal that which spares not the monuments of authentic history ! This is not improbably from the pen of Rev. Moody Pyram, who is mentioned by Hubbard as having been noted for a silver vein of poetry. If his papers be still extant, a copy might possibly be recovered.

THE BIGLOW PAPERS.

No. I.

A LETTER

FROM MR. EZEKIEL BIGLOW OF JAALAM TO THE HON.
JOSEPH T. BUCKINGHAM, EDITOR OF THE "BOSTON
COURIER," INCLOSING A POEM OF HIS SON, MR. HOSEA
BIGLOW.

JAYLEM, june 1846.

MISTER EDDYTER :—Our Hosea wuz down to Boston
last week, and he see a cruetin Sarjunt a struttin round as
popler as a hen with 1 chicking, with 2 fellers a drummin
and fifin arter him like all nater. the sarjunt he thout
Hosea hedn't gut his i teeth cut cos he looked a kindo's
though he'd jest com down, so he cal'lated to hook him in,
but Hosy woodn't take none o' his sarse for all he hed
much as 20 Rooster's tales stuck onto his hat and eenamost
enuf brass a bobbin up and down on his shoulders and
figureed onto his coat and trousis, let alone wut nater hed
sot in his featers, to make a 6 pounder out on.

wal, Hosea he com home considerabal riled, and arter
I'd gone to bed I heern Him a thrashin round like a short-
tailed Bull in fli-time. The old Woman ses she to me ses
she, Zekle, ses she, our Hosee's gut the chollery or suthin

another ses she, don't you Bee skeered, ses I, he's oney amakin pottery[1] ses i, he's ollers on hand at that ere busynes like Da & martin, and shure enuf, cum mornin, Hosy he cum down stares full chizzle, hare on eend and cote tales flyin, and sot rite of to go reed his varses to Parson Wilbur bein he haint aney grate shows o' book larnin himself, bimeby he cum back and sed the parson wuz dreffle tickled with 'em as I hoop you will Be, and said they wuz True grit.

Hosea ses taint hardly fair to call 'em hisn now, cos the parson kind o' slicked off sum o' the last varses, but he told Hosee he didnt want to put his ore in to tetch to the Rest on 'em, bein they wuz verry well As thay wuz, and then Hosy ses he sed suthin a nuther about Simplex Mundishes or sum sech feller, but I guess Hosea kind o' didn't hear him, for I never hearn o' nobody o' that name in this villadge, and I've lived here man and boy 76 year cum next tatur digging, and thar aint nowheres a kitting spryer'n I be.

If you print 'em I wish you'd jest let folks know who hosy's father is, cos my ant Keziah used to say it's nater to be curus ses she, she aint livin though and he's a likely kind o' lad.

EZEKIEL BIGLOW.

THRASH away, you'll *hev* to rattle
  On them kittle-drums o' yourn,—
'Taint a knowin' kind o' cattle
  Thet is ketched with mouldy corn;

[1] *Aut insanit, aut versos facit.*—H. W.

Put in stiff, you fifer feller,
　　Let folk see how spry you be,—
Guess you'll toot till you are yeller
　　'Fore you git ahold o' me !

Thet air flag's a leetle rotten,
　　Hope it aint your Sunday's best ;—
Fact ! it takes a sight o' cotton
　　To stuff out a soger's chest :
Sence we farmers hev to pay fer't,
　　Ef you must wear humps like these,
Sposin' you should try salt hay fer't,
　　It would du ez slick ez grease.

'Twouldn't suit them Southun fellers,
　　They're a dreffle graspin' set,
We must ollers blow the bellers
　　Wen they want their irons het ;
May be it's all right ez preachin',
　　But *my* narves it kind o' grates,
Wen I see the overreachin'
　　O' them nigger-drivin' States.

Them thet rule us, them slave-traders,
　　Haint they cut a thunderin' swarth,
(Helped by Yankee renegaders,)
　　Thru the vartu o' the North !
We begin to think it's nater
　　To take sarse an' not be riled ;—
Who'd expect to see a tater
　　All on eend at bein' biled ?

Ez fer war, I call it murder,—
　　There you hev it plain an' flat;
I don't want to go no furder
　　Than my Testyment fer that;
God hez said so plump an' fairly
　　It's ez long ez it is broad,
An' you've gut to git up airly
　　Ef you want to take in God.

'Taint your eppyletts an' feathers
　　Make the thing a grain more right;
'Taint afollerin' your bell-wethers
　　Will excuse ye in His sight;
Ef you take a sword an' dror it,
　　An' go stick a feller thru,
Guv'ment aint to answer for it,
　　God'll send the bill to you.

Wut's the use o' meetin'-goin'
　　Every Sabbath, wet or dry,
Ef it's right to go amowin'
　　Feller-men like oats an' rye?
I dunno but wut it's pooty
　　Trainin' round in bobtail coats,—
But it's curus Christian dooty
　　This 'ere cuttin' folks's throats.

They may talk o' Freedom's airy
　　Tell they're pupple in the face,—
It's a grand gret cemetary
　　Fer the barthrights of our race;

They jest want this Californy
   So's to lug new slave-states in
'To abuse ye, an' to scorn ye,
   An' to plunder ye like sin.

Aint it cute to see a Yankee
   Take sech everlastin' pains,
All to git the Devil's thankee,
   Helpin' on 'em weld their chains?
Wy, it's jest ez clear ez figgers,
   Clear ez one an' one make two,
Chaps thet make black slaves o' niggers
   Want to make wite slaves o' you.

Tell ye jest the eend I've come to
   Arter cipherin' plaguy smart,
An' it makes a handy sum, tu,
   Any gump could larn by heart;
Laborin' man an' laborin' woman
   Hev one glory an' one shame,
Ev'y thin' thet's done inhuman
   Injers all on 'em the same.

'Taint by turnin' out to hack folks;
   You're agoin' to git your right,
Nor by lookin' down on black folks
   Coz you're put upon by wite;
Slavery aint o' nary color,
   'Taint the hide thet makes it wus,
All it keers fer in a feller
   'S jest to make him fill its pus.

Want to tackle *me* in, du ye?
    I expect you'll hev to wait;
Wen cold lead puts daylight thru ye
    You'll begin to kal'late:
Spose the crows wun't fall to pickin'
    All the carkiss from your bones,
Coz you helped to give a lickin'
    To them poor half-Spanish drones?

Jest go home an' ask our Nancy
    Wether I'd be sech a goose
Ez to jine ye,—guess you'd fancy
    The etarnal bung wuz loose!
She wants me fer home consumption,
    Let alone the hay's to mow,—
Ef you're after folks o' gumption,
    You've a darned long row ta hoe.

Take them editors thet's crowin'
    Like a cockerel three months old,—
Don't ketch any on 'em goin',
    Though they *be* so blasted bold;
Aint they a prime lot o' fellers?
    'Fore they think on't they will sprout,
(Like a peach thet's got the yellers,)
    With the meanness bustin' out.

Wal, go 'long to help 'em stealin'
    Bigger pens to cram with slaves,
Help the men thet's ollers dealin'
    Insults on your fathers' graves;

Help the strong to grind the feeble,
    Help the many agin the few,
Help the men thet call your people
    Witewashed slaves an' peddlin' crew!

Massachusetts, God forgive her,
    She's akneelin' with the rest,
She, thet ough' to ha' clung fer ever
    In her grand old eagle-nest;
She thet ough' to stand so fearless
    Wile the wracks are round her hurled,
Holdin' up a beacon peerless
    To the oppressed of all the world!

Haint they sold your colored seamen?
    Haint they made your env'ys wiz?
Wut'll make ye act like freemen?
    Wut'll git your dander riz?
Come, I'll tell ye wut I'm thinkin'
    Is our dooty in this fix,
They'd ha' done 't ez quick ez winkin'
    In the days o' seventy-six.

Clang the bells in every steeple,
    Call all true men to disown
The tradoocers of our people,
    The enslavers o' their own;
Let our dear old Bay State proudly
    Put the trumpet to her mouth,
Let her ring this messidge loudly
    In the ears of all the South:—

" I'll return ye good fer evil
  Much ez we frail mortils can,
But I wun't go help the Devil
  Makin' man the cus o' man;
Call me coward, call me traiter,
  Jest ez suits your mean idees,—
Here I stand a tyrant-hater,
  An' the friend o' God an' Peace!"

Ef I'd *my* way I hed ruther
  We should go to work an' part,—
They take one way, we take t'other,—
  Guess it wouldn't break my heart;
Man had ough' to put asunder
  Them thet God has noways jined;
An' I shouldn't gretly wonder
  Ef there's thousands o' my mind.

[The first recruiting sergeant on record I conceive to have been that individual who is mentioned in the Book of Job as *going to and fro in the earth, and walking up and down in it.* Bishop Latimer will have him to have been a bishop, but to me that other calling would appear more congenial. The sect of Cainites is not yet extinct, who esteemed the first-born of Adam to be the most worthy, not only because of that privilege of primogeniture, but inasmuch as he was able to overcome and slay his younger brother. That was a wise saying of the famous Marquis Pescara to the Papal Legate, that *it was impossible for men to serve Mars and Christ at the same time.* Yet in time past the profession of arms was judged to be κατ' ἐξοχήν that of a gentleman, nor does this opinion want for strenuous upholders even in our day. Must we suppose, then, that the profession of Christianity was only intended for losels, or, at best, to afford an opening for plebeian ambition? Or shall we hold with that nicely metaphysical Pomeranian, Captain Vratz, who was Count Königsmark's chief instrument in the murder of Mr. Thynne, that the Scheme of Salvation has been arranged with an especial eye to the necessities of the upper classes, and that "God would consider *a gentleman* and deal with him suitably to the condition and profession he had placed him in"? It may be said of us all, *Exemplo plus quam ratione vivimus.*—H. W.]

No. II.

A LETTER

FROM MR. HOSEA BIGLOW TO THE HON. J. T. BUCKINGHAM, EDITOR OF THE "BOSTON COURIER," COVERING A LETTER FROM MR. B. SAWIN, PRIVATE IN THE MASSACHUSETTS REGIMENT.

[This letter of Mr. Sawin's was not originally written in verse. Mr. Biglow, thinking it peculiarly susceptible of metrical adornment, translated it, so to speak, into his own vernacular tongue. This is not the time to consider the question, whether rhyme be a mode of expression natural to the human race. If leisure from other and more important avocations be granted, I will handle the matter more at large in an appendix to the present volume. In this place I will barely remark that I have sometimes noticed in the unlanguaged prattlings of infants a fondness for alliteration, assonance, and even rhyme, in which natural predisposition we may trace the three degrees through which our Anglo-Saxon verse rose to its culmination in the poetry of Pope. I would not be understood as questioning in these remarks that pious theory which supposes that children, if left entirely to themselves, would naturally discourse in Hebrew. For this the authority of one experiment is claimed, and I could, with Sir Thomas Browne, desire its establishment, inasmuch as the acquirement of that sacred tongue would thereby be facilitated. I am aware that Herodotus states the conclusion of Psammeticus to have been in favour of a dialect of the Phrygian. But, beside the chance that a trial of this importance would hardly be blessed to a Pagan monarch whose only motive was curiosity, we have on the Hebrew side the comparatively recent investigation of James the Fourth of Scotland. I will add to this prefatory remark that Mr. Sawin, though a native of Jaalam, has never been a stated attendant on the religious exercises of my congregation. I consider my humble efforts prospered in that not one of my sheep hath ever indued the wolf's clothing of war, save for the comparatively innocent diversion of a militia training. Not that my flock are backward to undergo the hardships of *defensive* warfare. They serve cheerfully in the great army which fights even unto death *pro aris et focis,* accoutred with the spade, the axe, the plane, the sledge, the spelling-book, and other such effectual weapons against want and ignorance and unthrift. I have taught them (under God) to esteem our human institutions as but tents of a night, to be stricken whenever Truth puts the bugle to her lips and sounds a march to the heights of wider-viewed intelligence and more perfect organisation.—H. W.]

Mister Buckinum, the follerin Billet was writ hum by a Yung feller of our town that wuz cussed fool enuff to goe atrottin inter Miss Chiff arter a Drum and fife. it ain't Nater for a feller to let on that he's sick o' any bizness that He went intu off his own free will and a Cord, but I rather cal'late he's middlin tired o' voluntearin By this Time. I bleeve u may put dependunts on his statemence. For I never heerd nothin bad on him let Alone his havin what Parson Wilbur cals a *pongshong* for cocktales, and he ses it wuz a soshiashun of idees sot him agoin arter the Crootin Sargient cos he wore a cocktale onto his hat.

his Folks gin the letter to me and i shew it to parson Wilbur and he ses it oughter Bee printed. send It to mister Buckinum, ses he, i don't ollers agree with him, ses he, but by Time,[1] ses he, I *du* like a feller that ain't a Feared.

[1] In relation to this expression I cannot but think that Mr. Biglow has been too hasty in attributing it to me. Though Time be a comparatively innocent personage to swear by, and though Longinus in his discourse Περὶ Ὕψους has commended timely oaths as not only a useful but sublime figure of speech, yet I have always kept my lips free from that abomination. *Odi profanum vulgus,* I hate your swearing and hectoring fellows.—H. W.

I have intusspussed a Few refleckshuns hear and thair.
We're kind o' prest with Hayin.

Ewers respecfly

HOSEA BIGLOW.

THIS kind o' sogerin' aint a mite like our October trainin',
A chap could clear right out from there ef't only looked like
    rainin',
An' th' Cunnles, tu, could kiver up their shappoes with
    bandanners,
An' send the insines skootin' to the bar-room with their
    banners
(Fear o' gittin' on 'em spotted), an' a feller could cry quarter
Ef he fired away his ramrod arter tu much rum an' water.
Recollect wut fun we hed, you'n' I an' Ezry Hollis,
Up there to Waltham plain last fall, along o' the Corn-
    wallis?[1]
This sort o' thing aint *jest* like thet,—I wish thet I wuz
    furder,—[2]
Nimepunce a day fer killin' folks comes kind o' low fer murder,
(Wy I've worked out to slarterin' some fer Deacon Cephas
    Billins,
An' in the hardest times there wuz I ollers tetched ten
    shillins),
There's sutthin' gits into my throat thet makes it hard to
    swaller,
It comes so nateral to think about a hempen collar;
It's glory,—but, in spite o' all my tryin' to git callous,
I feel a kind o' in a cart, aridin' to the gallus.
But wen it comes to *bein'* killed,—I tell ye I felt streaked

---

[1] i hait the Site of a feller with a muskit as I do pizn But their *is* fun
to a cornwallis I aint agoin' to deny it.—H. B.

[2] he means Not quite so fur I guess.—H. B.

The fust time 'tever I found out wy baggonets wuz peaked;
Here's how it wuz: I started out to to go to a fandango,
The sentinul he ups an' sez, "Thet's furder 'an you can go."
"None o' your sarse," sez I; sez he, "Stan' back!" "Aint
    you a buster?"

Sez I, "I'm up to all thet air, I guess I've been to muster;
I know wy sentinuls air sot; you aint agoin' to eat us:
Caleb haint no monopoly to court the seenoreetas;
My folks to hum air full ez good ez hisn be, by golly!"
An' so ez I wuz goin' by, not thinkin' wut would folly,
The everlastin' cus he stuck his one-pronged pitchfork in me
An' made a hole right thru my close ez ef I wuz an in'my.

Wal, it beats all how big I felt hoorawin' in ole Funnel
Wen Mister Bolles he gin the sword to our Leftenant
    Cunnle,
(It's Mister Secondary Bolles,[1] thet writ the prize peace
    essay;
Thet's why he didn't list himself along o' us, I dessay),
An' Rantoul, tu, talked pooty loud, but don't put *his* foot
    in it,
Coz human life's so sacred thet he's principled agin it,—
Though I myself can't rightly see it's any wus achokin' on 'em,
Than puttin' bullets thru their lights, or with a bagnet
    pokin' on 'em;
How dreffle slick he reeled it off (like Blitz at our lyceum
Ahaulin' ribbins from his chops so quick you skeercely see
    'em),
About the Anglo-Saxon race (an' saxons would be handy
To du the buryin' down here upon the Rio Grandy),

---

[1] the ignerant creeter means Sekketary; but he ollers stuck to his books like cobbler's wax to an ile-stone.—H. B.

About our patriotic pas an' our star-spangled banner,
Our country's bird alookin' on an' singin' out hosanner,
An' how he (Mister B. himself) wuz happy fer Ameriky,—
I felt, ez sister Patience sez, a leetle mite histericky.
I felt, I swon, ez though it wuz a dreffle kind o' privilege
Atrampin' round thru Boston streets among the gutter's
  drivelage;
I act'lly thought it wuz a treat to hear a little drummin',
An' it did bonyfidy seem millanyum wuz acomin'
Wen all on us got suits (darned like them wore in the state
  prison)
An' every feller felt ez though all Mexico wuz hisn.[1]
This 'ere's about the meanest place a skunk could wal
  diskiver
(Saltillo's Mexican, I b'lieve, fer wut we call Salt-river);
The sort o' trash a feller gits to eat doos beat all nater,
I'd give a year's pay fer a smell o' one good blue-nose
  tater;
The country here thet Mister Bolles declared to be so
  charmin'
Throughout is swarmin' with the most alarmin' kind o'
  varmin.

He talked about delishis froots, but then it wuz a whopper
  all,
The holl on't's mud an' prickly pears, with here an' there a
  chapparal;
You see a feller peekin' out, an', fust you know, a lariat

---

[1] it must be aloud that thare's a streak o' nater in lovin' sho, but
it sartinly is 1 of the curusest things in nater to see a rispecktable dri
goods dealer (deekon off a chutch mayby) a riggin' himself out in the
Weigh they du and struttin' round in the Reign aspilin' his trowsis and
makin' wet goods of himself. Ef any thin's foolisher and more dicklus
than militerry gloary it is milishy gloary.—H. B.

Is round your throat an' you a copse, 'fore you can say,
    "Wut air ye at?"[1]
You never see sech darned gret bugs (it may not be
    irrelevant
To say I've seen a *scarabæus pilularius*[2] big ez a year old
    elephant),
The rigiment come up one day in time to stop a red bug
From runnin' off with Cunnle Wright,—'twuz jest a common
    cimex lectularius.

One night I started up on eend an' thought I wuz to hum
    agin,
I heern a horn, thinks I it's Sol the fisherman hez come agin,
His bellowses is sound enough,—ez I'm a livin' creeter,
I felt a thing go thru my leg,—'twuz nothin' more 'n a
    skeeter!
Then there's the yaller fever, tu, they call it here el
    vomito,—
(Come, thet wun't du, you landcrab there, I tell ye to le' *go*
    my toe!
My gracious! it's a scorpion thet's took a shine to play with't,
I darsn't skeer the tarnal thing fer fear he'd run away
    with't.)
Afore I cum away from hum I hed a strong persuasion
Thet Mexicans worn't human beans,[3]—an ourang-outang
    nation,

[1] these fellers are very proppilly called Rank Heroes, and the more
tha kill the ranker and more Herowick tha bekum.—H. B.

[2] it wuz "tumblebug" as he Writ it, but the parson put the Latten
instid. i sed tother maid better meeter, but he said tha was eddykated
peepl to Boston and tha wouldn't stan' it no how. idnow as tha *wood*
and idnow *as* tha wood.—H. B.

[3] he means human beins, that's wut he means. i spose he kinder
thought tha wuz human beans ware the Xisle Poles comes from.—H. B.

A sort o' folks a chap could kill an' never dream on't arter,
No more'n a feller'd dream o' pigs thet he hed hed to slarter,
I'd an idee thet they were built arter the darkie fashion all,
An' kickin' colored folks about, you know, 's a kind o'
    national ;
But wen I jined I wornt so wise ez thet air queen o' Sheby,
Fer, come to look at 'em, they aint much diff'rent from wut
    we be,
An' here we air ascrougin' 'em out o' thir own dominions,
Ashelterin' 'em, ez Caleb sez, under our eagle's pinions,
Wich means to take a feller up jest by the slack o' 's trowsis
An' walk him Spanish clean right out o' all his homes an'
    houses ;
Wal, it doos seem a curus way, but then hooraw fer Jack-
    son !
It must be right, fer Caleb sez it's reg'lar Anglo-Saxon.
The Mex'cans don't fight fair, they say, they piz'n all the
    water,
An' du amazin' lots o' things thet isn't wut they ough' to ;
Bein' they haint no lead, they make their bullets out o'
    copper
An' shoot the darned things at us, tu, wich Caleb sez aint
    proper ;
He sez they'd ough' to stan' right up an' let us pop 'em fairly
(Guess wen he ketches 'em at thet he'll hev to git up airly),
Thet our nation's bigger'n theirn an' so its rights air bigger,
An' thet it's all to make 'em free thet we air pullin' trigger,
Thet Anglo Saxondom's idee's abreakin' 'em to pieces,
An' thet idee's thet every man doos jest wut he damn
    pleases ;
Ef I don't make his meanin' clear, perhaps in some respex
    I can,
I know thet "every man" don't mean a nigger or a Mexican ;

An' there's another thing I know, an' thet is, ef these
    creeturs,
Thet stick an Anglo-Saxon mask onto State-prison feeturs,
Should come to Jaalam Centre fer to argify an' spout on't,
The gals 'ould count the silver spoons the minnit they
    cleared out on't.

This goin' ware glory waits ye haint one agreeable feetur,
An' ef it worn't fer wakin' snakes, I'd home agin short
    meter;
O, wouldn't I be off, quick time, ef't worn't thet I wuz
    sartin
They'd let the daylight into me to pay me fer desartin!
I don't approve o' tellin' tales, but jest to you I may state
Our ossifers aint wut they wuz afore they left the Bay state;
Then it wuz "Mister Sawin, sir, you're middlin' well now,
    be ye?
Step up an' take a nipper, sir; I'm dreffle glad to see ye;"
But now it's "Ware's my eppylet? here, Sawin, step an
    fetch it!
An' mind your eye, be thund'rin' spry, or, damn ye, you
    shall ketch it!"
Wal, ez the Doctor sez, some pork will bile so, but by
    mighty,
Ef I hed sum on 'em to hum, I'd give 'em linkum vity,
I'd play the rogue's march on their hides an' other music
    follerin'—
But I must close my letter here, fer one on 'em's ahollerin',
These Anglo-Saxon ossifers,—wal, taint no use ajawin',
I'm safe enlisted fer the war,

                            Yourn,
                    BIRDOFREDUM SAWIN.

[Those have not been wanting (as, indeed, when hath Satan been to seek for attorneys?) who have maintained that our late inroad upon Mexico was undertaken, not so much for the avenging of any national quarrel, as for the spreading of free institutions and of Protestantism. *Capita vix duabus Anticyris medenda!* Verily I admire that no pious sergeant among these new Crusaders beheld Martin Luther riding at the front of the host upon a tamed pontifical bull, as, in that former invasion of Mexico, the zealous Gomara (spawn though he were of the Scarlet Woman) was favoured with a vision of St. James of Compostella, skewering the infidels upon his apostolical lance. We read, also, that Richard of the lion heart, having gone to Palestine on a similar errand of mercy, was divinely encouraged to cut the throats of such Paynims as refused to swallow the bread of life (doubtless that they might be thereafter incapacitated for swallowing the filthy gobbets of Mahound) by angels of heaven, who cried to the king and his knights,—*Seigneurs, tuez! tuez!* providentially using the French tongue, as being the only one understood by their auditors. This would argue for the pantoglottism of these celestial intelligences, while, on the other hand, the Devil, *teste* Cotton Mather, is unversed in certain of the Indian dialects. Yet must he be a semeiologist the most expert, making himself intelligible to every people and kindred by signs; no other discourse, indeed, being needful, than such as the mackerel-fisher holds with his finned quarry, who, if other bait be wanting, can by a bare bit of white rag at the end of a string captivate those foolish fishes. Such piscatorial oratory is Satan cunning in. Before one he trails a hat and feather, or a bare feather without a hat; before another, a presidential chair, or a tidewaiter's stool, or a pulpit in the city, no matter what. To us, dangling there over our heads, they seem junkets dropped out of the seventh heaven, sops dipped in nectar; but, once in our mouths, they are all one, bits of fuzzy cotton.

This, however, by the way. It is time now *revocare gradum.* While so many miracles of this sort, vouched by eye-witnesses, have encouraged the arms of Papists, not to speak of Echetlæus at Marathon and those *Dioscuri* (whom we must conclude imps of the pit) who sundry times captained the pagan Roman soldiers, it is strange that our first American crusade was not in some such wise also signalised. Yet it is said that the Lord hath manifestly prospered our armies. This opens the question whether, when our hands are strengthened to make great slaughter of our enemies, it be absolutely and demonstratively certain that this might is added to us from above, or whether some Potentate from an opposite quarter may not have a finger in it, as there are few pies into which his meddling digits are not thrust. Would the Sanctifier and Setter-apart of the seventh day have assisted in a victory gained on the Sabbath, as was one in the late war? Or has that day become less an object of his especial care since the year 1697, when so manifest a providence occurred to Mr. William Trowbridge, in answer to whose prayers, when he and all on shipboard with him were starving, a dolphin was sent daily, "which was enough to serve 'em; only on *Saturdays* they still catched a couple, and on the *Lord's Days* they could catch none at all?" Haply they might have been permitted, by way of mortification, to take some few sculpins (those banes of the salt-water angler), which unseemly fish would, moreover, have conveyed to them a symbolical reproof for their breach of the day, being known in the rude dialect of our mariners as *Cape Cod Clergymen.*

It has been a refreshment to many nice consciences to know that our Chief Magistrate would not regard with eyes of approval the (by many esteemed) sinful pastime of dancing, and I own myself to be so far of that mind, that I could not but set my face against this Mexican Polka, though danced to the Presidential piping with a Gubernatorial second. If ever the country should be seized with another such mania *de propagandâ fide*, I think it would be wise to fill our bombshells with alternate copies of the Cambridge Platform and the Thirty-nine Articles, which would produce a mixture of the highest explosive power, and to wrap every one of our cannon-balls in a leaf of the New Testament, the reading of which is denied to those who sit in the darkness of Popery. Those iron evangelists would thus be able to disseminate vital religion and Gospel truth in quarters inaccessible to the ordinary missionary. I have seen lads, unimpregnate with the more sublimated punctiliousness of Walton, secure pickerel, taking their unwary *siesta* beneath the lily-pads too nigh the surface, with a gun and small shot. Why not, then, since gunpowder was unknown in the time of the Apostles (not to enter here upon the question whether it were discovered before that period by the Chinese), suit our metaphor to the age in which we live, and say *shooters* as well as *fishers* of men?

I do much fear that we shall be seized now and then with a Protestant fervour, as long as we have neighbour Naboths whose wallowings in Papistical mire excite our horror in exact proportion to the size and desirableness of their vineyards. Yet I rejoice that some earnest Protestants have been made by this war,—I mean those who protested against it. Fewer they were than I could wish, for one might imagine

America to have been colonised by a tribe of those nondescript African animals the Aye-Ayes, so difficult a word is *No* to us all. There is some malformation or defect of the vocal organs, which either prevents our uttering it at all, or gives it so thick a pronunciation as to be unintelligible. A mouth filled with the national pudding, or watering in expectation thereof, is wholly incompetent to this refractory monosyllable. An abject and herpetic Public Opinion is the Pope, the Anti-Christ, for us to protest against *e corde cordium.* And by what College of Cardinals is this our God's-vicar, our binder and looser, elected? Very like, by the sacred conclave of Tag, Rag, and Bobtail, in the gracious atmosphere of the grog-shop. Yet it is of this that we must all be puppets. This thumps the pulpit-cushion, this guides the editor's pen, this wags the senator's tongue. This decides what Scriptures are canonical, and shuffles Christ away into the Apocrypha. According to that sentence fathered upon Solon, Οὕτω δημόσιον κακὸν ἔρχεται οἴκαδ' ἑκάστῳ. This unclean spirit is skilful to assume various shapes. I have known it to enter my own study and nudge my elbow of a Saturday, under the semblance of a wealthy member of my congregation. It were a great blessing, if every particular of what in the sum we call popular sentiment could carry about the name of its manufacturer stamped legibly upon it. I gave a stab under the fifth rib to that pestilent fallacy,—" Our country, right or wrong,"—by tracing its original to a speech of Ensign Cilley at a dinner of the Bungtown Fencibles.—H. W.]

No. III.

WHAT MR. ROBINSON THINKS.

[A few remarks on the following verses will not be out of place. The satire in them was not meant to have any personal, but only a general, application. Of the gentleman upon whose letter they were intended as a commentary Mr. Biglow had never heard, till he saw the letter itself. The position of the satirist is oftentimes one which he would not have chosen, had the election been left to himself. In attacking bad principles, he is obliged to select some individual who has made himself their exponent, and in whom they are impersonate, to the end that what he says may not, through ambiguity, be dissipated *tenues in auras.* For what says Seneca? *Longum iter per præcepta, breve et efficace per exempla.* A bad principle is comparatively harmless while it continues to be an abstraction, nor can the general mind comprehend it fully till it is printed in that large type which all men can read at sight, namely, the life and character, the sayings and doings, of particular persons. It is one of the cunningest fetches of Satan, that he never exposes himself directly to our arrows, but, still dodging behind this neighbour or that acquaintance, compels us to wound him through them, if at all. He holds our affections as hostages, the while he patches up a truce with our conscience.

Meanwhile, let us not forget that the aim of the true satirist is not to be severe upon persons, but only upon falsehood, and, as Truth and Falsehood start from the same point, and sometimes even go along together for a little way, his business is to follow the path of the latter after it diverges, and to show her floundering in the bog at the end of it. Truth is quite beyond the reach of satire. There is so brave a simplicity in her, that she can no more be made ridiculous than an oak or a pine. The danger of the satirist is, that continual use may deaden his sensibility to the force of language. He becomes more and more liable to strike harder than he knows or intends. He may be careful to put on his boxing-gloves, and yet forget that the older they grow the more plainly may the knuckles inside be felt. Moreover, in the heat of contest, the eye is insensibly drawn to the crown of victory, whose tawdry tinsel glitters through that dust of the ring which obscures Truth's wreath of simple leaves. I have sometimes thought that my young friend, Mr. Biglow, needed a monitory hand laid on his arm,—*aliquid sufflaminandus erat.* I have never thought it good husbandry to water the tender plants of reform with *aqua fortis*, yet, where so much is to do in the beds, he were a sorry gardener who should wage a whole day's war with an iron scuffle on those ill weeds that make the garden-walks of life unsightly, when a sprinkle of Attic salt will wither them up. *Est ars etiam maledicendi*, says Scaliger, and truly it is a hard thing to say where the graceful gentleness of the lamb merges in downright sheepishness. We may conclude with worthy and wise Dr. Fuller, that "one may be a lamb in private wrongs, but in hearing general affronts to goodness they are asses which are not lions."—H. W.]

Guvener B. is a sensible man;
  He stays to his home an' looks arter his folks;
He draws his furrer ez straight ez he can,
  An' into nobody's tater-patch pokes;
          But John P.
          Robinson he
    Sez he wunt vote fer Guvener B.

My! aint it terrible? Wut shall we du?
  We can't never choose him, o' course,—thet's flat;
Guess we shall hev to come round (don't you?),
  An' go in for thunder an' guns, an' all that;
          Fer John P.
          Robinson he
    Sez he wunt vote fer Guvener B.

Gineral C. is a dreffle smart man:
  He's ben on all sides thet gives places or pelf;
But consistency still wuz a part of his plan,—
  He's ben true to *one* party,—an' thet is himself;—
          So John P.
          Robinson he
    Sez he shall vote fer Gineral C.

Gineral C. he goes in fer the war;
  He don't vally principle more'n an old cud;
What did God make us raytional creeturs fer,
  But glory an' gunpowder, plunder an' blood?
          So John P.
          Robinson he
    Sez he shall vote fer Gineral C.

We were gittin' on nicely up here to our village,
  With good old idees o' wut's right an' wut aint,
We kind o' thought Christ went agin war an' pillage,
  An' thet eppyletts worn't the best mark of a saint;
      But John P.
      Robinson he
  Sez this kind o' thing's an exploded idee.

The side of our country must ollers be took,
  An' Presidunt Polk, you know, *he* is our country;
An' the angel thet writes all our sins in a book
  Puts the *debit* to him, an' to us the *per contry;*
      An' John P.
      Robinson he
  Sez this is his view o' the thing to a T.

Parson Wilbur he calls all these argimunts lies;
  Sez they're nothin' on airth but jest *fee, faw, fum;*
An' thet all this big talk of our destinies
  Is half on it ignorance, an' t'other half rum;
      But John P.
      Robinson he
  Sez it ain't no sech thing; an', of course, so must we.

Parson Wilbur sez *he* never heerd in his life
  Thet th' Apostles rigged out in their swaller-tail coats,
An' marched round in front of a drum an' a fife,
  To git some on 'em office, an' some on 'em votes;
      But John P.
      Robinson he
  Sez they didn't know everythin' down in Judee.

Wal, it's a marcy we've gut folks to tell us
  The rights an' the wrongs o' these matters, I vow,—
God sends country lawyers, an' other wise fellers,
  To start the world's team wen it gits in a slough;
      Fer John P.
      Robinson he
  Sez the world'll go right, ef he hollers out Gee!

[The attentive reader will doubtless have perceived in the foregoing poem an allusion to that pernicious sentiment,—" Our country, right or wrong." It is an abuse of language to call a certain portion of land, much more certain personages, elevated for the time being to high station, our country. I would not sever nor loosen a single one of those ties by which we are united to the spot of our birth, nor minish by a tittle the respect due to the Magistrate. I love our own Bay State too well to do the one, and as for the other, I have myself for nigh forty years exercised, however unworthily, the function of Justice of the Peace, having been called thereto by the unsolicited kindness of that most excellent man and upright patriot, Caleb Strong. *Patriæ fumus igne alieno luculentior* is best qualified with this,—*Ubi libertas, ibi patria.* We are inhabitants of two worlds, and owe a double, but not a divided, allegiance. In virtue of our clay, this little ball of earth exacts a certain loyalty of us, while, in our capacity as spirits, we are admitted citizens of an invisible and holier fatherland. There is a patriotism of the soul whose claim absolves us from our other and terrene fealty. Our true country is that ideal realm which we represent to ourselves under the names of religion, duty, and the like. Our terrestrial organisations are but far-off approaches to so fair a model, and all they are verily traitors who resist not any attempt to divert them from this their original intendment. When, therefore, one would have us to fling up our caps and shout with the multitude,—" *Our country, however bounded!* " he demands of us that we sacrifice the larger to the less, the higher to the lower, and that we yield to the imaginary claims of a few acres of soil our duty and privilege as liegemen of Truth. Our true country is bounded on the north and the south, on the east and the west, by Justice, and when she oversteps that invisible boundary-line by so much as a hair's-breadth, she ceases to be our mother, and chooses rather to be looked upon *quasi noverca.* That is a hard choice when our earthly love of country calls upon us to tread one path and our duty points us to another. We must make as noble and becoming an election as did Penelope between Icarius and Ulysses. Veiling our faces, we must take silently the hand of Duty to follow her.

Shortly after the publication of the foregoing poem there appeared some comments upon it in one of the public prints which seemed to call for animadversion. I accordingly addressed to Mr. Buckingham, of the *Boston Courier*, the following letter :—

"JAALAM, November 4, 1847.

" *To the Editor of the Courier:*

"RESPECTED SIR,—Calling at the post-office this morning, our worthy and efficient postmaster offered for my perusal a paragraph in the *Boston Morning Post* of the 3d instant, wherein certain effusions of the pastoral muse are attributed to the pen of Mr. James Russell Lowell. For aught I know or can affirm to the contrary, this Mr. Lowell may be a very deserving person and a youth of parts (though I have seen verses of his which I could never rightly understand) ; and if he be such, he, I am certain, as well as I, would be free from any proclivity to appropriate to himself whatever of credit (or discredit) may honestly belong to another. I am confident that, in penning these few lines, I am only forestalling a disclaimer from that young gentleman, whose silence hitherto, when rumour pointed to himward, has excited in my bosom mingled emotions of sorrow and surprise. Well may my young parishioner, Mr. Biglow, exclaim with the poet—

' Sic vos non vobis,' etc. ;

though, in saying this, I would not convey the impression that he is a proficient in the Latin tongue,—the tongue, I might add, of a Horace and a Tully.

"Mr. B. does not employ his pen, I can safely say, for any lucre of worldly gain, or to be exalted by the carnal plaudits of men, *digito monstrari*, etc. He does not wait upon Providence for mercies, and in his heart mean *merces*. But I should esteem myself as verily deficient in my duty (who am his friend and in some unworthy sort his spiritual *fidus Achates*, etc.) if I did not step forward to claim for him whatever measure of applause might be assigned to him by the judicious.

"If this were a fitting occasion, I might venture here a brief dissertation touching the manner and kind of my young friend's poetry. But I dubitate whether this abstruser sort of speculation (though enlivened by some apposite instances from Aristophanes) would sufficiently interest your oppidan readers. As regards their satirical tone, and their plainness of speech, I will only say that, in my pastoral experience, I have found that the Arch-Enemy loves nothing better than to be treated as a religious, moral, and intellectual being, and that there is no *Apage Sathanas!* so potent as ridicule. But it is a kind of weapon that must have a button of good-nature on the point of it.

"The productions of Mr. B. have been stigmatised in some quarters as unpatriotic; but I can vouch that he loves his native soil with that hearty, though discriminating, attachment which springs from an intimate social intercourse of many years' standing. In the ploughing season no one has a deeper share in the well-being of the country than he. If Dean Swift were right in saying that he who makes two blades of grass grow where one grew before confers a greater benefit on the state than he who taketh a city, Mr. B. might exhibit a fairer claim to the Presidency than General Scott himself. I think that some of those disinterested lovers of the hard-handed democracy, whose fingers have never touched any thing rougher than the dollars of our common country, would hesitate to compare palms with him. It would do your heart good, respected Sir, to see that young man mow. He cuts a cleaner and wider swarth than any in this town.

"But it is time for me to be at my Post. It is very clear that my young friend's shot has struck the lintel, for the Post is shaken (Amos ix. 1). The editor of that paper is a strenuous advocate of the Mexican war, and a colonel, as I am given to understand. I presume that, being necessarily absent in Mexico, he has left his journal in some less judicious hands. At any rate, the Post has been too swift on this occasion. It could hardly have cited a more incontrovertible line from any poem than that which it has selected for animadversion, namely—

'We kind o' thought Christ went agin war an' pillage.'

"If the Post maintains the converse of this proposition, it can hardly be considered as a safe guide-post for the moral and religious portions of its party, however many other excellent qualities of a post it may be blessed with. There is a sign in London on which is painted,—'The Green Man.' It would do very well as a portrait of any individual who would support so unscriptural a thesis. As regards the language of the line in question, I am bold to say that He who readeth the hearts of men will not account any dialect unseemly which conveys a sound and pious sentiment. I could wish that such sentiments were more common, however uncouthly expressed. Saint Ambrose affirms that *veritas a quocunque* (why not, then, *quomodocunque?*) *dicatur, a spiritu sancto est.* Digest also this of Baxter :—' The plainest words are the most profitable oratory in the weightiest matters.'

" When the paragraph in question was shown to Mr. Biglow, the only part of it which seemed to give him any dissatisfaction was that which classed him with the Whig party. He says that, if resolutions are a nourishing kind of diet, that party must be in a very hearty and flourishing condition ; for that they have quietly eaten more good ones of their own baking than he could have conceived to be possible without repletion. He has been for some years past (I regret to say) an ardent opponent of those sound doctrines of protective policy which form so prominent a portion of the creed of that party. I confess that, in some discussions which I have had with him on this point in my study, he has displayed a vein of obstinacy which I had not hitherto detected in his composition. He is also (*horresco referens*) infected in no small measure with the peculiar notions of a print called the *Liberator*, whose heresies I take every proper opportunity of combating, and of which, I thank God, I have never read a single line.

" I did not see Mr. B.'s verses until they appeared in print, and there *is* certainly one thing in them which I consider highly improper. I allude to the personal references to myself by name. To confer notoriety on an humble individual who is labouring quietly in his vocation, and who keeps his cloth as free as he can from the dust of the political arena (though *væ mihi si non evangelizavero*), is no doubt an indecorum. The sentiments which he attributes to me I will not deny to be mine. They were embodied, though in a different form, in a discourse preached upon the last day of public fasting, and were acceptable to my entire people (of whatever political views), except the postmaster, who dissented *ex officio.* I observe that you sometimes devote a portion of your paper to a religious summary. I should be well pleased to furnish a copy of my discourse for insertion in this department of your instructive journal. By omitting the advertisements it might easily be got within the limits of a single number, and I venture to insure you the sale of some scores of copies in this town. I will cheerfully render myself responsible for ten. It might possibly be advantageous to issue it as an *extra.* But perhaps you will not esteem it an object, and I will not press it. My offer does not spring from any weak desire of seeing my name in print ; for I can enjoy this satisfaction at any time by turning to the Triennial Catalogue of the University, where it also possesses that added emphasis of Italics with which those of my calling are distinguished.

"I would simply add, that I continue to fit ingenuous youth for college, and that I have two spacious and airy sleeping apartments at this moment unoccupied. *Ingenuas didicisse*, etc. Terms, which vary according to the circumstances of the parents, may be known on application to me by letter, post paid. In all cases the lad will be expected to fetch his own towels. This rule, Mrs. W. desires me to add, has no exceptions.

"Respectfully, your obedient servant,

"HOMER WILBUR, A.M.

"P.S.—Perhaps the last paragraph may look like an attempt to obtain the insertion of my circular gratuitously. If it should appear to you in that light, I desire that you would erase it, or charge for it at the usual rates, and deduct the amount from the proceeds in your hands from the sale of my discourse, when it shall be printed. My circular is much longer and more explicit, and will be forwarded without charge to any who may desire it. It has been very neatly executed on a letter sheet, by a very deserving printer who attends upon my ministry, and is a creditable specimen of the typographic art. I have one hung over my mantelpiece in a neat frame, where it makes a beautiful and appropriate ornament, and balances the profile of Mrs. W., cut with her toe by the young lady born without arms.—H. W."

I have in the foregoing letter mentioned General Scott in connection with the Presidency, because I have been given to understand that he has blown to pieces and otherwise caused to be destroyed more Mexicans than any other commander. His claim would therefore be deservedly considered the strongest. Until accurate returns of the Mexicans killed, wounded, and maimed be obtained, it will be difficult to settle these nice points of precedence. Should it prove that any other officer has been more meritorious and destructive than General S., and has thereby rendered himself more worthy of the confidence and support of the conservative portion of our community, I shall cheerfully insert his name, instead of that of General S., in a future edition. It may be thought, likewise, that General S. has invalidated his claims by too much attention to the decencies of apparel, and the habits belonging to a gentleman. These abstruser points of statesmanship are beyond my scope. I wonder not that successful military achievement should attract the admiration of the multitude. Rather do I rejoice with wonder to behold how rapidly this sentiment is losing its hold upon the popular mind. It is related of Thomas Warton, the second of that honoured name who held the office of Poetry Professor at Oxford, that, when one wished to find him, being absconded, as was his wont, in some obscure alehouse, he was counselled to traverse the city with a drum and fife, the sound of which inspiring music would be sure to draw the Doctor from his retirement into the street. We are all more or less bitten with this martial insanity. *Nescio qua dulcedine . . . cunctos ducit.* I confess to some infection of that itch myself. When I see a Brigadier-General maintaining his insecure elevation in the saddle under the severe fire of the training-field, and when I remember that some military enthusiasts, through haste, inexperience, or an over-desire to lend reality to those fictitious combats, will sometimes discharge their ramrods, I cannot but admire, while I deplore, the mistaken devotion of those heroic officers. *Semel insanivimus omnes.* I was myself, during the late war with Great Britain, chaplain of a regiment which was fortunately never called to active military duty. I mention this circumstance with regret rather than pride. Had I been summoned to actual warfare, I trust that I might have been strengthened to bear myself after the manner of that reverend father in our New England Israel, Dr. Benjamin Colman, who, as we are told in Turell's life of him, when the vessel in which he had taken passage for England was attacked by a French privateer, " fought like a philosopher and a Christian, . . . and prayed all the while he charged and fired." As this note is already long, I shall not here enter upon a discussion of the question, whether Christians may lawfully be soldiers. I think it sufficiently evident that, during the first two centuries of the Christian era, at least, the two professions were esteemed incompatible. Consult Jortin on this head.—H. W.]

———————

No. IV.

REMARKS OF INCREASE D. O'PHACE, ESQUIRE, AT AN
EXTRUMPERY CAUCUS IN STATE STREET, REPORTED
BY MR. H. BIGLOW.

[The ingenious reader will at once understand that no such speech
as the following was ever *totidem verbis* pronounced. But there are
simpler and less guarded wits, for the satisfying of which such an
explanation may be needful. For there are certain invisible lines,
which as Truth successively overpasses, she becomes Untruth to one and
another of us, as a large river, flowing from one kingdom into another,
sometimes takes a new name, albeit the waters undergo no change,
how small soever. There is, moreover, a truth of fiction more veracious
than the truth of fact, as that of the poet, which represents to us things
and events as they ought to be, rather than servilely copies them as
they are imperfectly imaged in the crooked and smoky glass of our
mundane affairs. It is this which makes the speech of Antonius,
though originally spoken in no wider a forum than the brain of Shak-
speare, more historically valuable than that other which Appian has
reported, by as much as the understanding of the Englishman was
more comprehensive than that of the Alexandrian. Mr. Biglow, in the
present instance, has only made use of a licence assumed by all the
historians of antiquity, who put into the mouths of various characters
such words as seem to them most fitting to the occasion and to the
speaker. If it be objected that no such oration could ever have been
delivered, I answer that there are few assemblages for speech-making
which do not better deserve the title of *Parliamentum Indoctorum*
than did the sixth Parliament of Henry the Fourth, and that men still
continue to have as much faith in the Oracle of Fools as ever
Pantagruel had. Howell, in his letters, recounts a merry tale of a
certain ambassador of Queen Elizabeth, who, having written two
letters, one to her Majesty and the other to his wife, directed them at
cross-purposes, so that the Queen was beducked and bedeared, and
requested to send a change of hose, and the wife was beprincessed and
otherwise unwontedly besuperlatived, till the one feared for the wits of
her ambassador, and the other for those of her husband. In like
manner it may be presumed that our speaker has misdirected some of
his thoughts, and given to the whole theatre what he would have

wished to confide only to a select auditory at the back of the curtain. For it is seldom that we can get any frank utterance from men who address, for the most part, a Buncombe either in this world or the next. As for their audiences, it may be truly said of our people that they enjoy one political institution in common with the ancient Athenians: I mean a certain profitless kind of *ostracism*, wherewith, nevertheless, they seem hitherto well enough content. For in Presidential elections, and other affairs of the sort, whereas I observe that the *oysters* fall to the lot of comparatively few, the *shells* (such as the privileges of voting as they are told to do by the *ostrivori* aforesaid, and of huzzaing at public meetings) are very liberally distributed among the people, as being their prescriptive and quite sufficient portion.

The occasion of the speech is supposed to be Mr. Palfrey's refusal to vote for the Whig candidate for the Speakership.—H. W.]

No? Hez he? He haint, though? Wut? Voted agin him?
Ef the bird of our country could ketch him, she'd skin him;
I seem's though I see her, with wrath in each quill,
Like a chancery lawyer, afilin' her bill,
An' grindin' her talents ez sharp as all nater,
To pounce like a writ on the back o' the traitor.
Forgive me, my friends, ef I seem to be het,
But a crisis like this must with vigour be met;
Wen an Arnold the star-spangled banner bestains,
Holl Fourth o' Julys seem to bile in my veins.

Who ever'd ha' thought sech a pisonous rig
Would be run by a chap thet wuz chose fer a Wig?
"We knowed wut his principles wuz 'fore we sent him?"
Wut wuz ther in them from this vote to prevent him?
A marciful Providunce fashioned us holler
O' purpose thet we might our principles swaller;
It can hold any quantity on 'em, the belly can,
An' bring 'em up ready fer use like the pelican,
Or more like the kangaroo, who (wich is stranger)
Puts her family into her pouch wen there's danger.

Aint principle precious? then, who's goin' to use it
When there's resk o' some chap's gittin' up to abuse it?
I can't tell the wy on't, but nothin' is *so* sure
Ez thet principle kind o' gits spiled by exposure;[1]
A man that lets all sorts o' folks get a sight on't
Ough' to hev it all took right away, every mite on't;
Ef he can't keep it all to himself wen it's wise to,
He aint one it's fit to trust nothin' so nice to.
Besides, ther's a wonderful power in latitude
To shift a man's morril relations an' attitude;
Some flossifers think thet a fakkilty's granted
The minnit it's proved to be thoroughly wanted,
Thet a change o' demand makes a change o' condition,
An' thet everythin' 's nothin' except by position;
Ez, fer instance, thet rubber-trees fust begun bearin'
Wen p'litikle conshunces come into wearin',—
Thet the fears of a monkey, whose holt chanced to fail,
Drawed the vertibry out to a prehensile tail;
So, wen one's chose to Congriss, ez soon ez he's in it,
A collar grows right round his neck in a minnit,
An' sartin it is thet a man cannot be strict
In bein' himself, wen he gits to the Deestrict,
Fer a coat thet sets wal here in ole Massachusetts,
Wen it gits on to Washinton, somehow askew sets.

[1] The speaker is of a different mind from Tully, who, in his recently discovered tractate, *De Republica,* tells us, *Nec vero habere virtutem satis est, quasi artem aliquam, nisi utare,* and from our Milton, who says,— "I cannot praise a fugitive and cloistered virtue, unexercised and unbreathed, that never sallies out and sees her adversary, but slinks out of the race where that immortal garland is to be run for, *not without dust and heat.*"—*Areop.* He had taken the words out of the Roman's mouth, without knowing it, and might well exclaim with Austin (if a saint's name may stand sponsor for a curse), *Pereant qui ante nos nostra dixerint!*—H. W.

Resolves, do you say, o' the Springfield Convention?
Thet's percisely the pint I was goin' to mention;
Resolves air a thing we most gen'ally keep ill,
They're a cheap kind o' dust fer the eyes o' the people;
A parcel o' delligits jest get together
An' chat fer a spell o' the crops an' the weather,
Then, comin' to order, they squabble awile
An' let off the speeches they're ferful 'll spile;
Then—Resolve,—Thet we wunt hev an inch o' slave terri-
    tory;
Thet President Polk's holl perceedins air very tory;
Thet the war is a damned war, an' them thet enlist in it
Should hev a cravat with a dreffle tight twist in it;
Thet the war is a war fer the spreadin' o' slavery;
Thet our army desarves our best thanks fer their bravery;
Thet we're the original friends o' the nation,
All the rest air a paltry an' base fabrication;
Thet we highly respect Messrs. A, B, an' C,
An' ez deeply despise Messrs. E, F, an' G.
In this way they go to the eend o' the chapter,
An' then they bust out in a kind of a raptur
About their own vartoo, an' folks's stone-blindness
To the men thet 'ould actilly do 'em a kindness,—
The American eagle,—the Pilgrims thet landed,—
Till on ole Plymouth Rock they git finally stranded.
Wal, the people they listen and say, "Thet's the ticket;
Ez fer Mexico, t'aint no great glory to lick it,
But 'twould be a darned shame to go pullin' o' triggers
To extend the aree of abusin' the niggers."
So they march in percessions, an' git up hooraws,
An' tramp thru the mud fer the good o' the cause,
An' think they're a kind o' fulfillin' the prophecies,
Wen they're on'y jest changin' the holders of offices;

Ware A sot afore, B is comf'tably seated,
One humbug's victor'ous, an' t'other defeated,
Each honnable doughface gits jest wut he axes,
An' the people—their annooal soft-sodder an' taxes.

Now, to keep unimpaired all these glorious feeturs
Thet characterize morril an' reasonin' creeturs,
Thet give every paytriot all he can cram,
Thet oust the untrustworthy Presidunt Flam,
And stick honest Presidunt Sham in his place,
To the manifest gain o' the holl human race,
An' to some indervidgewals on't in partickler,
Who love Public Opinion an' know how to tickle her,
I say thet a party with great aims like these
Must stick jest ez close ez a hive full o' bees.

I'm willin' a man should go tollable strong
Agin wrong in the abstract, fer thet kind o' wrong
Is ollers unpop'lar an' never gits pitied,
Because it's a crime no one never committed;
But he mus'n't be hard on partickler sins,
Coz then he'll be kickin' the people's own shins;
On'y look at the Demmercrats, see wut they've done
Jest simply by stickin' together like fun;
They've sucked us right into a mis'able war
Thet no one on airth aint responsible for;
They've run us a hundred cool millions in debt,
(An' fer Demmercrat Horners ther's good plums left yet;)
They talk agin tayriffs, but act fer a high one,
An' so coax all parties to build up their Zion;
To the people they're ollers ez slick ez molasses,
An' butter their bread on both sides with The Masses,
Half o' whom they've persuaded, by way of a joke,
Thet Washinton's mantelpiece fell upon Polk.

Now all o' these blessin's the Wigs might enjoy,
Ef they'd gumption enough the right means to imploy;[1]
Fer the silver spoon born in Dermocracy's mouth
Is a kind of a scringe thet they hev to the South;
Their masters can cuss 'em an' kick 'em an' wale 'em,
An' they notice it less 'an the ass did to Balaam;
In this way they screw into second-rate offices
Wich the slaveholder thinks 'ould substract too much off
    his ease;
The file-leaders, I mean, du, fer they, by their wiles,
Unlike the old viper, grow fat on their files.
Wal, the Wigs hev been tryin' to grab all this prey frum 'em
An' to hook this nice spoon o' good fortin' away frum 'em,
An' they might ha' succeeded, ez likely ez not,
In lickin' the Demmercrats all round the lot,
Ef it warn't thet, wile all faithful Wigs were their knees on,
Some stuffy old codger would holler out,—"Treason!
You must keep a sharp eye on a dog thet hez bit you once,
An' *I* aint agoin' to cheat my constitoounts,"—
Wen every fool knows thet a man represents
Not the fellers thet sent him, but them on the fence,—
Impartially ready to jump either side
An' make the fust use of a turn o' the tide,—
The waiters on Providunce here in the city,
Who compose wut they call a State Centerl Committy.
Constitoounts air hendy to help a man in,
But arterwards don't weigh the heft of a pin.
Wy, the people can't all live on Uncle Sam's pus,
So they've nothin' to du with't fer better or wus:
It's the folks thet air kind o' brought up to depend on't
Thet hev any consarn in't, an' thet is the end on't.

[1] That was a pithy saying of Persius, and fits our politicians without
a wrinkle, *Magister artis, ingeniique largitor venter.*—H. W.

Now here wuz New England ahevin' the honour
Of a chance at the Speakership showered upon her;—
Do you say,—"She don't want no more Speakers, but
    fewer;
She's hed plenty o' them, wut she wants is a *doer*"?
Fer the matter o' thet, it's notorous in town
Thet her own representatives du her quite brown.
But thet's nothin' to du with it; wut right hed Palfrey
To mix himself up with fanatical small fry?
Warn't we gittin' on prime with our hot an' cold blowin'
Acondemnin' the war wilst we kep' it agoin'?
We'd assumed with gret skill a commandin' position,
On this side or thet, no one couldn't tell wich one,
So, wutever side wipped, we'd a chance at the plunder,
An' could sue fer infringin' our paytented thunder;
We were ready to vote fer whoever wuz eligible,
Ef on all pints at issoo he'd stay unintelligible.
Wal, sposin' we hed to gulp down our perfessions,
We were ready to come out next mornin' with fresh
    ones;
Besides, ef we did, 'twas our business alone,
Fer couldn't we du wut we would with our own?
An' ef a man can, wen pervisions hev riz so,
Eat up his own words, it's a marcy it is so.

Wy, these chaps frum the North, with back-bones to 'em,
    darn 'em,
'Ould be wuth more 'an Gennle Tom Thumb is to
    Barnum;
Ther's enough thet to office on this very plan grow,
By exhibitin' how very small a man can grow;
But an M.C. frum here ollers hastens to state he
Belongs to the order called invertebraty,

Wence some gret filologists judge primy fashy
Thet M.C. is M.T. by paronomashy ;
An' these few exceptions air *loosus naytury*
Folks 'ould put down their quarters to stare at, like fury.

It's no use to open the door o' success,
Ef a member can bolt so fer nothin' or less ;
Wy, all o' them grand constitootional pillers
Our forefathers fetched with 'em over the billers,
Them pillers the people so soundly hev slep' on,
Wile to slav'ry, invasion, an' debt they were swep' on,
Wile our Destiny higher an' higher kep' mountin',
(Though **I** guess folks 'll stare wen she hends her account
        in,)
Ef members in this way go kickin' agin 'em,
They wunt hev so much ez a feather left in 'em.

An', ez fer this Palfrey,[1] we thought wen we'd gut him in
He'd go kindly in wutever harness we put him in ;
Supposin' we *did* know thet he wuz a peace man ?
Doos he think he can be Uncle Sammle's policeman,
An' wen Sam gits tipsy an' kicks up a riot,
Lead him off to the lockup to snooze till he's quiet ?
Wy, the war is a war thet true paytriots can bear, ef
It leads to the fat promised land of a taryiff ;
We don't go an' fight it, nor aint to be driv on,
Nor Demmercrats nuther, thut hev wut to live on ;
Ef it aint jest the thing thet's well pleasin' to God,
It makes us thought highly on elsewhere abroad ;
The Rooshian black eagle looks blue in his eerie
An' shakes both his heads wen he hears o' Monteery ;

[1] There is truth yet in this of Juvenal,—
        " Dat veniam corvis, vexat censura columbas."

In the Tower Victory sets, all of a fluster,
An' reads, with locked doors, how we won Cherry Buster;
An' old Philip Lewis—thet come an' kep' school here
Fer the mere sake o' scornin' his ryalist ruler
On the tenderest part of our kings *in futuro*—
Hides his crown underneath an old shut in his bureau,
Breaks off in his brags to a suckle o' merry kings,
How he often hed hided young native Amerrikins,
An', turnin' quite faint in the midst of his fooleries,
Sneaks downstairs to bolt the front door o' the Tooleries.[1]

You say,—"We'd ha' scared 'em by growin' in peace,
A plaguy sight more then by bobberies like these"?
Who is it dares say thet "our naytional eagle
Wun't much longer be classed with the birds thet air regal,
Coz theirn be hooked beaks, an' she, arter this slaughter,
'll bring back a bill ten times longer'n she ough' to"?
Wut's your name? Come, I see ye, you upcountry feller,
You've put me out severil times with your beller;

[1] Jortin is willing to allow of other miracles besides those recorded in Holy Writ, and why not of other prophecies? It is granting too much to Satan to suppose him, as divers of the learned have done, the inspirer of the ancient oracles. Wiser, I esteem it, to give chance the credit of the successful ones. What is said here of Louis Philippe was verified in some of its minute particulars within a few months' time. Enough to have made the fortune of Delphi or Hammon, and no thanks to Beelzebub neither! That of Seneca in Medea will suit here:—

> " Rapida fortuna ac levis
> Præcepsque regno eripuit, exsilio dedit."

Let us allow, even to richly deserved misfortune, our commiseration, and be not over-hasty meanwhile in our censure of the French people, left for the first time to govern themselves, remembering that wise sentence of Æschylus,—

> Ἅπας δὲ τραχὺς ὅστις ἂν νέον κρατῇ.

H. W.

Out with it! Wut? Biglow? I say nothin' furder,
Thet feller would like nothin' better'n a murder;
He's a traiter, blasphemer, an' wut ruther worse is,
He puts all his ath'ism in dreffle bad verses;
Socity aint safe till sech monsters air out on it,
Refer to the Post, ef you hev the least doubt on it;
Wy, he goes agin war, agin indirect taxes,
Agin sellin' wild lands 'cept to settlers with axes,
Agin holdin' o' slaves, though he knows it's the corner
Our libbarty rests on, the mis'able scorner!
In short, he would wholly upset with his ravages
All thet keeps us above the brute critters an' savages,
An' pitch into all kinds o' briles an' confusions
The holl of our civilised, free institutions;
He writes fer thet ruther unsafe print, the Courier,
An' likely ez not hez a squintin' to Foorier;
I'll be ——, thet is, I mean I'll be blest,
Ef I hark to a word frum so noted a pest;
I shan't talk with *him*, my religion's too fervent.—
Good mornin', my friends, I'm your most humble servant.

[Into the question, whether the ability to express ourselves in articulate language has been productive of more good or evil, I shall not here enter at large. The two faculties of speech and speech-making are wholly diverse in their natures. By the first we make ourselves intelligible, by the last unintelligible, to our fellows. It has not seldom occurred to me (noting how in our national legislature every-thing runs to talk, as lettuces, if the season or the soil be unpropitious, shoot up lankly to seed, instead of forming handsome heads) that Babel was the first Congress, the earliest mill erected for the manufacture of gabble. In these days, what with Town Meetings, School Committees, Boards (lumber) of one kind and another, Congresses, Parliaments, Diets, Indian Councils, Palavers, and the like, there is scarce a village which has not its factories of this description driven by (milk-and-) water power. I cannot conceive the confusion of tongues to have been the curse of Babel, since I esteem my ignorance of other languages as a kind of Martello-tower, in which I am safe from the furious bombardments of foreign garrulity. For this reason I have ever preferred the study of the dead languages, those primitive formations being Ararats upon whose silent peaks I sit secure and watch this new deluge without fear, though it rain figures (*simulacra,* semblances) of speech forty days and nights together, as it not uncommonly happens. Thus is my coat, as it were, without buttons by which any but a vernacular wild bore can seize me. Is it not possible that the Shakers may intend to convey a quiet reproof and hint, in fastening their outer garments with hooks and eyes?

This reflection concerning Babel, which I find in no Commentary, was first thrown upon my mind when an excellent deacon of my congregation (being infected with the Second Advent delusion) assured me that he had received a first instalment of the gift of tongues, as a small earnest of larger possessions in the like kind to follow. For, of a truth, I could not reconcile it with my ideas of the Divine justice and mercy that the single wall which protected people of other languages from the incursions of this otherwise well-meaning propagandist should be broken down.

In reading Congressional debates, I have fancied that, after the subsidence of those painful buzzings in the brain which result from such exercises, I detected a slender residuum of valuable information. I made the discovery that *nothing* takes longer in the saying than anything else, for, as *ex nihilo nihil fit,* so from one polypus *nothing* any number of similar ones may be produced. I would recommend to the attention of *vivâ voce* debaters and controversialists the admirable example of the monk Copres, who, in the fourth century, stood for half-an-hour in the midst of a great fire, and thereby silenced a Manichæan antagonist who had less of the salamander in him. As for those who quarrel in print, I have no concern with them here, since the eyelids are a divinely-granted shield against all such. Moreover, I have observed in many modern books that the printed portion is becoming gradually smaller, and the number of blank or fly-leaves (as they are called) greater. Should this fortunate tendency of literature continue, books will grow more valuable from year to year, and the whole Serbonian bog yield to the advances of firm arable land.

The sagacious Lacedæmonians hearing that Tesephone had bragged that he could talk all day long on any given subject, made no more ado, but forthwith banished him, whereby they supplied him a topic and at the same time took care that his experiment upon it should be tried out of ear-shot.

I have wondered, in the Representatives' Chamber of our own Commonwealth, to mark how little impression seemed to be produced by that emblematic fish suspended over the heads of the members. Our wiser ancestors, no doubt, hung it there as being the animal which the Pythagoreans reverenced for its silence, and which certainly in that particular does not so well merit the epithet *cold-blooded*, by which naturalists distinguish it, as certain bipeds, afflicted with ditch-water on the brain, who take occasion to tap themselves in Fanueil Halls, meeting-houses, and other places of public resort.—H. W.]

No. V.

THE DEBATE IN THE SENNIT.

SOT TO A NUSRY RHYME.

[The incident which gave rise to the debate satirised in the following verses was the unsuccessful attempt of Drayton and Sayres to give freedom to seventy men and women, fellow-beings and fellow-Christians. Had Tripoli, instead of Washington, been the scene of this undertaking, the unhappy leaders in it would have been as secure of the theoretic as they now are of the practical part of martyrdom. I question whether the Dey of Tripoli is blessed with a District Attorney so benighted as ours at the seat of government. Very fitly is he named Key, who would allow himself to be made the instrument of locking the door of hope against sufferers in such a cause. Not all the waters of the ocean can cleanse the vile smutch of the gaoler's fingers from off that little Key *Ahenea clavis*, a brazen Key indeed!

Mr. Calhoun, who is made the chief speaker in this burlesque, seems to think that the light of the nineteenth century is to be put out as soon as he tinkles his little cow-bell curfew. Whenever slavery is touched, he sets up his scarecrow of dissolving the Union. This may do for the North, but I should conjecture that something more than a pumpkin-lantern is required to scare manifest and irretrievable Destiny out of her path. Mr. Calhoun cannot let go the apron-string of the Past. The Past is a good nurse, but we must be weaned from her sooner or later, even though, like Plotinus, we should run home from school to ask the breast, after we are tolerably well-grown youths. It will not do for us to hide our faces in her lap, whenever the strange Future holds out her arms and asks us to come to her.

But we are all alike. We have all heard it said, often enough, that little boys must not play with fire ; and yet, if the matches be taken away from us and put out of reach upon the shelf, we must needs get into our little corner, and scowl and stamp and threaten the dire revenge of going to bed without our supper. The world shall stop till we get our dangerous plaything again. Dame Earth, meanwhile, who has more than enough household matters to mind, goes bustling hither and thither as a hiss or a sputter tells her that this or that kettle of hers is boiling over, and before bedtime we are glad to eat our porridge cold, and gulp down our dignity along with it.

Mr. Calhoun has somehow acquired the name of a great statesman, and, if it be great statesmanship to put lance in rest and run a tilt at the Spirit of the Age with the certainty of being next moment hurled neck and heels into the dust amid universal laughter, he deserves the title. He is the Sir Kay of our modern chivalry. He should remember the old Scandinavian mythus. Thor was the strongest of gods, but he could not wrestle with Time, nor so much as lift up a fold of the great snake which knit the universe together ; and when he smote the Earth, though with his terrible mallet, it was but as if a leaf had fallen. Yet all the while it seemed to Thor that he had only been wrestling with an old woman, striving to lift a cat, and striking a stupid giant on the head.

And in old times, doubtless, the giants *were* stupid, and there was no better sport for the Sir Launcelots and Sir Gawains than to go about cutting off their great blundering heads with enchanted swords. But things have wonderfully changed. It is the giants, nowadays, that have the science and the intelligence, while the chivalrous Don Quixotes of Conservatism still cumber themselves with the clumsy armour of a bygone age. On whirls the restless globe through unsounded time, with its cities and its silences, its births and funerals, half light, half shade, but never wholly dark, and sure to swing round into the happy morning at last. With an involuntary smile, one sees Mr. Calhoun letting slip his pack-thread cable with a crooked pin at the end of it to anchor South Carolina upon the bank and shoal of the Past.—H. W.]

TO MR. BUCKENAM.

MR. EDITER, As i wuz kinder prunin round, in a little nussry sot out a year or 2 a go, the Dbait in the sennit cum inter my mine An so i took & Sot it to wut I call a nussry rime. I hev made sum onnable Gentlemun speak that dident speak in a Kind uv Poetikul lie sense the seeson is dreffle backerd up This way

ewers as ushul
HOSEA BIGLOW.

" HERE we stan' on the Constitution, by thunder!
　It's a fact o' wich ther's bushils o' proofs;
Fer how could we trample on't so, I wonder,
　Ef't worn't thet it's ollers under our hoofs?"
　　Sez John C. Calhoun, sez he;—
　　　" Human rights haint no more
　　　Right to come on this floor,
　　No more'n the man in the moon," sez he.

" The North haint no kind o' bisness with nothin',
　An' you've no idee how much bother it saves;
We aint none riled by their frettin' an' frothin',
　We're *used* to layin' the string on our slaves,"
　　Sez John C. Calhoun, sez he;—
　　　Sez Mister Foote,
　　　" I should like to shoot
　　The holl gang, by the gret horn spoon!" sez he.

" Freedom's Keystone is Slavery, thet ther's no doubt on,
　It's sutthin' thet's—wha' d' ye call it?—divine,—
An' the slaves thet we ollers *make* the most out on
　Air them north o' Mason an' Dixon's line,"

Sez John C. Calhoun, sez he ;—
  "Fer all thet," sez Mangum,
  "'Twould be better to hang 'em,
An' so git red on 'em soon," sez he.

"The mass ough' to labour an' we lay on soffies,
 Thet's the reason I want to spread Freedom's aree ;
It puts all the cunninest on us in office,
 An' reelises our Maker's orig'nal idee,"
  Sez John C. Calhoun, sez he ;—
   "Thet's ez plain," sez Cass,
   "Ez thet some one's an ass,
 It's ez clear ez the sun is at noon," sez he.

"Now don't go to say I'm the friend of oppression,
 But keep all your spare breath fer coolin' your broth,
Fer I ollers hev strove (at least thet's my impression)
 To make cussed free with the rights o' the North,"
  Sez John C. Calhoun, sez he ;—
   "Yes," sez Davis o' Miss.,
   "The perfection o' bliss
 Is in skinnin' thet same old coon," sez he.

"Slavery's a thing thet depends on complexion,
 It's God's law thet fetters on black skins don't
  chafe ;
Ef brains wuz to settle it (horrid reflection !)
 Wich of our onnable body'd be safe ?"
  Sez John C. Calhoun, sez he ;—
   Sez Mister Hannegan,
   Afore he began agin,
 "Thet exception is quite oppertoon," sez he.

" Gen'nle Cass, Sir, you needn't be twitchin' your collar,
   Your merit's quite clear by the dut on your knees,
At the North we don't make no distinctions o' colour;
   You can all take a lick at our shoes wen you please,"
      Sez John C. Calhoun, sez he;—
         Sez Mister Jarnagin,
         "They wunt hev to larn agin,
      They all on 'em know the old toon," sez he.

" The slavery question aint no ways bewilderin'.
   North an' South hev one int'rest, it's plain to a
      glance;
No'thern men, like us patriarchs, don't sell their childrin,
   But they *du* sell themselves, ef they git a good chance,"
      Sez John C. Calhoun, sez he;—
         Sez Atherton here,
         "This is gittin' severe,
      I wish I could dive like a loon," sez he.

" It'll break up the Union, this talk about freedom,
   An' your fact'ry gals (soon ez we split) 'll make head,
An' gittin' some Miss chief or other to lead 'em,
   'll go to work raisin' promiscoous Ned,"
      Sez John C. Calhoun, sez he;—
         "Yes, the North," sez Colquitt,
         "Ef we Southeners all quit,
      Would go down like a busted balloon," sez he.

" Jest look wut is doin', wut annyky's brewin'
   In the beautiful clime o' the olive an' vine,
All the wise aristoxy is tumblin' to ruin,
   An' the sankylots drorin' an' drinkin' their wine,"

Sez John C. Calhoun, sez he ;—
  "Yes," sez Johnson, "in France
  They're beginnin' to dance
Beelzebub's own rigadoon," sez he.

"The South's safe enough, it don't feel a mite skeery,
  Our slaves in their darkness an' dut air tu blest
Not to welcome with proud hallylugers the ery
  Wen our eagle kicks yourn from the naytional nest,"
    Sez John C. Calhoun, sez he ;—
      "O," sez Westcott o' Florida,
      "Wut treason is horrider
    Then our priv'leges tryin' to proon?" sez he.

"It's 'coz they're so happy, thet, wen crazy sarpints
  Stick their nose in our bizness, we git so darned riled ;
We think it's our dooty to give pooty sharp hints,
  Thet the last crumb of Edin on airth shan't be spiled,"
    Sez John C. Calhoun, sez he ;—
      "Ah," sez Dixon H. Lewis,
      "It perfectly true is
    Thet slavery's airth's grettest boon," sez he.

[It was said of old time that riches have wings; and, though this be not applicable in a literal strictness to the wealth of our patriarchal brethren of the South, yet it is clear that their possessions have legs, and an unaccountable propensity for using them in a northerly direction. I marvel that the grand jury of Washington did not find a true bill against the North Star for aiding and abetting Drayton and Sayres. It would have been quite of a piece with the intelligence displayed by the South on other questions connected with slavery. I think that no ship of state was ever freighted with a more veritable Jonah than this same domestic institution of ours. Mephistopheles himself could not feign so bitterly, so satirically sad a sight as this of three millions of human beings crushed beyond help or hope by this one mighty argument,—

Our fathers knew no better! Nevertheless, it is the unavoidable destiny of Jonahs to be cast overboard sooner or later. Or shall we try the experiment of hiding our Jonah in a safe place, that none may lay hands on him to make jetsam of him? Let us, then, with equal forethought and wisdom, lash ourselves to the anchor, and await in pious confidence the certain result. Perhaps our suspicious passenger is no Jonah after all, being black. For it is well known that a superintending Providence made a kind of sandwich of Ham and his descendants, to be devoured by the Caucasian race.

In God's name, let all who hear nearer and nearer the hungry moan of the storm and the growl of the breakers, speak out! But, alas! we have no right to interfere. If a man pluck an apple of mine, he shall be in danger of the justice; but if he steal my brother, I must be silent. Who says this? Our Constitution, consecrated by the callous consuetude of sixty years, and grasped in triumphant argument by the left hand of him whose right hand clutches the clotted slave-whip. Justice, venerable with the undethronable majesty of countless æons, says,—SPEAK! The Past, wise with the sorrows and desolations of ages, from amid her shattered fanes and wolf-housing palaces, echoes,—SPEAK! Nature, through her thousand trumpets of freedom, her stars, her sunrises, her seas, her winds, her cataracts, her mountains blue with cloudy pines, blows jubilant encouragement, and cries,—SPEAK! From the soul's trembling abysses the still, small voice not vaguely murmurs,—SPEAK! But, alas! the Constitution and the Honourable Mr. Bagowind, M.C., say,—BE DUMB!

It occurs to me to suggest, as a topic of inquiry in this connection, whether, on that momentous occasion when the goats and the sheep shall be parted, the Constitution and the Honourable Mr. Bagowind, M.C., will be expected to take their places on the left as our hircine vicars.

> " *Quid sum miser tunc dicturus?*
> *Quem patronum rogaturus?* "

There is a point where toleration sinks into sheer baseness and poltroonery. The toleration of the worst leads us to look on what is barely better as good enough, and to worship what is only moderately good. Woe to that man, or that nation, to whom mediocrity has become an ideal!

Has our experiment of self-government succeeded, if it barely manage to *rub and go?* Here, now, is a piece of barbarism which Christ and the nineteenth century say shall cease, and which Messrs. Smith, Brown, and others say shall *not* cease. I would by no means deny the eminent respectability of these gentlemen, but I confess that, in such a wrestling-match, I cannot help having my fears for them.

"Discite justitiam, moniti, et non temnere divos."

II. W.]

No. VI.

THE PIOUS EDITOR'S CREED.

[At the special instance of Mr. Biglow, I preface the following satire with an extract from a sermon preached during the past summer, from Ezekiel xxxiv. 2:—"Son of man, prophesy against the shepherds of Israel." Since the Sabbath on which this discourse was delivered, the editor of the *Jaalam Independent Blunderbuss* has unaccountably absented himself from our house of worship.

"I know of no so responsible position as that of the public journalist. The editor of our day bears the same relation to his time that the clerk bore to the age before the invention of printing. Indeed, the position which he holds is that which the clergyman should hold even now. But the clergyman chooses to walk off to the extreme edge of the world, and to throw such seed as he has clear over into that darkness which he calls the Next Life. As if *next* did not mean *nearest*, and as if any life were nearer than that immediately present one which boils and eddies all around him at the caucus, the ratification meeting, and the polls! Who taught him to exhort men to prepare for eternity, as for some future era of which the present forms no integral part? The furrow which Time is even now turning runs through the Everlasting, and in that must he plant, or nowhere. Yet he would fain believe and teach that we are *going* to have more of eternity than we have now. This *going* of his is like that of the auctioneer, on which *gone* follows before we have made up our minds to bid,—in which manner, not three months back, I lost an excellent copy of Chappelow on Job. So it has come to pass that the preacher, instead of being a living force, has faded into an emblematic figure at christenings, weddings, and funerals. Or, if he exercise any other function, it is as keeper and feeder of certain theologic dogmas, which, when occasion offers, he unkennels with a *staboy !* ' to bark and bite as 'tis their nature to,' whence that reproach of *odium theologicum* has arisen.

" Meanwhile, see what a pulpit the editor mounts daily, sometimes with a congregation of fifty thousand within reach of his voice, and never so much as a nodder, even, among them ! And from what a Bible can he choose his text,—a Bible which needs no translation, and which no priestcraft can shut and clasp from the laity, — the open volume of the world, upon which, with a pen of sunshine or destroying fire, the inspired Present is even now writing the annals of God ! Methinks the editor who should understand his calling, and be equal thereto, would truly deserve that title of ποιμὴν λαῶν, which Homer bestows upon princes. He would be the Moses of our nineteenth century ; and whereas the old Sinai, silent now, is but a common mountain stared at by the elegant tourist, and crawled over by the hammering geologist, he must find his tables of the new law here among factories and cities in this Wilderness of Sin (Numbers xxxiii. 12) called Progress of Civilisation, and be the captain of our Exodus into the Canaan of a truer social order.

" Nevertheless, our editor will not come so far within even the shadow of Sinai as Mahomet did, but chooses rather to construe Moses by Joe Smith. He takes up the crook, not that the sheep may be fed, but that he may never want a warm woollen suit and a joint of mutton.

" *Immemor, O, fidei, pecorumque oblite tuorum !*"

For which reason I would derive the name *editor* not so much from *edo*, to publish, as from *edo*, to eat, that being the peculiar profession to which he esteems himself called. He blows up the flames of political discord for no other occasion than that he may thereby handily boil his own pot. I believe there are two thousand of these mutton-loving shepherds in the United States, and of these how many have even the dimmest perception of their immense power, and the duties consequent thereon ? Here and there, haply, one. Nine hundred and ninety-nine labour to impress upon the people the great principles of *Tweedledum*, and other nine hundred and ninety-nine preach with equal earnestness the gospel according to *Tweedledee*."—H. W.]

I DU believe in Freedom's cause,
  Ez fur away ez Payris is ;
I love to see her stick her claws
  In them infarnal Phayrisees ;
It's wal enough agin a king
  To dror resolves an' triggers,—
But libbaty's a kind o' thing
  Thet don't agree with niggers.

I du believe the people want
  A tax on teas an' coffees,
Thet nothin' aint extravygunt,—
  Purvidin' I'm in office ;
Fer I hev loved my country sence
  My eye-teeth filled their sockets,
An' Uncle Sam I reverence,
  Partic'larly his pockets.

I du believe in *any* plan
  O' levyin' the taxes,
Ez long ez, like a lumberman,
  I git jest wut I axes :
I go free-trade thru thick an' thin,
  Because it kind o' rouses
The folks to vote,—an' keeps us in
  Our quiet custom-houses.

I du believe it's wise an' good
  To sen' out furrin missions,
Thet is, on sartin understood
  An' orthydox conditions ;—

I mean nine thousan' dolls. per ann.,
　　Nine thousan' more fer outfit,
An' me to recommend a man
　　The place 'ould jest about fit.

I du believe in special ways
　　O' prayin' an' convartin';
The bread comes back in many days,
　　An' buttered, tu, fer sartin;
I mean in preyin' till one busts
　　On wut the party chooses,
An' in convartin' public trusts
　　To very privit uses.

I du believe hard coin the stuff
　　Fer 'lectioneers to spout on;
The people's ollers soft enough
　　To make hard money out on;
Dear Uncle Sam pervides fer his,
　　An' gives a good-sized junk to all,—
I don't care *how* hard money is,
　　Ez long ez mine's paid punctooal.

I du believe with all my soul
　　In the great Press's freedom,
To pint the people to the goal
　　An' in the traces lead 'em;
Palsied the arm thet forges yokes
　　At my fat contracts squintin',
An' withered be the nose thet pokes
　　Inter the gov'ment printin'!

I du believe thet I should give
    Wut's his'n unto Cæsar,
Fer it's by him I move an' live,
    Frum him my bread an' cheese air ;
I du believe thet all o' me
    Doth bear his superscription,—
Will, conscience, honour, honesty,
    An' things o' thet description.

I du believe in prayer an' praise
    To him thet hez the grantin'
O' jobs,—in every thin' thet pays,
    But most of all in CANTIN' ;
This doth my cup with marcies fill,
    This lays all thought o' sin to rest,—
I *don't* believe in princerple,
    But O, I *du* in interest.

I du believe in bein' this
    Or thet, ez it may happen
One way or t'other hendiest is
    To ketch the people nappin' ;
It aint by princerples nor men
    My preudunt course is steadied,—
I scent wich pays the best, an' then
    Go into it baldheaded.

I du believe thet holdin' slaves
    Comes nat'ral tu a Presidunt,
Let 'lone the rowdedow it saves
    To hev a wal-broke precedunt ;

Fer any office, small or gret,
  I couldn't ax with no face,
Without I'd ben, thru dry an' wet,
  Th' unrizzest kind o' doughface.

I du believe wutever trash
  'll keep the people in blindness, —
Thet we the Mexicuns can thrash
  Right inter brotherly kindness,
Thet bombshells, grape, an' powder 'n' ball
  Air good-will's strongest magnets,
Thet peace, to make it stick at all,
  Must be druv in with bagnets.

In short, I firmly du believe
  In Humbug generally,
Fer it's a thing thet I perceive
  To hev a solid vally;
This heth my faithful shepherd ben,
  In pasturs sweet heth led me.
An' this'll keep the people green
  To feed ez they hev fed me.

[I subjoin here another passage from my before-mentioned discourse.

"Wonderful, to him that has eyes to see it rightly, is the newspaper. To me, for example, sitting on the critical front bench of the pit, in my study here in Jaalam, the advent of my weekly journal is as that of a strolling theatre, or rather of a puppet-show, on whose stage, narrow as it is, the tragedy, comedy, and farce of life are played in little. Behold the whole huge earth sent to me hebdomadally in a brown-paper wrapper!

"Hither, to my obscure corner, by wind or steam, on horseback or dromedary-back, in the pouch of the Indian runner, or clicking over the magnetic wires, troop all the famous performers from the four quarters of the globe. Looked at from a point of criticism, tiny puppets they seem all, as the editor sets up his booth upon my desk and officiates as showman. Now I can truly see how little and transitory is life. The earth appears almost as a drop of vinegar, on which the solar microscope of the imagination must be brought to bear in order to make out anything distinctly. That animalcule there, in the pea-jacket, is Louis Philippe, just landed on the coast of England. That other, in the grey surtout and cocked hat, is Napoleon Bonaparte Smith, assuring France that she need apprehend no interference from him in the present alarming juncture. At that spot, where you seem to see a speck of something in motion, is an immense mass-meeting. Look sharper, and you will see a mite brandishing his mandibles in an excited manner ; that is the great Mr. Soandso, defining his position amid tumultuous and irrepressible cheers. That infinitesimal creature, upon whom some score of others, as minute as he, are gazing in open-mouthed admiration, is a famous philosopher, expounding to a select audience their capacity for the Infinite. That scarce discernible pufflet of smoke and dust is a revolution. That speck there is a reformer, just arranging the lever with which he is to move the world. And lo, there creeps forward the shadow of a skeleton that blows one breath between its grinning teeth, and all our distinguished actors are whisked off the slippery stage into the dark Beyond.

"Yes, the little show-box has its solemner suggestions. Now and then we catch a glimpse of a grim old man, who lays down a scythe and hour-glass in the corner while he shifts the scenes. There, too, in the dim background, a weird shape is ever delving. Sometimes he leans upon his mattock, and gazes, as a coach whirls by, bearing the newly-married on their wedding jaunt, or glances carelessly at a babe brought home from christening. Suddenly (for the scene grows larger and larger as we look) a bony hand snatches back a performer in the midst of his part, and him, whom yesterday two infinities (past and future) would not suffice, a handful of dust is enough to cover and silence for ever. Nay, we see the same fleshless fingers opening to clutch the showman himself, and guess, not without a shudder, that they are lying in wait for spectator also.

"Think of it : for three dollars a year I buy a season-ticket to this great Globe Theatre, for which God would write the dramas (only that we like farces, spectacles, and the tragedies of Apollyon better), whose scene-shifter is Time, and whose curtain is rung down by Death.

"Such thoughts will occur to me sometimes as I am tearing off the wrapper of my newspaper. Then suddenly that otherwise too often vacant sheet becomes invested for me with a strange kind of awe. Look ! deaths and marriages, notices of inventions, discoveries, and books, lists of promotions, of killed, wounded, and missing, news of fires, accidents, of sudden wealth, and as sudden poverty. I hold in my hand the ends of myriad invisible electric conductors, along which tremble the joys, sorrows, wrongs, triumphs, hopes, and despairs of as many men and women everywhere. So that upon that mood of mind which seems to isolate me from mankind as a spectator of their puppet-pranks, another supervenes, in which I feel that I too, unknown and unheard of, am yet of some import to my fellows. For, through my newspaper here, do not families take pains to send me, an entire stranger, news of a death among them ? Are not here two who would have me know of their marriage ? And, strangest of all, is not this singular person anxious to have me informed that he has received a fresh supply of Dimitry Bruisgins ? But to none of us does the Present continue miraculous (even if for a moment discerned as such). We glance carelessly at the sunrise, and get used to Orion and the Pleiades. The wonder wears off, and to-morrow this sheet, in which a vision was let down to me from Heaven, shall be the wrappage to a bar of soap or the platter for a beggar's broken victuals."—H. W.]

No. VII.

A LETTER

FROM A CANDIDATE FOR THE PRESIDENCY IN ANSWER TO SUTTIN QUESTIONS PROPOSED BY MR. HOSEA BIGLOW, IN-CLOSED IN A NOTE FROM MR. BIGLOW TO S. H. GAY, ESQ., EDITOR OF THE "NATIONAL ANTI-SLAVERY STANDARD."

[Curiosity may be said to be the quality which pre-eminently distinguishes and segregates man from the lower animals. As we trace the scale of animated nature downward, we find this faculty (as it may truly be called) of the mind diminished in the savage, and quite extinct in the brute. The first object which civilised man proposes to himself I take to be the finding out whatsoever he can concerning his neighbours. *Nihil humanum a me alienum puto;* I am curious about even John

Smith. The desire next in strength to this (an opposite pole, indeed, of the same magnet) is that of communicating the unintelligence we have carefully picked up.

Men in general may be divided into the inquisitive and the communicative. To the first class belong Peeping Toms, eaves-droppers, navel-contemplating Brahmins, metaphysicians, travellers, Empedocleses, spies, the various societies for promoting Rhinothism, Columbuses, Yankees, discoverers, and men of science, who present themselves to the mind as so many marks of interrogation wandering up and down the world, or sitting in studies and laboratories. The second class I should again subdivide into four. In the first subdivision I would rank those who have an itch to tell us about themselves,—as keepers of diaries, insignificant persons generally, Montaignes, Horace Walpoles, autobiographers, poets. The second includes those who are anxious to impart information concerning other people,—as historians, barbers, and such. To the third belong those who labour to give us intelligence about nothing at all,—as novelists, political orators, the large majority of authors, preachers, lecturers, and the like. In the fourth come those who are communicative from motives of public benevolence,—as finders of mares'-nests and bringers of ill news. Each of us two-legged fowls without feathers embraces all these subdivisions in himself to a greater or less degree, for none of us so much as lays an egg, or incubates a chalk one, but straightway the whole barn-yard shall know it by our cackle or our cluck. *Omnibus hoc vitium est.* There are different grades in all these classes. One will turn his telescope toward a back-yard, another toward Uranus ; one will tell you that he dined with Smith, another that he supped with Plato. In one particular, all men may be considered as belonging to the first grand division, inasmuch as they all seem equally desirous of discovering the mote in their neighbour's eye.

To one or another of these species every human being may safely be referred. I think it beyond a peradventure that Jonah prosecuted some inquiries into the digestive apparatus of whales, and that Noah sealed up a letter in an empty bottle, that news in regard to him might not be wanting in case of the worst. They had else been super or subter human. I conceive, also, that, as there are certain persons who continually peep and pry at the key-hole of that mysterious door through which, sooner or later, we all make our exits, so there are doubtless ghosts fidgetting and fretting on the other side of it, because they have no means of conveying back to this world the scraps of news they have picked up in that. For there is an answer ready somewhere to every question, the great law of *give and take* runs through all nature, and if we see a hook, we may be sure that an eye is waiting for it. I read in every face I meet a standing advertisement of information wanted in regard to A. B., or that the friends of C. D. can hear something to his disadvantage by application to such a one.

It was to gratify the two great passions of asking and answering that epistolary correspondence was first invented. Letters (for by this usurped title epistles are now commonly known) are of several kinds. First, there are those which are not letters at all,—as letters-patent, letters dimissory, letters inclosing bills, letters of administration, Pliny's letters, letters of diplomacy, of Cato, of Mentor, of Lords Lyttelton, Chesterfield, and Orrery, of Jacob Behmen, Seneca (whom St. Jerome includes in his list of sacred writers), letters from abroad, from sons in college to their fathers, letters of marque and letters generally, which are in nowise letters of mark. Second, are real letters, such as those of Gray, Cowper, Walpole, Howel, Lamb, D. Y., the first letters from children (printed in staggering capitals), Letters from New York, letters of credit, and others, interesting for the sake of the writer or the thing written. I have read also letters from Europe by a gentleman named Pinto, containing some curious gossip, and which I hope to see collected for the benefit of the curious. There are, besides, letters addressed to posterity, —as epitaphs, for example, written for their own monuments by monarchs, whereby we have lately become possessed of the names of several great conquerors and kings of kings, hitherto unheard of and still unpronounceable, but valuable to the student of the entirely dark ages. The letter which St. Peter sent to King Pepin in the year of grace 755, that of the Virgin to the magistrates of Messina, that of St. Gregory Thaumaturgus to the D—l, and that of this last-mentioned active police-magistrate to a nun of Girgenti, I would place in a class by themselves, as also the letters of candidates, concerning which I shall dilate more fully in a note at the end of the following poem. At present, *sat prata biberunt.* Only, concerning the shape of letters, they are all either square or oblong, to which general figures circular letters and round-robins also conform themselves.—H. W.]

DEER SIR its gut to be the fashun now to rite letters to the candid 8s and i wus chose at a publick Meetin in Jaalam to du wut wus nessary fur that town. i writ to 271 ginerals and gut ansers to 209.   tha air called candid 8s but I don't see nothin candid about em.   this here 1 which I send wus thought satty's factory.   I dunno as it's ushle to print Pos-crips, but as all the ansers I got hed the saim, I sposed it wus best.   times has gretly changed.   Formaly to knock a man into a cocked hat wus to use him up, but now it ony gives him a chance fur the cheef madgustracy.—H. B.

DEAR SIR,—You wish to know my notions
    On sartin pints thet rile the land;
There's nothin' thet my natur so shuns
    Ez bein' mum or underhand;
I'm a straight-spoken kind o' creetur
    Thet blurts right out wut's in his head,
An' ef I've one pecooler feetur,
    It is a nose thet wunt be led.

So, to begin at the beginnin',
    An' come direcly to the pint,
I think the country's underpinnin'
    Is some consid'ble out o' jint;
I aint agoin' to try your patience
    By tellin' who done this or thet,
I don't make no insinooations,
    I jest let on I smell a rat.

Thet is, I mean, it seems to me so,
    But, ef the public think I'm wrong,
I wunt deny but wut I be so,—
    An', fact, it don't smell very strong;
My mind's tu fair to lose its balance
    An' say wich party hez most sense;
There may be folks o' greater talence
    That can't set stiddier on the fence.

I'm an eclectic; ez to choosin'
    'Twixt this an' thet, I'm plaguy lawth;
I leave a side thet looks like losin',
    But (wile there's doubt) I stick to both;
I stan' upon the Constitution,
    Ez preudunt statesmun say, who've planned
A way to git the most profusion
    O' chances ez to *ware* they'll stand.

Ez fer the war, I go agin it,—
    I mean to say I kind o' du,—
Thet is, I mean thet, bein' in it,
    The best way wuz to fight it thru;
Not but wut abstract war is horrid,
    I sign to thet with all my heart,—
But civlyzation *does* git forrid
    Sometimes upon a powder-cart.

About thet darned Proviso matter
    I never hed a grain o' doubt,
Nor I aint one my sense to scatter
    So'st no one couldn't pick it out;
My love fer North an' South is equil,
    So I'll jest answer plump an' frank,—
No matter wut may be the sequil,—
    Yes, Sir, I *am* agin a Bank.

Ez to the answerin' o' questions,
    I'm an off ox at bein' druv,
Though I aint one thet ary test shuns
    'll give our folks a helpin' shove;

Kind o' promiscoous I go it
  Fer the holl country, an' the ground
I take, ez nigh ez I can show it,
  Is pooty gen'ally all round.

I don't appruve o' givin' pledges;
  You'd ough' to leave a feller free,
An' not go knockin' out the wedges
  To ketch his fingers in the tree ;
Pledges air awfle breachy cattle
  Thet preudunt farmers don't turn out,—
Ez long 'z the people git their rattle,
  Wut is there fer'm to grout about ?

Ez to the slaves, there's no confusion
  In *my* idees consarnin' them,—
I think they air an Institution,
  A sort of—yes, jest so,—ahem :
Do *I* own any?   Of my merit
  On thet pint you yourself may jedge ;
All is, I never drink no sperit,
  Nor I haint never signed no pledge.

Ez to my princerples, I glory
  In hevin' nothin' o' the sort ;
I aint a Wig, I aint a Tory,
  I'm jest a candidate, in short;
Thet's fair an' square an' parpendicler,
  But, ef the Public cares a fig
To hev me an' thin' in particler,
  Wy, I'm a kind o' peri-wig.

P. S.

Ez we're a sort o' privateerin',
 O' course, you know, it's sheer an' sheer,
An' there is sutthin' wuth your hearin'
 I'll mention in *your* privit ear ;
Ef you git *me* inside the White House,
 Your head with ile I'll kin' o' 'nint
By gittin' *you* inside the Light-house
 Down to the eend o' Jaalam Pint.

An' ez the North hez took to brustlin'
 At bein' scrouged frum off the roost,
I'll tell ye wut'll save all tusslin'
 An' give our side a harnsome boost,—
Tell 'em thet on the Slavery question
 I'm RIGHT, although to speak I'm lawth ;
This gives you a safe pint to rest on,
 An' leaves me frontin' South by North.

[And now of epistles candidatial, which are of two kinds,—namely, letters of acceptance, and letters definitive of position. Our republic, on the eve of an election, may safely enough be called a republic of letters. Epistolary composition becomes then an epidemic, which seizes one candidate after another, not seldom cutting short the thread of political life. It has come to such a pass that a party dreads less the attacks of its opponents than a letter from its candidate. *Litera scripta manet*, and it will go hard if something bad cannot be made of it. General Harrison, it is well understood, was surrounded, during his candidacy, with the *cordon sanitaire* of a vigilance committee. No prisoner in Spielberg was ever more cautiously deprived of writing materials. The soot was scraped carefully from the chimney-places ; outposts of expert rifle-shooters rendered it sure death for any goose (who came clad in feathers) to approach within a certain limited distance of North Bend ; and all domestic fowls about the premises were reduced to the condition of Plato's original man. By these precautions the General was saved. *Parva componere magnis,* I remember that, when party-spirit once ran high among my people, upon occasion of the choice of a new deacon, I, having my preferences, yet not caring too openly to express them, made use of an innocent fraud to bring about that result which I deemed most desirable. My stratagem was no other than the throwing a copy of the Complete Letter-Writer in the way of the candidate whom I wished to defeat. He caught the infection, and addressed a short note to his constituents, in which the opposite party detected so many and so grave improprieties (he had modelled it upon the letter of a young lady accepting a proposal of marriage), that he not only lost his election, but, falling under a suspicion of Sabellianism and I know not what (the widow Endive assured me that he was a Paralipomenon, to her certain knowledge), was forced to leave the town. Thus it is that the letter killeth.

The object which candidates propose to themselves in writing is to convey no meaning at all. And here is a quite unsuspected pitfall into which they successively plunge headlong. For it is precisely in such cryptographies that mankind are prone to seek for and find a wonderful amount and variety of significance. *Omne ignotum pro mirifico.* How do we admire at the antique world striving to crack those oracular nuts from Delphi, Hammon, and elsewhere, in only one of which can I so much as surmise that any kernel had ever lodged ; that, namely, wherein Apollo confessed that he was mortal. One Didymus is, moreover, related to have written six thousand books on the single subject of grammar, a topic rendered only more tenebrific by the labours of his successors, and which seems still to possess an attraction for authors in proportion as they can make nothing of it. A singular loadstone for theologians, also, is the Beast in the Apocalypse, whereof, in the course of my studies, I have noted two hundred and three several interpretations, each lethiferal to all the rest. *Non nostrum est tantas componere lites,* yet I have myself ventured upon a two hundred and fourth, which I embodied in a discourse preached on occasion of the demise of the late usurper, Napoleon Bonaparte, and which quieted, in a large measure, the minds of my people. It is true that my views on this important point were ardently controverted by Mr. Shearjashub Holden, the then preceptor of our academy, and in other particulars a very deserving and sensible young man, though possessing a somewhat limited knowledge of the Greek tongue. But his heresy struck down no deep root, and, he having been lately removed by the hand of Providence, I had the satisfaction of re-affirming my cherished sentiments in a sermon preached upon the Lord's day immediately succeeding his funeral. This might seem like taking an unfair advantage, did I not add that he had made provision in his last will (being celibate) for the publication of a posthumous tractate in support of his own dangerous opinions.

I know of nothing in our modern times which approaches so nearly to the ancient oracle as the letter of a Presidential candidate. Now, among the Greeks, the eating of beans was strictly forbidden to all such as had it in mind to consult those expert amphibologists, and this same prohibition on the part of Pythagoras to his disciples is understood to imply an abstinence from politics, beans having been used as ballots. That other application, *quod videlicet sensus eo cibo obtundi existimaret,* though supported *pugnis et calcibus* by many of the learned, and not wanting the countenance of Cicero, is confuted by the larger experience of New England. On the whole, I think it safer to apply here the rule of interpretation which now generally obtains in regard to antique cosmogonies, myths, fables, proverbial expressions, and knotty points generally, which is, to find a common-sense meaning, and then select whatever can be imagined the most opposite thereto. In this way we arrive at the conclusion, that the Greeks objected to the questioning of candidates. And very properly, if, as I conceive, the chief point be not to discover what a person in that position is, or what he will do, but whether he can be elected. *Vos exemplaria Græca nocturna versate manu, versate diurna.*

But, since an imitation of the Greeks in this particular (the asking of questions being one chief privilege of freemen) is hardly to be hoped for, and our candidates will answer whether they are questioned or not, I would recommend that these ante-electionary dialogues should be carried on by symbols, as were the diplomatic correspondences of the Scythians and Macrobii, or confined to the language of signs, like the famous interview of Panurge and Goatsnose. A candidate might then convey a suitable reply to all committees of inquiry by closing one eye, or by presenting them with a phial of Egyptian darkness to be speculated upon by their respective constituencies. These answers would be susceptible of whatever retrospective construction the exigencies of the political campaign might seem to demand, and the candidate could take his position on either side of the fence with entire consistency. Or, if letters must be written, profitable use might be made of the Dighton rock hieroglyphic or the cuneiform script, every fresh decipherer of which is enabled to educe a different meaning, whereby a sculptured stone or two supplies us, and will probably continue to supply posterity, with a very vast and various body of authentic history. For even the briefest epistle in the ordinary chirography is dangerous. There is scarce any style so compressed that superfluous words may not be detected in it. A severe critic might curtail that famous brevity of Cæsar's by two-thirds, drawing his pen through the supererogatory *veni* and *vidi*. Perhaps, after all, the surest footing of hope is to be found in the rapidly increasing tendency to demand less and less of qualification in candidates. Already have statesmanship, experience, and the possession (nay, the profession, even) of principles been rejected as superfluous, and may not the patriot reasonably hope that the ability to write will follow? At present, there may be death in pot-hooks as well as pots, the loop of a letter may suffice for a bow-string, and all the dreadful heresies of Anti-slavery may lurk in a flourish.—H. W.]

No. VIII.

A SECOND LETTER FROM B. SAWIN, ESQ.

[In the following epistle, we behold Mr. Sawin returning, a *miles emeritus*, to the bosom of his family. *Quantum mutatus!* The good Father of us all had doubtless intrusted to the keeping of this child of his certain faculties of a constructive kind. He had put in him a share of that vital force, the nicest economy of every minute atom of which is necessary to the perfect development of Humanity. He had given him a brain and heart, and so had equipped his soul with the two strong wings of knowledge and love, whereby it can mount to hang its nest under the eaves of heaven. And this child, so dowered, he had intrusted to the keeping of his vicar, the State. How stands the account of that stewardship? The State, or Society (call her by what name you will), had taken no manner of thought of him till she saw him swept out into the street, the pitiful leavings of last night's debauch, with cigar-ends, lemon-parings, tobacco-quids, slops, vile stenches, and the whole loathsome next-morning of the bar-room,—an own child of the Almighty God! I remember him as he was brought to be christened, a ruddy, rugged babe; and now there he wallows, reeking, seething,—the dead corpse, not of a man, but of a soul,—a putrefying lump, horrible for the life that is in it. Comes the wind of heaven, that good Samaritan, and parts the hair upon his forehead, nor is too nice to kiss those parched, cracked lips; the morning opens upon him her eyes full of pitying sunshine, the sky yearns down to him,—and there he lies fermenting. O sleep! let me not profane thy holy name by calling that stertorous unconsciousness a slumber! By-and-by comes along the State, God's vicar. Does she say,—" My poor, forlorn foster-child! Behold here a force which I will make dig and plant and build for me?" Not so, but,—" Here is a recruit ready-made to my hand, a piece of destroying energy lying unprofitably idle." So she claps an ugly grey suit on him, puts a musket in his grasp, and sends him off, with Gubernatorial and other godspeeds, to do duty as a destroyer.

I made one of the crowd at the last Mechanics' Fair, and, with the rest, stood gazing in wonder at a perfect machine with its soul of fire, its boiler-heart that sent the hot blood pulsing along the iron arteries, and its thews of steel. And while I was admiring the adaptation of means to end, the harmonious involutions of contrivance, and the never-bewildered complexity, I saw a grimed and greasy fellow, the imperious engine's lackey and drudge, whose sole office was to let fall, at intervals, a drop or two of oil upon a certain joint. Then my soul said within me, See there a piece of mechanism to which that other you marvel at is but as the rude first effort of a child,—a force which not merely suffices to set a few wheels in motion, but which can send an impulse all through the infinite future,—a contrivance, not for turning out pins, or stitching button-holes, but for making Hamlets and Lears. And yet this thing of iron shall be housed, waited on, guarded from rust and dust, and it shall be a crime but so much as to scratch it with a pin; while the other, with its fire of God in it, shall be buffeted hither and thither, and finally sent carefully a thousand miles to be the target for a Mexican cannon-ball. Unthrifty Mother State! My heart burned within me for pity and indignation, and I renewed this covenant with my own soul,—*In aliis mansuetus ero, at, in blasphemiis contra Christum, non ita.*—H. W.]

I SPOSE you wonder ware I be; I can't tell, fer the soul o' me,
Exacly ware I be myself,—meanin' by thet the holl o' me.
Wen I left hum, I hed two legs, an' they worn't bad ones
    neither
(The scaliest trick they ever played wuz bringin' on me
    hither),

Now one on 'em's I dunno ware;—they thought I wuz
　　adyin',
An' sawed it off because they said 'twuz kin' o' mortifyin';
I'm willin' to believe it wuz, an' yit I don't see, nuther,
Wy one should take to feelin' cheap a minnit sooner 'n
　　t'other,
Sence both wuz equilly to blame; but things is ez they be;
It took on so they took it off, an' thet's enough fer me:
There's one good thing, though, to be said about my
　　wooden nev one,—
The liquor can't git into it ez't used to in the true one;
So it saves drink; an' then, besides, a feller couldn't beg
A gretter blessin' then to hev one ollers sober peg;
It's true a chap's in want o' two fer follerin' a drum,
But all the march I'm up to now is jest to Kingdom Come.

I've lost one eye, but thet's a loss it's easy to supply
Out o' the glory thet I've gut, fer thet is all my eye;
An' one is big enough, I guess, by diligently usin' it,
To see all I shall ever git by way o' pay fer losin' it;
Off'cers, I notice, who git paid fer all our thumps an'
　　kickins,
Du wal by keepin' single eyes arter the fattest pickins;
So, ez the eye's put fairly out I'll larn to go without it,
An' not allow *myself* to be no gret put out about it.
Now, le' me see, thet isn't all; I used, 'fore leavin' Jalaam,
To count things on my finger-eends, but sutthin' seems to
　　ail 'em:
Ware's my left hand? O, darn it, yes, I recollect wut's
　　come on't;
I haint no left arm but my right, an' thet's gut jest a thumb
　　on't;
It aint so hendy ez it wuz to cal'late a sum on't.

I've hed some ribs broke,—six (I b'lieve),—I haint kep' no
    account on 'em ;
Wen pensions git to be the talk, I'll settle the amount on
    'em.
An' now I'm speakin' about ribs, it kin' o' brings to mind
One thet I couldn't never break,—the one I lef' behind ;
Ef you should see her, jest clear out the spout o' your
    invention
An' pour the longest sweetnin' in about an annooal pension,
An' kin' o' hint (in case, you know, the critter should refuse
    to be
Consoled) I aint so 'xpensive now to keep ez wut I used to
    be ;
There's one arm less, ditto one eye, an' then the leg thet's
    wooden
Can be took off an' sot away wenever ther's a puddin'.

I spose you think I'm comin' back ez opperlunt ez thunder,
With shiploads o' gold images an' varus sorts o' plunder ;
Wal, 'fore I vullinteered, I thought this country wuz a sort o'
Canaan, a reg'lar Promised Land flowin' with rum an' water,
Ware propaty growed up like time, without no cultivation,
An' gold wuz dug ez taters be among our Yankee nation,
Ware nateral advantages were pufficly amazin',
Ware every rock there wuz about with precious stuns wuz
    blazin',
Ware mill-sites filled the country up ez thick ez you could
    cram 'em,
An' desput rivers run about abeggin' folks to dam 'em ;
Then there were meetinhouses, tu, chockful o' gold an'
    silver
Thet you could take, an' no one couldn't hand ye in no bill
    fer ;—

Thet's wut I thought afore I went, thet's wut them fellers
    told us
Thet stayed to hum an' speechified an' to the buzzards sold
    us;
I thought thet gold mines could be gut cheaper than Chiny
    asters,
An' see myself acomin' back like sixty Jacob Astors;
But sech idees soon melted down an' didn't leave a grease-
    spot;
I vow my holl sheer o' the spiles wouldn't come nigh a V
    spot;
Although, most anywares we've ben, you needn't break no
    locks,
Nor run no kin' o' risks, to fill your pocket full o' rocks.

I guess I mentioned in my last some o' the nateral feeturs
O' this all-fiered buggy hole in th' way o' awfle creeturs,
But I fergut to name (new things to speak on so abounded)
How one day you'll most die o' thust, an' 'fore the next git
    drownded.
The clymit seems to me jest like a teapot made o' pewter
Our Prudence hed, thet wouldn't pour (all she could du) to
    suit her;
Fust place the leaves 'ould choke the spout, so's not a drop
    'ould dreen out,
Then Prude 'ould tip an' tip an' tip, till the holl kit bust
    clean out,
The kiver-hinge-pin bein' lost, tea-leaves an' tea an' kiver
'ould all come down *kerswosh!* ez though the dam broke in
    a river.
Jest so 't is here; holl months there aint a day o' rainy
    weather,
An' jest ez th' officers 'ould be alayin' heads together

Ez t' how they'd mix their drink at sech a milingtary
 deepot,—

'T 'ould pour ez though the lid wuz off the everlastin' teapot.

The cons'quence is, thet I shall take, wen I'm allowed to
 leave here,

One piece o' propaty along,—an' thet's the shakin' fever;

It's reggilar employment, though, an' thet aint thought to
 harm one,

Nor 't aint so tiresome ez it wuz with t'other leg an' arm on;

An' it's a consolation, tu, although it doosn't pay,

To hev it said you're some gret shakes in any kin' o' way.

'Tworn't very long, I tell ye wut, I thought o' fortin-
 makin',—

One day a reg'lar shiver-de-freeze, an' next ez good ez
 bakin',—

One day abrilin' in the sand, then smoth'rin' in the
 mashes,—

Git up all sound, be put to bed a mess o' hacks an' smashes

But then, thinks I, at any rate there's glory to be hed,—

Thet's an investment, arter all, thet mayn't turn out so bad;

But somehow, wen we'd fit an' licked, I ollers found the
 thanks

Gut kin' o' lodged afore they come ez low down ez the
 ranks;

The Gin'rals gut the biggest sheer, the Cunnles next, an' so
 on,—

We never gut a blasted mite o' glory ez I know on;

An' spose we hed, I wonder how you're goin' to contrive its

Division so's to give a piece to twenty thousand privits;

Ef you should multiply by ten the portion o' the brav'st
 one,

You wouldn't git more'n half enough to speak of on a grave-
 stun;

We git the licks,—we're jest the grist thet's put into War's
    hoppers;
Leftenants is the lowest grade thet helps pick up the
    coppers.
It may suit folks thet go agin a body with a soul in't,
An' aint contented with a hide without a bagnet hole
    in't;
But glory is a kin' o' thing *I* shan't persue no furder,
Coz thet's the off'cers parquisite,—yourn's on'y jest the
    murder.

Wal, arter I gin glory up, thinks I at least there's one
Thing in the bills we aint hed yit, an' thet's the GLORIOUS
    FUN;
Ef once we git to Mexico, we fairly may presume we
All day an' night shall revel in the halls o' Montezumy.
I'll tell ye wut *my* revels wuz, an' see how you would like
    'em;
We never gut inside the hall: the nighest ever *I* come
Wuz stan'in' sentry in the sun (an', fact, it *seemed* a
    cent'ry)
A ketchin' smells o' biled an' roast thet come out thru the
    entry,
An' hearin' ez I sweltered thru my passes an' repasses,
A rat-tat-too o' knives an' forks, a clinkty-clink o' glasses:
I can't tell off the bill o' fare the Gin'rals hed inside;
All I know is, thet out o' doors a pair o' soles wuz
    fried,
An' not a hunderd miles away frum ware this child wuz
    posted,
A Massachusetts citizen wuz baked, an' biled, an' roasted;
The on'y thing like revellin' thet ever come to me
Wuz bein' routed out o' sleep by thet darned revelee.

They say the quarrel's settled now; fer my part I've some
    doubt on't,
'T 'll take more fish-skin than folks think to take the rile
    clean out on't;
At any rate, I'm so used up I can't do no more fightin',
The on'y chance thet's left to me is politics or writin';
Now, ez the people's gut to hev a milingtary man,
An' I aint nothin' else jest now, I've hit upon a plan;
The can'idatin' line, you know, 'ould suit me to a T,
An' ef I lose, 'twunt hurt my ears to lodge another flea;
So I'll set up ez can'idate for any kin' o' office
(I mean fer any thet includes good easy-cheers an' soffies;
Fer ez to runnin' fer a place ware work's the time o' day,
You know thet's wut I never did,—except the other way);
Ef it's the Presidential cheer fer wich I'd better run,
Wut two legs anywares about could keep up with my one?
There aint no kin' o' quality in can'idates, it's said,
So useful ez a wooden leg,—except a wooden head;
There's nothin' aint so poppylar—(wy, it's a parfect sin
To think wut Mexico hez paid fer Santy Anny's pin;)—
Then I haint gut no princerples, an', sense I wuz knee-high,
I never *did* hev any gret, ez you can testify;
I'm a decided peace-man, tu, an' go agin the war,—
Fer now the holl on't's gone an' past, wut is there to go *for?*
Ef, wile you're 'lectioneerin' round, some curus chaps should
    beg
To know my views o' state affairs, jest answer WOODEN
    LEG!
Ef they aint settisfied with thet, an' kin' o' pry an' doubt,
An' ax fer sutthin' deffynit, jest say ONE EYE PUT OUT!
Thet kin' o' talk I guess you'll find'll answer to a charm,
An' when you're druv tu nigh the wall, hol' up my missin'
    arm;

Ef they should nose round fer a pledge, put on a vartoous
 look
An' tell 'em thet's percisely wut I never gin nor—took!

Then you can call me "Timbertoes,"—thet's wut the people
 likes ;
Sutthin' combinin' morril truth with phrases sech ez strikes;
Some say the people's fond o' this, or thet, or wut you
 please,—
I tell ye wut the people want is jest correct idees ;
"Old Timbertoes," you see, 's a creed it's safe to be quite
 bold on,
There's nothin' in't the other side can any ways git hold
 on;
It's a good tangible idee, a sutthin' to embody
Thet valooable class o' men who look thru brandy-toddy ;
It gives a Party Platform, tu, jest level with the mind
Of all right-thinkin', honest folks thet mean to go it blind ;
Then there air other good hooraws to dror on ez you need
 'em,
Sech ez the ONE-EYED SLATERER, the BLOODY BIRDOFREDUM;
Them's wut takes hold o' folks thet think, ez well ez o' the
 masses,
An' makes you sartin o' the aid o' good men of all classes.

There's one think I'm in doubt about; in order to be
 Presidunt,
It's absolutely ne'ssary to be a Southern residunt ;
The Constitution settles thet, an' also thet a feller
Must own a nigger o' some sort, jet black, or brown, or
 yeller.
Now I haint no objections agin partickler climes,
Nor agin ownin' anythin' (except the truth sometimes),

8

But, ez I haint no capital, up there among ye, may be,
You might raise funds enough fer me to buy a low-priced
  baby,
An' then, to suit the No'thern folks, who feel obleeged to say
They hate an' cuss the very thing they vote fer every day,
Say you're assured I go full butt fer Libbaty's diffusion
An' made the purchis on'y jest to spite the Institootion;—
But, golly! there's the currier's hoss upon the pavement
  pawin'!
I'll be more 'xplicit in my next.

    Yourn,
       BIRDOFREDUM SAWIN.

[We have now a tolerably fair chance of estimating how the balance-sheet stands between our returned volunteer and glory. Supposing the entries to be set down on both sides of the account in fractional parts of one hundred, we shall arrive at something like the following result :—

   B. SAWIN, Esq., in account with (BLANK) GLORY.

Cr.   Dr.

By loss of one leg . . 20	To one 675th three cheers in	
,, do. one arm . . 15	Faneuil Hall . .	30
,, do. four fingers . 5	,, do. do. on occasion	
,, do. one eye . . 10	of presentation of sword	
,, the breaking of six ribs . 6	to Colonel Wright . .	25
,, having served under Colo-	,, one suit of grey clothes	
nel Cushing one month . 44	(ingeniously unbecoming)	15
	,, musical entertainments	
	(drum and fife six months)	5
	,, one dinner after return .	1
	,, chance of pension . .	1
	,, privilege of drawing long-	
	bow during rest of natural	
	life	23

        100   100

E. E.

It would appear that Mr. Sawin found the actual feast curiously the reverse of the bill of fare advertised in Faneuil Hall and other places. His primary object seems to have been the making of his fortune. *Quærenda pecunia primum, virtus post nummos.* He hoisted sail for Eldorado, and shipwrecked on Point Tribulation. *Quid non mortalia pectora cogis, auri sacra fames?* The speculation has sometimes crossed my mind, in that dreary interval of drought which intervenes between quarterly stipendiary showers, that Providence, by the creation of a money-tree, might have simplified wonderfully the sometimes perplexing problem of human life. We read of bread-trees, the butter for which lies ready churned in Irish bogs. Milk-trees we are assured of in South America, and stout Sir John Hawkins testifies to water-trees in the Canaries. Boot-trees bear abundantly in Lynn and elsewhere; and I have seen, in the entries of the wealthy, hat-trees with a fair show of fruit. A family-tree I once cultivated myself, and found therefrom but a scanty yield, and that quite tasteless and innutritious. Of trees bearing men we are not without examples; as those in the park of Louis the Eleventh of France. Who has forgotten, moreover, that olive-tree, growing in the Athenian's back garden, with its strange uxorious crop, for the general propagation of which, as of a new and precious variety, the philosopher Diogenes, hitherto uninterested in arboriculture, was so zealous? In the *sylva* of our own Southern States the females of my family have called my attention to the china-tree. Not to multiply examples, I will barely add to my list the birch-tree, in the smaller branches of which has been implanted so miraculous a virtue for communicating the Latin and Greek languages, and which may well, therefore, be classed among the trees producing necessaries of life,—*venerabile donum fatalis virgæ.* That money-trees existed in the golden age there want not prevalent reasons for our believing. For does not the old proverb, when it asserts that money does not grow on *every* bush, imply *a fortiori* that there were certain bushes which did produce it? Again, there is another ancient saw to the effect that money is the *root* of all evil. From which two adages it may be safe to infer that the aforesaid species of tree first degenerated into a shrub, then absconded underground, and finally, in our iron age, vanished altogether. In favourable exposures it may be conjectured that a specimen or two survived to a great age, as in the garden of the Hesperides; and, indeed, what else could that tree in the Sixth Æneid have been, with a branch whereof the Trojan hero procured admission to a territory, for the entering of which money is a surer passport than to a certain other more profitable (too) foreign kingdom? Whether these speculations of mine have any force in them, or whether they will not rather, by most readers, be deemed impertinent to the matter in hand, is a question which I leave to the determination of an indulgent posterity. That there were, in more primitive and happier times, shops where money was sold,—and that, too, on credit and at a bargain,—I take to be matter of demonstration. For what but a dealer in this article was that Æolus who supplied Ulysses with motive power for his fleet in bags? What that Ericus, king of Sweden, who is said to have kept the winds in his cap? What, in more recent times, those Lapland Nornas who traded in favourable breezes? All which will appear the more clearly when we consider that, even to this day, *raising the wind* is proverbial for raising money, and that brokers and banks were invented by the Venetians at a later period.

And now for the improvement of this digression. I find a parallel to Mr. Sawin's fortune in an adventure of my own. For, shortly after I had first broached to myself the before-stated natural-historical and archæological theories, as I was passing, *hæc negotia penitus mecum revolvens*, through one of the obscure suburbs of our New England metropolis, my eye was attracted by these words upon a sign-board,— CHEAP CASH-STORE. Here was at once the confirmation of my speculations, and the substance of my hopes. Here lingered the fragment of a happier past, or stretched out the first tremulous organic filament of a more fortunate future. Thus glowed the distant Mexico to the eyes of Sawin, as he looked through the dirty pane of the recruiting-office window, or speculated from the summit of that mirage-Pisgah which the imps of the bottle are so cunning in raising up. Already had my Alnaschar-fancy (even during that first half-believing glance) expended in various useful directions the funds to be obtained by pledging the manuscript of a proposed volume of discourses. Already did a clock ornament the tower of the Jaalam meeting-house, a gift appropriately, but modestly, commemorated in the parish and town records, both, for now many years, kept by myself. Already had my son Seneca completed his course at the University. Whether, for the moment, we may not be considered as actually lording it over those Baratarias with the viceroyalty of which Hope invests us, and whether we are ever so warmly housed as in our Spanish castles, would afford matter of argument. Enough that I found that sign-board to be no other than a bait to the trap of a decayed grocer. Nevertheless, I bought a pound of dates (getting short weight by reason of immense flights of harpy flies, who pursued and lighted upon their prey even in the very scales), which purchase I made not only with an eye to the little ones at home, but also as a figurative reproof of that too frequent habit of my mind, which, forgetting the due order of chronology, will often persuade me that the happy sceptre of Saturn is stretched over this Astræa-forsaken nineteenth century.

Having glanced at the ledger of Glory under the title *Sawin, B.*, let us extend our investigations, and discover if that instructive volume does not contain some charges more personally interesting to ourselves. I think we should be more economical of our resources, did we thoroughly appreciate the fact that, whenever Brother Jonathan seems to be thrusting his hand into his own pocket, he is, in fact, picking ours. I confess that the late *muck* which the country has been running has materially changed my views as to the best method of raising revenue. If, by means of direct taxation, the bills for every extraordinary outlay were brought under our immediate eye, so that, like thrifty house-keepers, we could see where and how fast the money was going, we should be less likely to commit extravagancies. At present these things are managed in such a hugger-mugger way, that we know not what we pay for ; the poor man is charged as much as the rich ; and, while we are saving and scrimping at the spigot, the government is drawing off at the bung. If we could know that a part of the money we expend for tea and coffee goes to buy powder and balls, and that it is Mexican blood which makes the clothes on our backs more costly, it would set some of us athinking. During the present fall I have often pictured to myself a government official entering my study and handing me the following bill :—

WASHINGTON, Sept. 30, 1848.

REV. HOMER WILBUR to 𝔘𝔫𝔠𝔩𝔢 𝔖𝔞𝔪𝔲𝔢𝔩.   Dr.

To his share of work done in Mexico on partnership account, sundry jobs, as below :—

,, killing, maiming, and wounding about 5000 Mexicans .	$2.00
,, slaughtering one woman carrying water to wounded .	.10
,, extra work on two different Sabbaths (one bombardment and one assault) whereby the Mexicans were prevented from defiling themselves with the idolatries of high mass.	3.50
,, throwing an especially fortunate and Protestant bombshell into the Cathedral at Vera Cruz, whereby several female Papists were slain at the altar	.50

To his proportion of cash paid for conquered territory	.	.	$1.75
,, do. do. for conquering do.	.	.	1.50
,, manuring do. with new superior compost called "American Citizen"	.	.	.50
,, extending the area of freedom and Protestantism	.	.	.01
,, glory	.	.	.01

Immediate payment is requested. $9.87

N.B.—Thankful for former favours, U. S. requests a continuance of patronage.   Orders executed with neatness and despatch.   Terms as low as those of any other contractor for the same kind and style of work.

I can fancy the official answering my look of horror with,—"Yes, Sir, it looks like a high charge, Sir; but in these days slaughtering is slaughtering."   Verily, I would that every one understood that it was; for it goes about obtaining money under the false pretence of being glory.   For me, I have an imagination which plays me uncomfortable tricks.   It happens to me sometimes to see a slaughterer on his way home from his day's work, and forthwith my imagination puts a cocked-hat upon his head and epaulettes upon his shoulders, and sets him up as a candidate for the Presidency.   So, also, on a recent public occasion, as the place assigned to the "Reverend Clergy" is just behind that of "Officers of the Army and Navy" in processions, it was my fortune to be seated at the dinner-table over against one of these respectable persons.   He was arrayed as (out of his own profession) only kings, court-officers, and footmen are in Europe, and Indians in America.   Now what does my over-officious imagination but set to work upon him, strip him of his gay livery, and present him to me coatless, his trousers thrust into the tops of a pair of boots thick with clotted blood, and a basket on his arm, out of which lolled a gore-smeared axe, thereby destroying my relish for the temporal mercies upon the board before me !—H. W.]

No. IX.

A THIRD LETTER FROM B. SAWIN, ESQ.

[Upon the following letter slender comment will be needful. In what river Selemnus has Mr. Sawin bathed, that he has become so swiftly oblivious of his former loves? From an ardent and (as befits a soldier) confident wooer of that coy bride, the popular favour, we see him subside of a sudden into the (I trust not jilted) Cincinnatus, returning to his plough with a goodly-sized branch of willow in his hand; figuratively returning, however, to a figurative plough, and from no profound affection for that honoured implement of husbandry (for which, indeed, Mr. Sawin never displayed any decided predilection), but in order to be gracefully summoned therefrom to more congenial labours. It would seem that the character of the ancient Dictator had become part of the recognised stock of our modern political comedy, though, as our term of office extends to a quadrennial length, the parallel is not so minutely exact as could be desired. It is sufficiently so, however, for purposes of scenic representation. An humble cottage (if built of logs, the better) forms the Arcadian background of the stage. This rustic paradise is labelled Ashland, Jaalam, North Bend, Marshfield, Kinderhook, or Bâton Rouge, as occasion demands. Before the door stands a something with one handle (the other painted in proper perspective), which represents, in happy ideal vagueness, the plough. To this the defeated candidate rushes with delirious joy, welcomed as a father by appropriate groups of happy labourers, or from it the successful one is torn with difficulty, sustained alone by a noble sense of public duty. Only I have observed that, if the scene be laid at Bâton Rouge or Ashland, the labourers are kept carefully in the background, and are heard to shout from behind the scenes in a singular tone resembling ululation, and accompanied by a sound not unlike vigorous clapping. This, however, may be artistically in keeping with the habits of the rustic population of those localities. The precise connection between agricultural pursuits and statesmanship I have not been able, after diligent inquiry, to discover. But that my investigations may not be barren of all fruit, I will mention one curious statistical fact, which I consider thoroughly established, namely, that no real farmer ever attains practically beyond a seat in General Court, however theoretically qualified for more exalted station.

It is probable that some other prospect has been opened to Mr.

Sawin, and that he has not made this great sacrifice without some definite understanding in regard to a seat in the cabinet or a foreign mission. It may be supposed that we of Jaalam were not untouched by a feeling of villatic pride in beholding our townsman occupying so large a space in the public eye. And to me, deeply revolving the qualifications necessary to a candidate in these frugal times, those of Mr. S. seemed peculiarly adapted to a successful campaign. The loss of a leg, an arm, an eye, and four fingers, reduced him so nearly to the condition of a *vox et præterea nihil*, that I could think of nothing but the loss of his head by which his chance could have been bettered. But since he has chosen to baulk our suffrages, we must content ourselves with what we can get, remembering *lactucas non esse dandas, dum cardui sufficiant.*—H. W.]

I spose you recollect thet I explained my gennle views
In the last billet thet I writ, 'way down from Veery Cruze,
Jest arter I'd a kind o' ben spontanously sot up
To run unanimously fer the Presidential cup;
O' course it worn't no wish o' mine, 'twuz ferflely distressin',
But poppiler enthusiasm gut so almighty pressin'
Thet, though like sixty all along I fumed an' fussed an' sorrered,
There didn't seem no ways to stop their bringin' on me forrerd:
Fact is, they udged the matter so, I couldn't help admittin'
The Father o' his Country's shoes no feet but mine 'ould fit in,
Besides the savin' o' the soles for ages to succeed,
Seein' thet with one wannut foot, a pair 'd be more 'n I need;
An', tell ye wut, them shoes 'll want a thund'rin sight o' patchin',
Ef this 'ere fashion is to last we've gut into o' hatchin'
A pair o' second Washintons fer every new election,—
Though, fur ez number one's consarned, I don't make no objection.

I wuz agoin' on to say thet wen at fust I saw
The masses would stick to't I wuz the Country's father-'n-
    law,
(They would ha' hed it *Father*, but I told 'em 't wouldn't du,
Coz thet wuz sutthin' of a sort they couldn't split in tu,
An' Washinton hed hed the thing laid fairly to his door
Nor darsn't say 'twon't his'n, much ez sixty year afore),
But 'taint no matter ez to thet; wen I wuz nomernated,
'Twon't natur but wut I should feel consid'able elated,
An' wile the hooraw o' the thing wuz kind o' noo an' fresh,
I thought our ticket would ha' caird the country with a resh.

Sence I've come hum, though, an' looked round, I think I
    seem to find
Strong argimunts ez thick ez fleas to make me change my
    mind;
It's clear to any one whose brain aint fur gone in a phthisis,
Thet hail Columby's happy land is goin' thru a crisis,
An' 'twouldn't noways du to hev the people's mind dis-
    tracted
By bein' all to once by sev'ral pop'lar names attackted;
'Twould save holl haycartloads o' fuss an' three four months
    o' jaw,
Ef some illustrous paytriot should back out an' withdraw;
So, ez I aint a crooked stick, jest like—like ole (I swow,
I dunno ez I know his name)—I'll go back to my plough.

Wenever an Amerikin distinguished politishin
Begins to try et wut they call definin' his posishin,
Wal, I, fer one, feel sure he aint gut nothin' to define;
It's so nine cases out o' ten, but jest that tenth is mine;
An' 'taint no more'n is proper 'n' right in sech a sitooation
To hint the course you think 'll be the savin' o' the nation;

To funk right out o' p'lit'cal strife aint thought to be the
    thing,
Without you deacon off the toon you want your folks should
    sing;
So I edvise the noomrous friends thet's in one boat with me
To jest up killock, jam right down their hellum hard a lee,
Haul the sheets taut, an', laying out upon the Suthun tack,
Make fer the safest port they can, wich, *I* think, is Ole Zack.

Next thing you'll want to know, I spose, wut argimunts I
    seem
To see thet makes me think this ere'll be the strongest
    team;
Fust place, I've ben consid'ble round in bar-rooms an'
    saloons
Agethrin' public sentiment, 'mongst Demmercrats and
    Coons,
An' 'taint ve'y offen thet I meet a chap but wut goes in
Fer Rough an' Ready, fair an' square, hufs, taller, horns,
    an' skin;
I don't deny but wut, fer one, ez fur ez I could see,
I didn't like at fust the Pheladelphy nomernee:
I could ha' pinted to a man thet wuz, I guess, a peg
Higher than him,—a soger, tu, an' with a wooden leg;
But every day with more an' more o' Taylor zeal I'm
    burnin',
Seein' wich way the tide thet sets to office is aturnin';
Wy, into Bellers's we notched the votes down on three
    sticks,—
'Twuz Birdofredum *one*, Cass *aught*, an' Taylor *twenty-six*,
An' bein' the on'y canderdate thet wuz upon the ground,
They said 'twuz no more'n right thet I should pay the
    drinks all round;

Ef I'd expected sech a trick, I wouldn't ha' cut my foot
By goin' an' votin' fer myself like a consumed coot;
It didn't make no diff'rence, though; I wish I may be cust,
Ef Bellers wuzn't slim enough to say he wouldn't trust!

Another pint thet influences the minds o' sober jedges
Is thet the Gin'ral hezn't gut tied hand an' foot with
    pledges;
He hezn't told ye wut he is, an' so there aint no knowin'
But wut he may turn out to be the best there is agoin';
This, at the on'y spot thet pinched, the shoe directly eases,
Coz every one is free to 'xpect percisely wut he pleases:
I want free-trade; you don't; the Gin'ral isn't bound to
    neither;—
I vote my way; you, yourn; an' both air sooted to a T
    there.
Ole Rough an' Ready, tu, 's a Wig, but without bein' ultry
(He's like a holsome hayinday, thet's warm, but isn't
    sultry);
He's jest wut I should call myself, a kin' o' *scratch*, ez
    'tware,
Thet aint exacly all a wig nor wholly your own hair;
I've ben a Wig three weeks myself, jest o' this mod'rate sort,
An' don't find them an' Demmercrats so different ez I
    thought;
They both act pooty much alike, an' push an' scrouge an'
    cus;
They're like two pickpockets in league fer Uncle Samwell's
    pus;
Each takes a side, an' then they squeeze the old man in
    between 'em,
Turn all his pockets wrong side out an' quick ez lightnin'
    clean 'em;

To nary one on 'em I'd trust a secon'-handed rail
No furder off 'an I could sling a bullock by the tail.

Webster sot matters right in thet air Mashfiel' speech o'
    his'n ;—
"Taylor," sez he, "aint nary ways the one thet I'd a
    chizzen,
Nor he aint fittin' fer the place, an' like ez not he aint
No more'n a tough old bullethead, an' no gret of a saint ;
But then," sez he, "obsarve my pint, he's jest ez good to
    vote fer
Ez though the greasin' on him worn't a thing to hire Choate
    fer ;
Aint it ez easy done to drop a ballot in a box
Fer one ez't is fer t'other, fer the bulldog ez the fox ?"
It takes a mind like Dannel's, fact, ez big ez all ou' doors,
To find out thet it looks like rain arter it fairly pours ;
I 'gree with him, it aint so dreffle troublesome to vote
Fer Taylor arter all,—it's jest to go an' change your coat ;
Wen he's once greased, you'll swaller him an' never know
    on't scurce,
Unless he scratches, goin' down, with them 'ere Gin'ral's
    spurs.
I've ben a votin' Demmercrat, ez reg'lar ez a clock,
But don't find goin' Taylor gives my narves no gret 'f a
    shock ;
Truth is, the cutest leadin' Wigs, ever sence fust they found
Wich side the bread gut buttered on, hev kep' a edgin'
    round ;
They kin' o' slipt the planks frum out th' ole platform one
    by one
An' made it gradooally noo, 'fore folks know'd wut wuz
    done,

Till, fur'z I know, there aint an inch thet I could lay my
　　han' on
But I, or any Demmercrat, feels comf'table to stan' on,
An' ole Wig doctrines act'lly look, their occ'pants bein'
　　gone,
Lonesome ez staddles on a mash without no hayricks on.

I spose it's time now I should give my thoughts upon the
　　plan,
Thet chipped the shell at Buffalo, o' settin' up ole Van.
I used to vote fer Martin, but, I swan, I'm clean disgusted, —
He aint the man thet I can say is fittin' to be trusted ;
He aint half antislav'ry 'nough, nor I aint sure, ez some be,
He'd go in fer abolishin' the Deestrick o' Columby ;
An', now I come to recollect, it kin' o' makes me sick'z
A horse, to think o' wut he wuz in eighteen thirty-six.
An' then, another thing ;—I guess, though mebby I am
　　wrong,
This Buff'lo plaster aint agoin' to dror almighty strong ;
Some folks, I know, hev gut th' idee thet No'thun dough 'll
　　rise,
Though, 'fore I see it riz an' baked, I wouldn't trust my
　　eyes ;
'Twill take more emptins, a long chalk, than this noo party's
　　gut,
To give sech heavy cakes ez them a start, I tell ye wut.
But even ef they caird the day, there wouldn't be no
　　endurin'
To stan' upon a platform with sech critters ez Van Buren ;—
An' his son John, tu, I can't think how thet 'ere chap
　　should dare
To speak ez he doos ; wy, they say he used to cuss an'
　　swear !

I spose he never read the hymn thet tells how down the
    stairs
A feller with long legs wuz throwed thet wouldn't say his
    prayers.
This brings me to another pint : the leaders o' the party
Aint jest sech men ez I can act along with free an' hearty ;
They aint not quite respectable, an' wen a feller's morrils
Don't toe the straightest kin' o' mark, wy, him an' me jest
    quarrils.
I went to a free soil meetin' once, an' wut d'ye think I see ?
A feller was aspoutin' there thet act'lly come to me,
About two year ago last spring, ez nigh ez I can jedge,
An' axed me ef I didn't want to sign the Temprunce pledge !
He's one o' them that goes about an' sez you hedn't ough' ter
Drink nothin', mornin', noon, or night, stronger 'an Taunton
    water.
There's one rule I've been guided by, in settlin' how to
    vote, ollers,—
I take the side thet *isn't* took by them consarned teetotallers.

Ez fer the niggers, I've ben South, an' thet hez changed my
    mind ;
A lazier, more ongrateful set you couldn't nowers find.
You know I mentioned in my last thet I should buy a nigger,
Ef I could make a purchase at a pooty mod'rate figger ;
So, ez there's nothin' in the world I'm fonder of 'an
    gunnin',
I closed a bargin finally to take a feller runnin'.
I shou'dered queen's-arm an' stumped out, an' wen I come
    t' th' swamp,
'Twor'n't very long afore I gut upon the nest o' Pomp ;
I come acrost a kin' o' hut, an', playin' round the door,
Some little woolly-headed cubs, ez many'z six or more.

At fust I thought o' firin', but *think twice* is safest ollers ;
There aint, thinks I, not one on 'em but's wuth his twenty
    dollars,
Or would be, ef I hed 'em back into a Christian land,—
How temptin' all on 'em would look upon an auction-stand !
(Not but wut *I* hate Slavery in th' abstract, stem to starn,—
I leave it ware our fathers did, a privit State consarn.)
Soon'z they see me, they yelled an' run, but Pomp wuz out
    ahoein'
A leetle patch o' corn he hed, or else there aint no knowin'
He wouldn't ha' took a pop at me ; but I hed gut the start,
An' wen he looked, I vow he groaned ez though he'd broke
    his heart ;
He done it like a white man, tu, ez nat'ral ez a pictur,
The imp'dunt, pis'nous hypocrite ! wus 'an a boy constrictur.
"You can't gum *me*, I tell ye now, an' so you needn't try,
I 'xpect my eye-teeth every mail, so jest shet up," sez I.
"Don't go to actin' ugly now, or else I'll jest let strip,
You'd best draw kindly, seein' 'z how I've gut ye on the
    hip ;
Besides, you darned ole fool, it aint no gret of a disaster
To be benev'lently druv back to a contented master,
Ware you hed Christian priv'ledges you don't seem quite
    aware of,
Or you'd ha' never run away from bein' well took care of ;
Ez fer kin' treatment, wy, he wuz so fond on ye, he said
He'd give a fifty spot right out, to git ye, 'live or dead ;
Wite folks aint sot by half ez much ; 'member I run away,
Wen I wuz bound to Cap'n Jakes, to Mattysqumscot bay ;
Don' know him, likely ? Spose not ; wal, the mean ole
    codger went
An' offered—wut reward, think ? Wal, it worn't no *less* 'n a
    cent."

Wal, I jest gut 'em into line, an' druv 'em on afore me,
The pis'nous brutes, I'd no idee o' the ill-will they bore me;
We walked till som'ers about noon, an' then it grew so hot
I thought it best to camp awile, so I chose out a spot
Jest under a magnoly tree, an' there right down I sot;
Then I unstrapped my wooden leg, coz it begun to chafe,
An' laid it down 'long side o' me, supposin' all wuz safe;
I made my darkies all set down around me in a ring,
An' sot an' kin' o' ciphered up how much the lot would
        bring;
But, wile I drinked the peaceful cup of a pure heart an'
        mind
(Mixed with some wiskey, now an' then), Pomp he snaked
        up behind,
An' creepin' grad'lly close tu, ez quiet ez a mink,
Jest grabbed my leg, and then pulled foot, quicker 'an you
        could wink,
An', come to look, they each on 'em hed gut behin' a tree,
An' Pomp poked out the leg a piece, jest so ez I could
        see,
An' yelled to me to throw away my pistils an' my gun,
Or else thet they'd cair off the leg, an' fairly cut an' run.
I vow I didn't b'lieve there wuz a decent alligatur
Thet hed a heart so destitoot o' common human natur;
However, ez there worn't no help, I finally give in
An' heft my arms away to git my leg safe back agin.
Pomp gethered all the weapins up, an' then he come an'
        grinned,
He showed his ivory some, I guess, an' sez, "You're fairly
        pinned;
Jest buckle on your leg agin, an' git right up an' come,
'Twunt du fer fammerly men like me to be so long from
        hum."

At fust I put my foot right down an' swore I wouldn't
    budge.
" Jest ez you choose," sez he, quite cool, "either be shot or
    trudge."
So this black-hearted monster took an' act'lly druv me
    back
Along the very feetmarks o' my happy mornin track,
An' kep' me pris'ner 'bout six months, an' worked me, tu,
    like sin,
Till I hed gut his corn an' his Carliny taters in ;
He made me larn him readin', tu (although the crittur saw
How much it hut my morril sense to act agin the law),
So'st he could read a Bible he'd gut ; an' axed ef I could
    pint
The North Star out ; but there I put his nose some out o'
    jint,
Fer I weeled roun' about sou'west, an', lookin' up a bit,
Picked out a middlin' shiny one an' tole him thet wuz it.
Fin'lly, he took me to the door, an' givin' me a kick,
Sez,—" Ef you know wut's best fer ye, be off, now, double-
    quick ;
The winter-time's a comin' on, an', though I gut ye cheap,
You're so darned lazy, I don't think you're hardly wuth
    your keep ;
Besides, the childrin's growin' up, an' you aint jest the
    model
I'd like to hev 'em immertate, an' so you'd better toddle ! "

Now is there any thin' on airth 'll ever prove to me
Thet renegader slaves like him air fit fer bein' free ?
D'you think they'll suck me in to jine the Buff'lo chaps, an'
    them
Rank infidels thet go agin the Scriptur'l cus o' Shem ?

Not by a jugfull! sooner'n thet, I'd go thru fire an' water;
Wen I hev once made up my mind, a meet'nhus aint sotter;
No, not though all the crows thet flies to pick my bones wuz
          cawin',—
I guess we're in a Christian land,—

                              Yourn,
                    BIRDOFREDUM SAWIN.

[Here, patient reader, we take leave of each other, I trust with some
mutual satisfaction. I say *patient*, for I love not that kind which skims
dippingly over the surface of the page, as swallows over a pool before
rain. By such no pearls shall be gathered. But if no pearls there be
(as, indeed, the world is not without example of books wherefrom the
longest-winded diver shall bring up no more than his proper handful
of mud), yet let us hope that an oyster or two may reward adequate
perseverance. If neither pearls nor oysters, yet is patience itself a gem
worth diving deeply for.

It may seem to some that too much space has been usurped by my
own private lucubrations, and some may be fain to bring against me
that old jest of him who preached all his hearers out of the meeting-
house save only the sexton, who, remaining for yet a little space, from
a sense of official duty, at last gave out also, and, presenting the keys,
humbly requested our preacher to lock the doors, when he should have
wholly relieved himself of his testimony. I confess to a satisfaction in
the self act of preaching, nor do I esteem a discourse to be wholly
thrown away even upon a sleeping or unintelligent auditory. I cannot
easily believe that the Gospel of Saint John, which Jacques Cartier
ordered to be read in the Latin tongue to the Canadian savages, upon
his first meeting with them, fell altogether upon stony ground. For
the earnestness of the preacher is a sermon appreciable by dullest
intellects and most alien ears. In this wise did Episcopius convert
many to his opinions, who yet understood not the language in which he
discoursed. The chief thing is, that the messenger believe that he has
an authentic message to deliver. For counterfeit messengers that mode
of treatment which Father John de Plano Carpini relates to have pre-
vailed among the Tartars would seem effectual, and, perhaps, deserved
enough. For my own part, I may lay claim to so much of the spirit
of martyrdom as would have led me to go into banishment with those

clergymen whom Alphonso the Sixth of Portugal drave out of his kingdom for refusing to shorten their pulpit eloquence. It is possible that, having been invited into my brother Biglow's desk, I may have been too little scrupulous in using it for the venting of my own peculiar doctrines to a congregation drawn together in the expectation and with the desire of hearing him.

I am not wholly unconscious of a peculiarity of mental organisation which impels me, like the railroad-engine with its train of cars, to run backward for a short distance in order to obtain a fairer start. I may compare myself to one fishing from the rocks when the sea runs high, who, misinterpreting the suction of the undertow for the biting of some larger fish, jerks suddenly, and finds that he has *caught bottom*, hauling in upon the end of his line a trail of various *algæ*, among which, nevertheless, the naturalist may haply find somewhat to repay the disappointment of the angler. Yet have I conscientiously endeavoured to adapt myself to the impatient temper of the age, daily degenerating more and more from the high standard of our pristine New England. To the catalogue of lost arts I would mournfully add also that of listening to two-hour sermons. Surely we have been abridged into a race of pigmies. For, truly, in those of the old discourses yet subsisting to us in print, the endless spinal column of divisions and subdivisions can be likened to nothing so exactly as to the vertebræ of the saurians, whence the theorist may conjecture a race of Anakim proportionate to the withstanding of these other monsters. I say Anakim rather than Nephelim, because there seem reasons for supposing that the race of those whose heads (though no giants) are constantly enveloped in clouds (which that name imports) will never become extinct. The attempt to vanquish the innumerable *heads* of one of those aforementioned discourses may supply us with a plausible interpretation of the second labour of Hercules, and his successful experiment with fire affords us a useful precedent.

But while I lament the degeneracy of the age in this regard, I cannot refuse to succumb to its influence. Looking out through my study-window, I see Mr. Biglow at a distance busy in gathering his Baldwins, of which, to judge by the number of barrels lying about under the trees, his crop is more abundant than my own,—by which sight I am admonished to turn to those orchards of the mind wherein my labours may be more prospered, and apply myself diligently to the preparation of my next Sabbath's discourse.—H. W.]

THE BIGLOW PAPERS.

(Second Series.)

BIRDOFREDUM SAWIN, ESQ., TO MR. HOSEA BIGLOW.

LETTER FROM THE REVEREND HOMER WILBUR, M.A.,
INCLOSING THE EPISTLE AFORESAID.

JAALAM, 15th Nov. 1861.

It is not from any idle wish to obtrude my humble person with undue prominence upon the public view that I resume my pen upon the present occasion. *Juniores ad labores.* But having been a main instrument in rescuing the talent of my young parishioner from being buried in the ground, by giving it such warrant with the world as would be derived from a name already widely known by several printed discourses (all of which I may be permitted without immodesty to state have been deemed worthy of preservation in the Library of Harvard College by my esteemed friend Mr. Sibley), it seemed becoming that I should not only testify to the genuineness of the following production, but call attention to it, the more as Mr. Biglow had so long been silent as to be in danger of absolute oblivion. I insinuate no claim to any share in the authorship (*vix ea nostra voco*) of the works already published by Mr. Biglow, but merely take to myself the credit of having fulfilled toward them the office of taster (*experto crede*), who, having first tried, could afterwards bear witness—an office always arduous, and sometimes even dangerous, as in the case of those devoted persons who venture their lives in the deglutition of patent medicines (*dolus latet in generalibus,* there is deceit in the most of them), and thereafter are wonderfully preserved long enough to append their signatures to testimonials in the diurnal and hebdomadal prints. I say not this as covertly glancing at the authors of certain manuscripts which have been submitted to my literary judgment (though an epic in twenty-four books on the " Taking of Jericho " might, save for the prudent forethought of Mrs. Wilbur in secreting the same just as I had arrived beneath the walls, and was beginning a catalogue of the various horns and their blowers, too ambitiously emulous in longanimity of Homer's list of ships, might, I say, have rendered frustrate any hope I could entertain *vacare Musis* for the small remainder of my days), but only further to secure myself against any imputation of unseemly forthputting. I will barely subjoin, in this connection, that, whereas Job was left to desire, in the soreness of his heart, that his adversary had written a book, as perchance misanthropically wishing to indite a review thereof, yet was not Satan allowed so far to tempt him as to send Bildad, Eliphaz, and Zophar each with an unprinted work in his wallet to be submitted to his censure. But of this enough. Were I in need of other excuse, I might add that I write by the express desire of Mr. Biglow himself, whose entire winter leisure is occupied, as he assures me, in answering demands for autographs, a labour exacting enough in itself, and egregiously so to him, who, being no ready penman, cannot sign so much as his name without strange contortions of the face (his nose, even, being essential to complete success), and painfully suppressed Saint-Vitus-dance of every muscle in his body. This, with his having been put in the commission of the Peace by our excellent Governor (*O, si sic omnes!*) immediately on his accession to office, keeps him continually employed. *Haud inexpertus loquor*, having for many years written myself J.P., and being not seldom applied to for specimens of my chirography, a request to which I have sometimes too weakly assented, believing as I do that nothing written of set purpose can properly be called an autograph, but only those unpremeditated sallies and lively runnings which betray the fireside Man instead of the hunted Notoriety doubling on his pursuers. But it is time that I should bethink me of Saint Austin's prayer, *Libera me a meipso*, if I would arrive at the matter in hand.

Moreover, I had yet another reason for taking up the pen myself. I am informed that the *Atlantic Monthly* is mainly indebted for its success to the contributions and editorial supervision of Dr. Holmes, whose excellent *Annals of America* occupy an honoured place upon my shelves. The journal itself I have never seen ; but if this be so, it should seem that the recommendation of a brother clergyman (though *par magis quam similis*) would carry a greater weight. I suppose that you have a department for historical lucubrations, and should be glad, if deemed desirable, to forward for publication my " Collections for the Antiquities of Jaalam," and my (now happily complete) pedigree of the Wilbur family from its *fons et origo*, the Wild Boar of Ardennes.

Withdrawn from the active duties of my profession by the settlement of a colleague-pastor, the Reverend Jeduthun Hitchcock, formerly of Brutus-Four-Corners, I might find time for further contributions to general literature on similar topics. I have made large advances towards a completer genealogy of Mrs. Wilbur's family, the Pilcoxes, not, if I know myself, from any idle vanity, but with the sole desire of rendering myself useful in my day and generation. *Nulla dies sine lineâ.* I inclose a meteorological register, a list of the births, deaths, and marriages, and a few *memorabilia* of longevity in Jaalam East Parish for the last half-century. Though spared to the unusual period of more than eighty years, I find no diminution of my faculties or abatement of my natural vigour, except a scarcely sensible decay of memory, and a necessity of recurring to younger eyesight for the finer print in Cruden. It would gratify me to make some further provision for declining years from the emoluments of my literary labours—I had intended to effect an insurance on my life, but was deterred therefrom by a circular from one of the offices, in which the sudden deaths of so large a proportion of the insured was set forth as an inducement, that it seemed to me little less than the tempting of Providence. *Neque in summâ inopiâ levis esse senectus potest, ne sapienti quidem.*

Thus far concerning Mr. Biglow; and so much seemed needful (*brevis esse laboro*) by way of preliminary, after a silence of fourteen years. He greatly fears lest he may in this essay have fallen below himself, well knowing that, if exercise be dangerous on a full stomach, no less so is writing on a full reputation. Beset as he has been on all sides, he could not refrain, and would only imprecate patience till he shall again have "got the hang" (as he calls it) of an accomplishment long disused. The letter of Mr. Sawin was received some time in last June, and others have followed, which will in due season be submitted to the public. How largely his statements are to be depended on I more than merely dubitate. He was always distinguished for a tendency to exaggeration—it might almost be qualified by a stronger term. *Fortiter mentire, aliquid hæret*, seemed to be his favourite rule of rhetoric. That he is actually where he says he is, the postmark would seem to confirm; that he was received with the public demonstrations he describes would appear consonant with what we know of the habits of those regions; but further than this I venture not to decide. I have sometimes suspected a vein of humour in him which leads him to speak by contraries; but since, in the unrestrained intercourse of private life, I have never observed in him any striking powers of invention, I am the more willing to put a certain qualified faith in the incidents and the details of life and manners which give to his narrative some of the interest and entertainment which characterises a Century Sermon.

It may be expected of me that I should say something to justify myself with the world for a seeming inconsistency with my well-known principles in allowing my youngest son to raise a company for the war, a fact known to all through the medium of the public prints. I did reason with the young man, but *expellas naturam furcâ, tamen usque recurrit.* Having myself been a chaplain in 1812, I could the less wonder that a man of war had sprung from my loins. It was, indeed, grievous to send my Benjamin, the child of my old age; but after the discomfiture of Manassas, I with my own hands did buckle on his armour, trusting in the great Comforter for strength according to my need. For truly the memory of a brave son dead in his shroud were a greater staff of my declining years than a coward, though his days might be long in the land, and he should get much goods. It is not till our earthen vessels are broken that we find and truly possess the treasure that was laid up in them. *Migravi in animam meam,* I have sought refuge in my own soul; nor would I be shamed by the heathen comedian with his *Nequam illud verbum, bene vult, nisi bene facit.* During our dark days I read constantly in the inspired book of Job, which I believe to contain more food to maintain the fibre of the soul for right living and high thinking than all Pagan literature together, though I would by no means vilipend the study of the classics. There I read that Job said in his despair, even as the fool saith in his heart there is no God—"The tabernacles of robbers prosper, and they that provoke God are secure" (Job xii. 6). But I sought farther till I found this Scripture also, which I would have those perpend who have striven to turn our Israel aside to the worship of strange gods—"If I did despise the cause of my man-servant or of my maid-servant when they contended with me, what then shall I do when God riseth up? and when he visiteth, what shall I answer him?" (Job xxxi. 13, 14). On this text I preached a discourse on the last day of Fasting and Humiliation with general acceptance, though there were not wanting one or two Laodiceans who said that I should have waited till the President announced his policy. But let us hope and pray, remembering this of Saint Gregory, *Vult Deus rogari, vult cogi, vult quâdam importunitate vinci.*

We had our first fall of snow on Friday last. Frosts have been unusually backward this fall. A singular circumstance occurred in this town on the 20th October, in the family of Deacon Pelatiah Tinkham. On the previous evening, a few moments before family prayers,

.   .   .   .

[The editors of the *Atlantic* find it necessary here to cut short the letter of their valued correspondent, which seemed calculated rather on the rates of longevity in Jaalam than for less favoured localities. They have every encouragement to hope that he will write again.]

With esteem and respect,

Your obedient Servant,

HOMER WILBUR, A.M.

IT'S some consid'ble of a spell sence I hain't writ no letters,
An' ther' 's gret changes hez took place in all polit'cle
    metters :
Some canderdates air dead an' gone, an' some hez ben
    defeated,
Which 'mounts to pooty much the same ; fer it's ben proved
    repeated
A betch o' bread thet hain't riz once ain't goin' to rise agin,
An' it's jest money throwed away to put the emptins in :
But thet's wut folks wun't never larn ; they dunno how to go,
Arter you want their room, no more'n a bullet-headed beau ;
Ther' 's ollers chaps a-hangin' roun' thet can't see pea-time's
    past,
Mis'ble as roosters in a rain, heads down an' tails half-mast :
It ain't disgraceful bein' beat, when a holl nation doos it,
But Chance is like an amberill,—it don't take twice to lose it.

I spose you're kin' o' cur'ous, now, to know why I hain't
    writ.
Wal, I've ben where a litt'ry taste don't somehow seem to git
Th' encouragement a feller 'd think, thet's used to public
    schools,
An' where sech things ez paper 'n' ink air clean agin the
    rules :

A kind o' vicyvarsy house, built dreffle strong an' stout,
So 's 't honest people can't git in, ner t' other sort git out,
An' with the winders so contrived, you'd prob'ly like the
　　　view
Better a-lookin' in than out, though it seems sing'lar, tu;
But then the landlord sets by ye, can't bear ye out o'
　　　sight,
And locks ye up ez reg'lar ez an outside door at night.

This world is awfle contrary: the rope may stretch your
　　　neck
Thet mebby kep' another chap frum washin' off a wreck;
An' you will see the taters grow in one poor feller's patch,
So small no self-respectin' hen thet vallied time 'ould scratch,
So small the rot can't find 'em out, an' then agin, nex'
　　　door,
Ez big ez wut hogs dream on when they're 'most too fat to
　　　snore.
But groutin' ain't no kin' o' use; an' ef the fust throw fails,
Why, up an' try agin, thet's all,—the coppers ain't all tails;
Though I *hev* seen 'em when I thought they hedn't no
　　　more head
Than 'd sarve a nussin' Brigadier thet gits some ink to shed.

When I writ last, I'd ben turned loose by thet blamed
　　　nigger, Pomp,
Ferlorner than a musquash, ef you'd took an' dreened his
　　　swamp:
But I ain't o' the meechin' kind, thet sets an' thinks fer
　　　weeks
The bottom's out o' th' univarse coz their own gill-pot leaks.
I hed to cross bayous an' criks (wal, it did beat all natur'),
Upon a kin' o' corderoy, fust log, then alligator:

Luck'ly the critters warn't sharp-sot; I guess 't wuz overruled
They'd done their mornin's marketin' an' gut their hunger
  cooled;
Fer missionaries to the Creeks an' runaways are viewed
By them an' folks ez sent express to be their reg'lar food:
Wutever 't wuz, they laid an' snoozed ez peacefully ez
  sinners,
Meek ez disgestin' deacons be at ordination dinners;
Ef any on 'em turned an' snapped, I let 'em kin' o' taste
My live-oak leg, an' so, ye see, ther' warn't no gret o' waste.
Fer they found out in quicker time than ef they'd ben to
  college
'T warn't heartier food than though 't wuz made out o' the
  tree o' knowledge.
But *I* tell *you* my other leg hed larned wut pizon-nettle
  meant,
An' var'ous other usefle things, afore I reached a settlement,
An' all o' me thet wuzn't sore an' sendin' prickles thru me
Wuz jest the leg I parted with in lickin' Montezumy:
A usefle limb it's ben to me, an' more of a support
Than wut the other hez ben,—coz I dror my pension for 't.

Wal, I gut in at last where folks wuz civerlized an' white,
Ez I diskivered to my cost afore 't wuz hardly night;
Fer 'z I wuz settin' in the bar a-takin' sunthin' hot,
An' feelin' like a man agin, all over in one spot,
A feller thet sot opposite, arter a squint at me,
Lep up an' drawed his peacemaker, an', "Dash it, Sir,"
  suz he,
"I'm doubledashed ef you ain't him thet stole my yeller
  chettle
(You're all the stranger thet's around), so now you've gut to
  settle;

It ain't no use to argerfy ner try to cut up frisky,
I know ye ez I know the smell o' ole chain-lightnin'
    whisky;
We're lor-abidin' folks down here, we'll fix ye so 's 't a bar
Would n' tech ye with a ten-foot pole; (Jedge, you jest warm
    the tar;)
You'll think you'd better ha' gut among a tribe o' Mongrel
    Tartars,
'Fore we've done showin' how we raise our Southun prize
    tar-martyrs;
A moultin' fallen cherubim, ef he should see ye, 'd snicker,
Thinkin' he hedn't nary chance. Come, genlemun, le' 's
    liquor;
An', Gin'ral, when you've mixed the drinks an' chalked 'em
    up, tote roun'
An' see ef ther' 's a feather-bed (thet's borryable) in town.
We'll try ye fair, Ole Grafted-Leg, an' ef the tar wun't
    stick,
Th' ain't not a juror here but wut 'll 'quit ye double-quick."
To cut it short, I wun't say sweet, they gi' me a good dip
(They ain't *perfessin'* Bahptists here), then give the bed a
    rip,—
The jury 'd sot, an' quicker 'n a flash they hetched me out,
    a livin'
Extemp'ry mammoth turkey-chick fer a Feejee Thanksgivin'.

Thet I felt some stuck up is wut it's nat'ral to suppose,
When poppylar enthusiasm hed furnished me sech clo'es;
(Ner 't ain't without edvantiges, this kin' o' suit, ye see,
It's water-proof, an' water 's wut I like kep' out o' me;)
But nut content with thet, they took a kerridge from the
    fence
An' rid me roun' to see the place, entirely free 'f expense,

With forty-'leven new kines o' sarse without no charge
    acquainted me,
Gi' me three cheers, an' vowed thet I wuz all their fahncy
    painted me ;
They treated me to all their eggs; (they keep 'em I should
    think,
Fer sech ovations, pooty long, for they wuz mos' distinc' ;)
They starred me thick 'z the Milky-Way with indiscrim'nit
    cherity,
Fer wut we call reception eggs air sunthin' of a rerity ;
Green ones is plentifle anough, skurce wuth a nigger's
    getherin',
But your dead-ripe ones ranges high fer treatin' Nothun
    bretherin :
A spotteder, ringstreakeder child the' warn't in Uncle Sam's
Holl farm,—a cross of stripèd pig an' one o' Jacob's lambs ;
'T wuz Dannil in the lions' den, new an' enlarged edition,
An' everythin' fust-rate o' 'ts kind, the' warn't no impersition.
People 's impulsiver down here than wut our folks to home
    be,
An' kin' o' go it 'ith a resh in raisin' Hail Columby :
Thet's *so :* an' they swarmed out like bees, for your real
    Southun men's
Time isn't o' much more account than an ole settin'
    hen's ;
(They jest work semioccashnally or else don't work at
    all,
An' so their time an' 'tention both air et saci'ty's call).
Talk about hospitality ! wut Nothun town d'ye know
Would take a totle stranger up an' treat him gratis so ?
You'd better b'lieve ther' 's nothin' like this spendin' days
    an' nights
Along 'ith a dependent race fer civerlisin' whites.

But this wuz all prelim'nary ; it's so Gran' Jurors here
Fin' a true bill, a hendier way than ourn, an' nut so dear ;
So arter this they sentenced me, to make all tight 'n' snug,
Afore a reg'lar court o' law, to ten years in the Jug.
I did n' make no gret defence : you don't feel much like
    speakin',
When, ef you let your clamshells gape, a quart o' tar will
    leak in :
I *hev* hearn tell o' wingèd words, but pint o' fact it tethers
The spoutin' gift to hev your words tu thick sot on with
    feathers,
An' Choate ner Webster wouldn't ha' made an A1 kin' o'
    speech
Astride a Southun chestnut horse sharper 'n a baby's
    screech.

Two year ago they ketched the thief, 'n' seein' I wuz
    innercent,
They jest oncorked an' le' me run, an' in my stid the sinner
    sent
To see how *he* liked pork 'n' pone flavored with wa'nut
    saplin',
An' nary social priv'ledge but a one-hoss, starn-wheel
    chaplin.
When I come out, the folks behaved mos' gen'manly an'
    harnsome ;
They 'lowed it wouldn't be more 'n right, ef I should cuss
    'n' darn some :
The Cunnle he apolergised ; suz he, " I'll du wut's right,
I'll give ye settisfection now by shootin' ye at sight,
An' give the nigger (when he's caught), to pay him fer his
    trickin'
In gittin' the wrong man took up, a most H fired lickin',—

It's jest the way with all on 'em, the inconsistent critters,

They're 'most enough to make a man blaspheme his
    mornin' bitters;

I'll be your frien' thru thick an' thin an' in all kines o'
    weathers,

An' all you'll hev to pay fer 's jest the waste o' tar an'
    feathers :

A lady owned the bed, ye see, a widder, tu, Miss Shennon;

It wuz her mite; we would ha' took another, ef ther 'd ben
    one :

We don't make *no* charge for the ride an' all the other fixins.

Le' 's liquor; Gin'ral, you can chalk our friend for all the
    mixins."

A meetin' then wuz called, where they "RESOLVED, Thet
    we respec'

B. S. Esquire for quallerties o' heart an' intellec'

Peculiar to Columby's sile, an' not to no one else's,

Thet makes Európean tyrans scringe in all their gilded
    pel'ces,

An' doos gret honor to our race an' Southun institootions

(I give ye jest the substance o' the leadin' resolootions :)

RESOLVED, Thet we revere in him a soger 'thout a flor,

A martyr to the princerples o' libbaty an' lor :

RESOLVED, Thet other nations all, ef sot 'longside o' us,

For vartoo, larnin', chivverlry, ain't noways wuth a cuss."

They gut up a subscription, tu, but no gret come o' *that*,

I 'xpect in cairin' of it roun' they took a leaky hat;

Though Southun genelmun ain't slow at puttin' down their
    name

(When they can write), fer in the eend it comes to jest the
    same,

Because, ye see, 't 's the fashion here to sign an' not to think

A critter 'd be so sordid ez to ax 'em for the chink :

10

I didn't call but jest on one, an' *he* drawed toothpick on
    me,
An' reckoned he warn't goin' to stan' no sech doggauned
    econ'my;
So nothin' more wuz realised, 'ceptin' the good-will shown,
Than ef 't had ben from fust to last a reg'lar Cotton Loan.
It's a good way, though, come to think, coz ye enjy the
    sense
O' lendin' lib'rally to the Lord, an' nary red o' 'xpense:
Sence then I've gut my name up for a gin'rous-hearted
    man
By jes' subscribin' right an' left on this high-minded plan;
I've gin away my thousans so to every Southun sort
O' missions, colleges, an' sech, ner ain't no poorer for 't.

I warn't so bad off, arter all; I needn't hardly mention
Thet Guv'ment owed me quite a pile for my arrears o'
    pension,—
I mean the poor, weak thing we *hed:* we run a new one
    now,
Thet strings a feller with a claim up tu the nighest bough,
An' *prectises* the rights o' man, purtects down-trodden
    debtors,
Ner wun't hev creditors about a-scrougin' o' their betters:
Jeff 's got the last idees ther' is, poscrip', fourteenth edition,
He knows it takes some enterprise to run an oppersition;
Ourn 's the fust thru-by-daylight train, with all ou'doors for
    deepot,
Yourn goes so slow, you'd think 'twuz drawed by a last
    cent'ry teapot;—
Wal, I gut all on 't paid in gold afore our State seceded,
An' done wal, for Confed'rit bonds warn't jest the cheese I
    needed:

Nut but wut they're ez *good* ez gold, but then it's hard
    a-breakin' on 'em,

An' ignorant folks is ollers sot an' wun't git used to takin'
    on 'em;

They're wuth ez much ez wut they wuz afore ole Mem'nger
    signed 'em,

An' go off middlin' wal for drinks, when ther' 's a knife
    behind 'em;

We *du* miss silver, jest fer thet an' ridin' in a bus,

Now we've shook off the despots thet was suckin' at our pus;

An' it's *because* the South's so rich; 'twuz nat'ral to expec'

Supplies o' change wuz jest the things we shouldn't recollec';

We'd ough' to ha' thought aforehan', though, o' thet good
    rule o' Crockett's,

For 't 's tiresome cairin' cotton-bales an' niggers in your
    pockets,

Ner 't ain't quite hendy to pass off one o' your six-foot
    Guineas

An' git your halves an' quarters back in gals an' pickaninnies:

Wal, 't ain't quite all a feller 'd ax, but then ther' 's this to
    say,

It's on'y jest among ourselves thet we expec' to pay;

Our system would ha' caird us thru in any Bible cent'ry,

'Fore this onscripterl plan come up o' books by double entry;

We go the patriarkle here out o' all sight an' hearin',

For Jacob warn't a circumstance to Jeff at financierin';

He never 'd thought o' borryin' from Esau like all nater

An' then cornfiscatin' all debts to sech a small pertater;

There's p'litickle econ'my, now, combined 'ith morril beauty

Thet saycrifices privit eends (your in'my's, tu) to dooty!

Wy, Jeff 'd ha' gin him five an' won his eye-teeth 'fore he
    knowed it,

An', stid o' wastin' pottage, he'd ha' eat it up an' owed it.

But I wuz goin' on to say how I come here to dwall;—
'Nough said, thet, arter lookin' roun', I liked the place so
    wal,
Where niggers doos a double good, with us atop to stiddy
    'em,
By bein' proofs o' prophecy an' cirkleatin' medium,
Where a man's sunthin' cos he's white, an' whiskey's cheap
    ez fleas,
An' the financial pollercy jest sooted my idees,
Thet I friz down right where I wuz, married the Widder
    Shennon,
(Her thirds wuz part in cotton-land, part in the curse o'
    Canaan,)
An' here I be ez lively ez a chipmunk on a wall,
With nothin' to feel riled about much later 'n Eddam's
    fall.

Ez fur ez human foresight goes, we made an even trade:
She gut an overseer, an' I a fem'ly ready-made
(The youngest on 'em 's 'most growed up), rugged an' spry
    ez weazles,
So 's 't ther' 's no resk o' doctors' bills fer hoopin' cough
    an' measles.
Our farm 's at Turkey-Buzzard Roost, Little Big Boosy
    River,
Wal located in all respex—fer 't ain't the chills 'n' fever
Thet makes my writin' seem to squirm; a Southuner 'd
    allow I'd
Some call to shake, for I've jest hed to meller a new cow-
    hide.
Miss S. is all 'f a lady; th' ain't no better on Big Boosy,
Ner one with more accomplishmunts 'twixt here an'
    Tuscaloosy;

She's an F. F., the tallest kind, an' prouder 'n the Gran'
    Turk,
An' never hed a relative thet done a stroke o' work ;
Hern ain't a scrimpin' fem'ly sech ez *you* git up Down East,
Th' ain't a growed member on 't but owes his thousuns et
    the least :
She *is* some old; but then agin ther' 's drawbacks in my
    sheer :
Wut 's left o' me ain't more 'n enough to make a Brigadier :
The wust is, she hez tantrums; she is like Seth Moody's gun
(Him thet wuz nicknamed frum his limp Ole Dot an' Kerry
    One) ;
He'd left her loaded up a spell, an' hed to git her clear,
So he onhitched,—Jeerusalem ! the middle o' last year
Wuz right nex' door compared to where she kicked the
    critter tu
(Though *jest* where he brought up wuz wut no human never
    knew) ;
His brother Asaph picked her up an' tied her to a tree,
An' then she kicked an hour 'n' a half afore she'd let it be :
Wal, Miss S. *doos* hev cuttins-up an' pourins-out o' vials,
But then she hez her widder's thirds, an' all on uz hez
    trials.
My objec', though, in writin' now warn't to allude to sech,
But to another suckemstance more dellykit to tech,—
I want thet you should grad'lly break my merriage to
    Jerushy,
An' there's a heap of argymunts thet's emple too indooce ye:
Fust place, State's Prison,—wal, it's true it warn't fer crime,
    o' course,
But then it's jest the same fer her in gittin' a disvorce ;
Nex' place, my State's secedin' out hez leg'lly lef' me free
To merry any one I please, pervidin' it's a she ;

Fin'lly, I never wun't come back, she needn't hev no fear
    on't,
But then it's wal to fix things right fer fear Miss S. should
    hear on't;
Lastly, I've gut religion South, an' Rushy she's a pagan
Thet sets by th' graven imiges o' the gret Nothun Dagon;
(Now I hain't seen one in six munts, for, sence our Treasbry
    Loan,
Though yaller boys is thick anough, eagles hez kind o'
    flown;)
An' ef J. wants a stronger pint than them thet I hev stated,
Wy, she's an aliun in'my now, an' I've ben cornfiscated,—
For sence we've entered on th' estate o' the late nayshnul
    eagle,
She haint' no kin' o' right but jest wut I allow ez legle:
Wut *doos* Secedin' mean, ef 't ain't thet nat'rul rights hez
    riz, 'n'
Thet wut is mine 's my own, but wut's another man's ain't
    his'n?

Besides, I couldn't do no else; Miss S. suz she to me,
"You've sheered my bed," [Thet's when I paid my
    interduction fee
To Southun rites,] "an' kep' your sheer," [Wal, I allow it
    sticked
So 's 't I wuz most six weeks in gaol afore I gut me picked.]
"Ner never paid no demmiges; but thet wun't do no harm,
Pervidin' thet you'll ondertake to oversee the farm;
(My eldes' boy is so took up, wut with the Ringtail
    Rangers
An settin' in the Jestice-Court for welcomin' o' strangers";)
[He sot on *me* ;] "an' so, ef you'll jest ondertake the care
Upon a mod'rit sellery, we'll up an' call it square;

But ef you *can't* conclude," suz she, an' give a kin' o' grin,
"Wy, the Gran' Jury, I expect, 'll hev to set agin."
Thet's the way metters stood at fust; now wut wuz I to du,
But jest to make the best on't an' off coat an' buckle tu?
Ther' ain't a livin' man thet finds an income necessarier
Than me,—bimeby I'll tell ye how I fin'lly come to merry
    her.

She hed another motive, tu; I mention of it here
T' encourage lads thet's growin' up to study 'n' persevere,
An' show 'em how much better 't pays to mind their winter-
    schoolin'
Than to go off on benders 'n' sech, an' waste their time in
    foolin'
Ef 't warn't for studyin' evenins, I never 'd ha' been here
An orn'ment o' society, in my approprut spear:
She wanted somebody, ye see, o' taste an' cultivation,
To talk along o' preachers when they stopt to the planta-
    tion;
For folks in Dixie th't read an' write, onless it is by jarks
Is skurce ez wut they wuz among th' oridgenal patriarchs;
To fit a feller f' wut they call the soshle higherarchy,
All thet you've gut to know is jest beyund an evrage
    darky;
Schoolin' 's wut they can't seem to stan', they're tu con-
    sarned high-pressure,
An' knowin' t' much might spile a boy for bein' a Secesher.
We hain't no settled preachin' here, ner ministeril taxes;
The min'ster's only settlement 's the carpet-bag he packs
    his
Razor an' soap-brush intu, with his hymbook an' his
    Bible,—
But they *du* preach, I swan to man, it's puf'kly indescrib'le!

They go it like an Ericsson's ten-hoss-power coleric ingine,
An' make Ole Split-Foot winch an' squirm, for all he's
    used to singein';
Hawkins's whetstone ain't a pinch o' primin' to the innards
To hearin' on 'em put free grace t' a lot o' tough old sin-
    hards!
But I must eend this letter now: 'fore long I'll send a fresh
    un:
I've lots o' things to write about, perticklerly Seceshun:
I'm called off now to mission-work, to let a leetle law in
To Cynthy's hide: an' so, till death,

               Yourn,
               BIRDOFREDUM SAWIN.

MASON AND SLIDELL: A YANKEE IDYLL.

TO THE EDITORS OF THE "ATLANTIC MONTHLY."

                     JAALAM, 6th Jan. 1862.

  GENTLEMEN,—I was highly gratified by the insertion of a portion of my letter in the last number of your valuable and entertaining Miscellany, though in a type which rendered its substance inaccessible even to the beautiful new spectacles presented to me by a Committee of the Parish on New Year's Day. I trust that I was able to bear your very considerable abridgment of my lucubrations with a spirit becoming a Christian. My third grand-daughter, Rebekah, aged fourteen years, and whom I have trained to read slowly and with proper emphasis (a practice too much neglected in our modern systems of education), read aloud to me the excellent essay upon " Old Age," the author of which I cannot help suspecting to be a young man who has never yet known what it was to have snow (*canities morosa*) upon his own roof. *Dissolve frigus, largè super foco ligna reponens* is a rule for the young; whose wood-pile is yet abundant for such cheerful lenitives. A good life behind him is the best thing to keep an old man's shoulders from shivering at every breath of sorrow or ill-fortune. But methinks it were easier for an old man to feel the disadvantages of youth than the advantages of age. Of these latter I reckon one of the chiefest to be this: that we attach a less inordinate value to our own productions, and, distrusting daily more and more our own wisdom (with the conceit whereof at twenty we wrap ourselves away from knowledge as with a garment), do reconcile ourselves with the wisdom of God. I could have wished, indeed, that room might have been made for the residue of the anecdote relating to Deacon Tinkham, which would not only have gratified a natural curiosity on the part of the public (as I have reason to know from several letters of inquiry already received), but would also, as I think, have largely increased the circulation of your Magazine in this town. *Nihil humani alienum*, there is a curiosity about the affairs of our neighbours which is not only pardonable, but even commendable. But I shall abide a more fitting season.

As touching the following literary effort of Esquire Biglow, much might be profitably said on the topic of Idyllic and Pastoral Poetry, and concerning the proper distinctions to be made between them, from Theocritus, the inventor of the former, to Collins, the latest author I know of who has emulated the classics in the latter style. But in the time of civil war worthy a Milton to defend and a Lucan to sing, it may be reasonably doubted whether the public, never too studious of serious instruction, might not consider other objects more deserving of present attention. Concerning the title of Idyll, which Mr. Biglow has adopted at my suggestion, it may not be improper to animadvert, that the name properly signifies a poem somewhat rustic in phrase (for, though the learned are not agreed as to the particular dialect employed by Theocritus, they are universanimous both as to its rusticity and its capacity of rising now and then to the level of more elevated sentiments and expressions), while it is also descriptive of real scenery and manners. Yet it must be admitted that the production now in question (which here and there bears perhaps too plainly the marks of my correcting hand) does partake of the nature of a Pastoral, inasmuch as the interlocutors therein are purely imaginary beings, and the whole is little better than καπνοῦ σκιᾶς ὄναρ. The plot was, as I believe, suggested by the "Twa Briggs" of Robert Burns, a Scottish poet of the last century, as that found its prototype in the "Mutual Complaint of Plainstanes and Causey," by Fergusson, though the metre of this latter be different by a foot in each verse. I reminded my talented young parishioner and friend that Concord Bridge had long since yielded to the edacious tooth of Time. But he answered me to this effect: that there was no greater mistake of an author than to suppose the reader had no fancy of his own; that, if once that faculty was to be called into activity, it were *better* to be in for the whole sheep than the shoulder; and that he knew Concord like a book—an expression questionable in propriety, since there are few things with which he is not more familiar than with the printed page. In proof of what he affirmed, he showed me some verses which with others he had stricken out as too much delaying the action, but which I communicate in this place because they rightly define "punkin-seed" (which Mr. Bartlett would have a kind of perch—a creature to which I have found a rod or pole not to be so easily equivalent in our inland waters as in the books of arithmetic), and because it conveys an eulogium on the worthy son of an excellent father, with whose acquaintance (*eheu, fugaces anni!*) I was formerly honoured.

> "But nowadays the Bridge ain't wut they show,
> So much ez Em'som, Hawthorne, an' Thoreau.
> I know the village, though: was sent there once
> A-schoolin', coz to home I played the dunce;
> An' I've ben sence a-visitin' the Jedge,
> Whose garding whispers with the river's edge,
> Where I've sot mornin's lazy as the bream,
> Whose only business is to head up-stream
> (We call 'm punkin-seed), or else in chat
> Along 'th the Jedge, who covers with his hat
> More wit an' gumption an' shrewd Yankee sense
> Than there is mosses on an ole stone fence."

Concerning the subject-matter of the verses, I have not the leisure at present to write so fully as I could wish, my time being occupied with the preparation of a discourse for the forthcoming bi-centenary celebration of the first settlement of Jaalam East Parish. It may gratify the public interest to mention the circumstance, that my investigations to this end have enabled me to verify the fact (of much historic importance, and hitherto hotly debated) that Shearjashub Tarbox was the first child of white parentage born in this town, being named in his father's will under date August 7th or 9th, 1662. It is well known that those who advocate the claims of Mehetable Goings, are unable to find

any trace of her existence prior to October of that year.   As respects
the settlement of the Mason and Slidell question, Mr. Biglow has not
incorrectly stated the popular sentiment, so far as I can judge by its
expression in this locality.   For myself, I feel more sorrow than resent-
ment; for I am old enough to have heard those talk of England who
still, even after the unhappy estrangement, could not unschool their lips
from calling her the Mother Country.   But England has insisted on
ripping up old wounds, and has undone the healing work of fifty years;
for nations do not reason, they only feel, and the *spretæ injuria formæ*
rankles in their minds as bitterly as in that of a woman.   And because
this is so, I feel the more satisfaction that our Government has acted
(as all Governments should, standing as they do between the people
and their passions) as if it had arrived at years of discretion.   There
are three short and simple words, the hardest of all to pronounce in any
language (and I suspect they were no easier before the confusion of
tongues), but which no man or nation that cannot utter can claim to
have arrived at manhood.   Those words are, *I was wrong;* and I am
proud that, while England played the boy, our rulers had strength
enough from below and wisdom enough from above to quit themselves
like men.   Let us strengthen the hands of those in authority over us,
and curb our own tongues,[1] remembering that General Wait commonly

---

[1] And not only our own tongues, but the pens of others, which are
swift to convey useful intelligence to the enemy.   This is no new
inconvenience; for, under date 3rd June 1745, General Pepperell
wrote thus to Governor Shirley from Louisbourg:—"What your
Excellency observes of the *army's being made acquainted with any
plans proposed, until ready to be put in execution,* has always been
disagreeable to me, and I have given many cautions relating to it.
But when your Excellency considers that *our Council of War consists
of more than twenty members,* I am persuaded you will think it *impossible for me to hinder it,* if any of them will persist in communicating to
inferior officers and soldiers what ought to be kept secret.   I am
informed that the Boston newspapers are filled with paragraphs from
private letters relating to the expedition.   Will your Excellency permit
me to say I think it may be of ill consequence?   Would it not be
convenient, if your Excellency should forbid the printers inserting such
news?"   Verily, if *tempora mutantur,* we may question the *et nos
mutemur in illis;* and if tongues be leaky, it will need all hands at the

proves in the end more than a match for General Headlong, and that the Good Book ascribes safety to a multitude, indeed, but not to a mob, of counsellors. Let us remember and perpend the words of Paulus Emilius to the people of Rome: that, "if they judged they could manage the war to more advantage by any other, he would willingly yield up his charge; but if they confided in him, *they were not to make themselves his colleagues in his office, or raise reports, or criticise his actions, but, without talking, supply him with means and assistance necessary to the carrying on of the war; for, if they proposed to command their own commander, they would render this expedition more ridiculous than the former.*" (Vide *Plutarchum in vitâ P. E.*) Let us also not forget what the same excellent author says concerning Perseus's fear of spending money, and not permit the covetousness of Brother Jonathan to be the good fortune of Jefferson Davis. For my own part, till I am ready to admit the Commander-in-Chief to my pulpit, I shall abstain from planning his battles. Patience is the armour of a nation; and in our desire for peace let us never be willing to surrender the Constitution bequeathed us by fathers at least as wise as ourselves (even with Jefferson Davis to help us), and, with those degenerate Romans, *tuta et præsentia quam vetera et periculosa malle.*

With respect,

Your ob[t] humble serv[t],

HOMER WILBUR, A.M.

I love to start out arter night's begun,
An' all the chores about the farm are done,
The critters milked an' foddered, gates shet fast,
Tools cleaned aginst to-morrer, supper past,
An' Nancy darnin' by her ker'sene lamp,—
I love, I say, to start upon a tramp,
To shake the kinkles out o' back an' legs,
An' kind o' rack my life off from the dregs

---

pumps to save the Ship of State. Our history dotes and repeats itself. If Sassycus (rather than Alcibiades) find a parallel in Beauregard, so Weakwash, as he is called by the brave Lieutenant Lion Gardiner, need not seek far among our own Sachems for his antitype.

Thet's apt to settle in the buttery-hutch
Of folks thet foller in one rut too much:
Hard work is good an' wholesome, past all doubt;
But 't ain't so, ef the mind gets tuckered out.

Now, bein' born in Middlesex, you know,
There's certin spots where I like best to go:
The Concord road, for instance (I, for one,
Most gin'lly ollers call it *John Bull's Run*),—
The field o' Lexin'ton, where England tried
The fastest colours thet she ever dyed,—
An' Concord Bridge, thet Davis, when he came,
Found was the bee-line track to heaven an' fame,—
Ez all roads be by natur', ef your soul
Don't sneak thru shun-pikes so's to save the toll.

They're 'most too fur away, take too much time
To visit often, ef it ain't in rhyme;
But there's a walk thet's hendier, a sight,
An' suits me fust-rate of a winter's night,—
I mean the round whale's-back o' Prospect Hill.
I love to loiter there while night grows still,
An' in the twinklin' villages about,
Fust here, then there, the well-saved lights goes out,
An' nary sound but watch-dogs' false alarms,
Or muffled cock-crows from the drowsy farms,
Where some wise rooster (men act jest thet way)
Stands to 't thet moon-rise is the break o' day:
So Mister Seward sticks a three-months pin
Where the war 'd oughto end, then tries agin;—
My gran'ther's rule was safer n' 't is to crow:
Don't never prophesy—onless ye know.

I love to muse there till it kind o' seems
Ez ef the world went eddyin' off in dreams.
The Northwest wind thet twitches at my baird
Blows out o' sturdier days not easy scared,
An' the same moon thet this December shines
Starts out the tents an' booths o' Putnam's lines;
The rail-fence posts, acrost the hill thet runs,
Turn ghosts o' sogers should'rin' ghosts o' guns;
Ez wheels the sentry, glints a flash o' light
Along the firelock won at Concord Fight,
An' 'twixt the silences, now fur, now nigh,
Rings the sharp chellenge, hums the low reply.

Ez I was settin' so, it warn't long sence,
Mixin' the perfect with the present tense,
I heerd two voices som'ers in the air,
Though, ef I was to die, I can't tell where:
Voices I call 'em: 'twas a kind o' sough
Like pine-trees thet the wind is geth'rin' through;
An', fact, I thought it *was* the wind a spell,—
Then some misdoubted,—couldn't fairly tell,—
Fust sure, then not, jest as you hold an eel,—
I knowed, an' didn't,—fin'lly seemed to feel
'Twas Concord Bridge a-talkin' off to kill
With the Stone Spike thet's druv thru Bunker Hill:
Whether 'twas so, or ef I only dreamed,
I couldn't say; I tell it ez it seemed.

THE BRIDGE.

Wal, neighbor, tell us, wut's turned up thet's new?
You're younger 'n I be,—nigher Boston, tu:
An' down to Boston, ef you take their showin',

Wut they don't know ain't hardly wuth the knowin'.
There's *sunthin'* goin' on, I know: las' night
The British sogers killed in our gret fight
(Nigh fifty year they hedn't stirred nor spoke)
Made sech a coil you'd thought a dam hed broke:
Why, one he up an' beat a revellee
With his own crossbones on a holler tree,
Till all the graveyards swarmed out like a hive
With faces I hain't seen sence Seventy-five.
Wut *is* the news? 'Tain't good, or they'd be cheerin'.
Speak slow an' clear, for I'm some hard o' hearin'.

THE MONIMENT.

I don't know hardly ef it's good or bad,——

THE BRIDGE.

At wust, it can't be wus than wut we've had.

THE MONIMENT.

You know them envys thet the Rebbles sent,
An' Cap'n Wilkes he borried o' the Trent?

THE BRIDGE.

Wut! hev they hanged 'em? Then their wits is gone;
Thet's a sure way to make a goose a swan!

THE MONIMENT.

No: England she *would* hev 'em, *Fee, Faw, Fum!*
(Ez though she hedn't fools enough to home),
So they've returned 'em——

THE BRIDGE.

                       Hev they?   Wal, by heaven,
Thet's the wust news I've heerd sence Seventy-seven!
By George, I meant to say, though I declare
It's 'most enough to make a deacon swear.

THE MONIMENT.

Now don't go off half-cock: folks never gains
By usin' pepper-sarse instid o' brains.
Come, neighbor, you don't understand——

THE BRIDGE.

                             How?   Hey?

Not understand?   Why, wut's to hender, pray?
Must I go huntin' round to find a chap
To tell me when my face hez had a slap?

THE MONIMENT.

See here: the British they found out a flaw
In Cap'n Wilkes's readin' o' the law:
(They *make* all laws, you know, an' so, o' course,
It's nateral they should understand their force:)
He'd oughto took the vessel into port,
An' hed her sot on by a reg'lar court;
She was a mail-ship, an' a steamer, tu,
An' thet, they say, hez changed the pint o' view
Coz the old practice, bein' meant for sails,
Ef tried upon a steamer, kind o' fails;
You *may* take out despatches, but you mus'n't
Take nary man——

THE BRIDGE.

                    You mean to say, you dus'n't.
Changed pint o' view! No, no,—it's overboard
With law an' gospel, when their ox is gored!
I tell ye, England's law, on sea an' land,
Hez ollers ben, *"I've gut the heaviest hand."*
Take nary man? Fine preachin' from *her* lips!
Why, she hez taken hundreds from our ships,
An' would agin, an' swear she had a right to,
Ef we warn't strong enough to be perlite to.
Of all the sarse thet I can call to mind,
England *doos* make the most onpleasant kind:
It's you're the sinner ollers, she's the saint;
Wut's good 's all English, all thet isn't ain't;
Wut profits her is ollers right an' just,
An' ef you don't read Scriptur so, you must;
She's praised herself ontil she fairly thinks
There ain't no light in Natur when she winks;
Hain't she the Ten Comman'ments in her pus?
Could the world stir 'thout she went, tu, ez nus?
She ain't like other mortals, thet's a fact:
She never stopped the habus-corpus act,
Nor specie payments, nor she never yet
Cut down the int'rest on her public debt;
She don't put down rebellions, lets 'em breed,
An' 's ollers willin' Ireland should secede;
She's all thet's honest, honnable, an' fair,
An' when the vartoos died, they made her heir.

THE MONIMENT.

Wal, wal, two wrongs don't never make a right;
Ef we're mistaken, own it, an' don't fight:

For gracious' sake, hain't we enough to du
'Thout gittin' up a fight with England, tu?
She thinks we're rabble-rid——

THE BRIDGE.

        An' so we can't
Distinguish 'twixt *You oughtn't* an' *You shan't :*
She jedges by herself; she's no idear
How 't stiddies folks to give 'em their fair sheer :
The odds 'twixt her an' us is plain 's a steeple,—
Her People's turned to Mob, our Mob's turned People.

THE MONIMENT.

She's riled jes' now——

THE BRIDGE.

        Plain proof her cause ain't strong,—
The one thet fust gits mad 's most ollers wrong.

THE MONIMENT.

You're ollers quick to set your back aridge,—
Though 't suits a tom-cat more 'n a sober bridge :
Don't you git het : they thought the thing was
    planned ;
They'll cool off when they come to understand.

THE BRIDGE.

Ef *thet*'s wut you expect, you'll *hev* to wait ;
Folks never understand the folks thet hate.
She'll fin' some other grievance jest ez good,
'Fore the month's out, to git misunderstood.

England cool off! She'll do it, ef she sees
She's run her head into a swarm o' bees.
I ain't so prejudiced ez wut you spose:
I hev thought England was the best thet goes;
Remember (no, you can't), when *I* was reared,
God save the King was all the tune you heerd:
But it's enough to turn Wachuset roun',
This stumpin' fellers when you think they're down.

THE MONIMENT.

But, neighbor, ef they prove their claim at law,
The best way is to settle, an' not jaw.
An' don't le' 's mutter 'bout the awfle bricks
We'll give 'em, ef we ketch 'em in a fix:
That 'ere's most frequently the kin' o' talk
Of critters can't be kicked to toe the chalk;
Your "You'll see *nex'* time!" an' "Look out bimeby!"
Most ollers ends in eatin' umble-pie.
'T wun't pay to scringe to England: will it pay
To fear thet meaner bully, old "They'll say"?
Suppose they *du* say: words are dreffle bores,
But they ain't quite so bad ez seventy-fours.
Wut England wants is jest a wedge to fit
Where it'll help to widen out our split:
She's found her wedge, an' 't ain't for us to come
An' lend the beetle thet's to drive it home.
For growed-up folks like us 'twould be a scandle,
When we git sarsed, to fly right off the handle.
England ain't *all* bad, coz she thinks us blind:
Ef she can't change her skin, she can her mind;
An' you will see her change it double-quick,
Soon ez we've proved thet we're a-goin' to lick.

She an' Columby 's gut to be fas' friends;
For the world prospers by their privit ends:
'Twould put the clock back all o' fifty years,
Ef they should fall together by the ears.

THE BRIDGE.

You may be right; but hearken in your ear,—
I'm older 'n you,—Peace wun't keep house with Fear:
Ef you want peace, the thing you've gut to du
Is jest to show you're up to fightin', tu.
I recollect how sailors' rights was won
Yard locked in yard, hot gun-lip kissin' gun:
Why, afore thet, John Bull sot up thet he
Hed gut a kind o' mortgage on the sea;
You'd thought he held by Gran'ther Adam's will,
An' ef you knuckle down, *he*'ll think so still.
Better thet all our ships an' all their crews
Should sink to rot in ocean's dreamless ooze,
Each torn flag wavin' chellenge ez it went,
An' each dumb gun a brave man's moniment,
Than seek sech peace ez only cowards crave:
Give *me* the peace of dead men or of brave!

THE MONIMENT.

I say, ole boy, it ain't the Glorious Fourth:
You'd oughto learned 'fore this wut talk wuz worth.
It ain't *our* nose thet gits put out o' jint;
It's England thet gives up her dearest pint.
We've gut, I tell ye now, enough to du
In our own fem'ly fight, afore we're thru.
I hoped, las' spring, jest arter Sumter's shame,
When every flag-staff flapped its tethered flame,

An' all the people, startled from their doubt,
Come must'rin' to the flag with sech a shout,—
I hoped to see things settled 'fore this fall,
The Rebbles licked, Jeff Davis hanged, an' all ;
Then come Bull Run, an' *sence* then I've ben waitin'
Like boys in Jennooary thaw for skatin',
Nothin' to du but watch my shadder's trace
Swing, like a ship at anchor, roun' my base,
With daylight's flood an' ebb : it's gittin' slow,
An' I 'most think we'd better let 'em go.
I tell ye wut, this war's a-goin' to cost——

THE BRIDGE.

An' I tell *you* it wun't be money lost ;
Taxes milks dry, but, neighbor, you'll allow
Thet havin' things onsettled kills the cow:
We've gut to fix this thing for good an' all ;
It's no use buildin' wut's a-goin' to fall.
I'm older 'n you, an' I've seen things an' men,
An' here's wut my experience hez ben:
Folks thet worked thorough was the ones thet thriv,
But bad work follers ye ez long's ye live ;
You can't git red on't ; jest ez sure ez sin,
It's ollers askin' to be done agin :
Ef we should part, it wouldn't be a week
'Fore your soft-soddered peace would spring aleak.
We've turned our cuffs up, but, to put her thru,
We must git mad an' off with jackets, tu ;
'T wun't du to think thet killin' ain't perlite,—
You've gut to be in airnest, ef you fight ;
Why, two-thirds o' the Rebbles 'ould cut dirt,
Ef they once thought thet Guv'ment meant to hurt ;

An' I *du* wish our Gin'rals hed in mind
The folks in front more than the folks behind;
You wun't do much ontil you think it's God,
An' not constitoounts, thet holds the rod;
We want some more o' Gideon's sword, I jedge,
For proclamations hain't no gret of edge;
There's nothin' for a cancer but the knife,
Onless you set by 't more than by your life.
I've seen hard times; I see a war begun
Thet folks thet love their bellies never'd won,—
Pharo's lean kine hung on for seven long year,—
But when 't was done, we didn't count it dear.
Why, law an' order, honor, civil right,
Ef they *ain't* wuth it, wut *is* wuth a fight?
I'm older 'n you: the plough, the axe, the mill,
All kinds o' labor an' all kinds o' skill,
Would be a rabbit in a wile-cat's claw,
Ef 't warn't for thet slow critter, 'stablished law;
Onsettle *thet*, an' all the world goes whiz,
A screw is loose in everythin' there is:
Good buttresses once settled, don't you fret
An' stir 'em: take a bridge's word for thet!
Young folks are smart, but all ain't good thet's new:
I guess the gran'thers they knowed sunthin', tu.

THE MONIMENT.

Amen to thet! build sure in the beginnin',
An' then don't never tech the underpinnin':
Th' older a Guv'ment is, the better 't suits;
New ones hunt folks's corns out like new boots:
Change jest for change is like those big hotels
Where they shift plates, an' let ye live on smells.

THE BRIDGE.

Wal, don't give up afore the ship goes down:
It's a stiff gale, but Providence wun't drown;
An' God wun't leave us yet to sink or swim,
Ef we don't fail to du wut's right by Him.
This land o' ourn, I tell ye, 's gut to be
A better country than man ever see.
I feel my sperit swellin' with a cry
Thet seems to say, "Break forth an' prophesy!"
O strange New World, thet yet wast never young,
Whose youth from thee by gripin' need was wrung,—
Brown foundlin' o' the woods, whose baby-bed
Was prowled round by the Injun's cracklin' tread,
An' who grew'st strong thru shifts an' wants an' pains
Nussed by stern men with empires in their brains,
Who saw in vision their young Ishmel strain
With each hard hand a vassal ocean's mane,—
Thou, skilled by Freedom an' by gret events
To pitch new States ez Old-World men pitch tents,—
Thou, taught by Fate to know Jehovah's plan
Thet only manhood ever makes a man,
An' whose free latch-string never was drawed in
Aginst the poorest child o' Adam's kin,—
The grave's not dug where traitor hands shall lay
In fearful haste thy murdered corse away!
I see——
          Jest here some dogs began to bark,
So thet I lost old Concord's last remark:
I listened long, but all I seemed to hear
Was dead leaves goss'pin' on some birch-trees near;
But ez they hedn't no gret things to say,
An' said 'em often, I *come* right away.

An', walkin' home'ards, jest to pass the time,
I put some thoughts thet bothered me in rhyme:
I hain't hed time to fairly try 'em on,
But here they be,—it's

JONATHAN TO JOHN.

It don't seem hardly right, John,
   When both my hands was full,
To stump me to a fight, John,—
   Your cousin, tu, John Bull.
      Ole Uncle S. sez he, "I guess
      We know it now," sez he,
      "The lion's paw is all the law,
      Accordin' to J. B.,
      Thet's fit for you an' me!"

Blood ain't so cool as ink, John:
   It's likely you'd ha' wrote,
An' stopped a spell to think, John,
   Arter they'd cut your throat?
      Ole Uncle S. sez he, "I guess
      He'd skurce ha' stopped," sez he,
      "To mind his p's an' q's, ef thet weasan
      Hed b'longed to ole J. B.,
      Instid o' you an' me!"

Ef *I* turned mad dogs loose, John,
   On *your* front-parlor stairs,
Would it jest meet your views, John,
   To wait an' sue their heirs?

Ole Uncle S. sez he, " I guess,
I on'y guess," sez he,
" Thet, ef Vattel on *his* toes fell,
'Twould kind o' rile J. B.,
Ez wal ez you an' me ! "

Who made the law thet hurts, John,
   Heads I win,—ditto, tails?
"*J. B.*" was on his shirts, John,
  Onless my memory fails.
     Ole Uncle S. sez he, " I guess
     (I'm good at thet)," sez he,
     " Thet sauce for goose ain't *jest* the juice
     For ganders with J. B.,
     No more than you or me ! "

When your rights was our wrongs, John,
  You didn't stop for fuss,—
Britanny's trident-prongs, John,
  Was good 'nough law for us.
     Ole Uncle S. sez he, " I guess,
     Though physic's good," sez he,
     " It doesn't foller thet he can swaller
     Prescriptions signed '*J. B.*,'
     Put up by you an' me ! "

We own the ocean, tu, John :
  You mus' n't take it hard,
Ef we can't think with you, John,
  It's jest your own back-yard.

Ole Uncle S. sez he, "I guess,
  Ef *thet*'s his claim," sez he,
"The fencin'-stuff 'll cost enough
  To bust up friend J. B.,
    Ez wal ez you an' me!"

Why talk so dreffle big, John,
  Of honor, when it meant
You didn't care a fig, John,
  But jest for *ten per cent.?*
    Ole Uncle S. sez he, "I guess,
      He's like the rest," sez he:
    "When all is done, it's number one
      Thet's nearest to J. B.,
        Ez wal ez you an' me!"

We give the critters back, John,
  Cos Abram thought 'twas right;
It warn't your bullyin' clack, John,
  Provokin' us to fight.
    Ole Uncle S. sez he, "I guess,
      We've a hard row," sez he,
    "To hoe jest now; but thet, somehow,
      May heppen to J. B.,
        Ez wal ez you an' me!"

We ain't so weak an' poor, John,
  With twenty million people,
An' close to every door, John,
  A school-house an' a steeple.

Ole Uncle S. sez he, " I guess
It is a fact," sez he,
" The surest plan to make a Man
Is, Think him so, J. B.,
Ez much ez you or me ! "

Our folks believe in Law, John ;
  An' it's for her sake, now,
They've left the axe an' saw, John,
  The anvil an' the plough.
     Ole Uncle S. sez he, " I guess,
     Ef 't warn't for law," sez he,
     "There 'd be one shindy from here to Indy;
     An' thet don't suit J. B.
     (When 'tain't 'twixt you an' me) ! "

We know we've gut a cause, John,
  Thet's honest, just, an' true;
We thought 't would win applause, John,
  Ef nowheres else, from you.
     Ole Uncle S. sez he, " I guess
     His love of right," sez he,
     " Hangs by a rotten fibre o' cotton:
     There's natur' in J. B.,
     Ez wal ez you an' me ! "

The South says, "*Poor folks down !* " John,
  An' "*All men up !* " say we,—
White, yaller, black, an' brown, John:
  Now which is your idee ?

Ole Uncle S. sez he, "I guess,
   John preaches wal," sez he;
" But, sermon thru, an' come to *du,*
   Why, there's the old J. B.
   A crowdin' you an' me ! "

Shall it be love, or hate, John?
   It's you thet's to decide;
Ain't *your* bonds held by Fate, John,
   Like all the world's beside?
      Ole Uncle S. sez he, " I guess,
      Wise men forgive," sez he,
      " But not forget; an' some time yet
      Thet truth may strike J. B.,
      Ez wal ez you an' me ! "

God means to make this land, John,
   Clear thru, from sea to sea,
Believe an' understand, John,
   The *wuth* o' bein' free.
      Ole Uncle S. sez he, " I guess,
      God's price is high," sez he;
      " But nothin' else than wut He sells
      Wears long, an' thet J. B.
      May learn like you an' me ! "

BIRDOFREDUM SAWIN, ESQ., TO MR. HOSEA BIGLOW.

With the following Letter from the REVEREND HOMER WILBUR, A.M.

TO THE EDITORS OF THE "ATLANTIC MONTHLY."

JAALAM, 7th Feb. 1862.

RESPECTED FRIENDS,—If I know myself, and surely a man can hardly be supposed to have overpassed the limit of fourscore years without attaining to some proficiency in that most useful branch of learning (*e cælo descendit*, says the pagan poet), I have no great smack of that weakness which would press upon the public attention any matter pertaining to my private affairs. But since the following letter of Mr. Sawin contains not only a direct allusion to myself, but that in connection with a topic of interest to all those engaged in the public ministrations of the sanctuary, I may be pardoned for touching briefly thereupon. Mr. Sawin was never a stated attendant upon my preaching—never, as I believe, even an occasional one, since the erection of the new house (where we now worship) in 1845. He did, indeed, for a time, supply a not unacceptable bass in the choir; but, whether on some umbrage (*omnibus hoc vitium est cantoribus*) taken against the bass-viol, then, and till his decease in 1850 (*æt.* 77), under the charge of Mr. Asaph Perley, or, as was reported by others, on account of an imminent subscription for a new bell, he thenceforth absented himself from all outward and visible communion. Yet he seems to have preserved (*altâ mente repostum*), as it were, in the pickle of a mind soured by prejudice, a lasting *scunner*, as he would call it, against our staid and decent form of worship; for I would rather in that wise interpret his fling, than suppose that any chance tares sown by my pulpit discourses should survive so long, while good seed too often fails to root itself. I humbly trust that I have no personal feeling in the matter; though I know that, if we sound any man deep enough, our lead shall bring up the mud of human nature at last. The Bretons believe in an evil spirit which they call *ar c'houskezik*, whose office it is to make the congregation drowsy; and though I have never had reason to think that he was specially busy among my flock, yet have I seen enough to make me sometimes regret the hinged seats of the ancient meeting-house, whose lively clatter, not unwillingly intensified by boys beyond eyeshot of the tithing-man, served at intervals as a wholesome *réveil.* It is true, I have numbered among my parishioners some whose gift of somnolence rivalled that of the Creton Rip van Winkle, Epimenides, and who, nevertheless, complained not so much of the substance as of the length of my (by them unheard) discourses. Happy Saint Anthony of Padua, whose finny acolytes, however they might profit, could never murmur ! *Quare fremuerunt gentes?* Who is he that can twice a week be inspired, or has eloquence (*ut ita dicam*) always on tap ? A good man, and, next to David, a sacred poet (himself, haply, not inexpert of evil in this particular), has said—

> "The worst speak something good : if all want sense,
> God takes a text and preacheth patience."

There are one or two other points in Mr. Sawin's letter which I would also briefly animadvert upon. And first concerning the claim he sets up to a certain superiority of blood and lineage in the people of our Southern States, now unhappily in rebellion against lawful authority and their own better interests. There is a sort of opinions, anachronisms and anachorisms, foreign both to the age and the country, that maintain a feeble and buzzing existence, scarce to be called life, like winter flies, which in mild weather crawl out from obscure nooks and crannies to expatiate in the sun, and sometimes acquire vigour enough to disturb with their enforced familiarity the studious hours of the scholar. One of the most stupid and pertinacious of these is the theory that the Southern States were settled by a class of emigrants from the Old World socially superior to those who founded the institutions of New England. The Virginians especially lay claim to this generosity of lineage, which were of no possible account, were it not for the fact that such superstitions are sometimes not without their effect on the course of human affairs. The early adventurers to Massachusetts at least paid their passages ; no felons were ever shipped thither ; and though it be true that many deboshed younger brothers of what are called good families may have sought refuge in Virginia, it is equally certain that a great part of the early deportations thither were the sweepings of the London streets and the leavings of the London stews. On what the heralds call the spindle side, some, at least, of the oldest Virginian families are descended from matrons who were exported and sold for so many hogsheads of tobacco the head. So notorious was this, that it became one of the jokes of contemporary playwrights, not only that men bankrupt in purse and character were "Food for the Plantations" (and this before the settlement of New England), but also that any drab would suffice to wive such pitiful adventurers. "Never choose a wife as if you were going to Virginia," says Middleton in one of his comedies. The mule is apt to forget all but the equine side of his pedigree. How early the counterfeit nobility of the Old Dominion became a topic of ridicule in the Mother Country may be learned from a play of Mrs. Behn's founded on the Rebellion of Bacon : for even these kennels of literature may yield a fact or two to pay the raking. Mrs. Flirt, the keeper of a Virginia ordinary, calls herself the daughter of a baronet "undone in the late rebellion,"— her father having in truth been a tailor,—and three of the Council, assuming to themselves an equal splendour of origin, are shown to have been, one "a broken exciseman who came over a poor servant," another a tinker transported for theft, and the third "a common pick-pocket often flogged at the cart's tail." The ancestry of South Carolina will as little pass muster at the Herald's Visitation, though I hold them to have been more reputable, inasmuch as many of them were honest tradesmen and artisans, in some measure exiles for conscience' sake, who would have smiled at the high-flying nonsense of their descendants. Some of the more respectable were Jews. The absurdity of supposing a population of eight millions all sprung from gentle loins in the course of a century and a half is too manifest for confutation. The aristocracy of the South, such as it is, has the shallowest of all foundations, for it is only skin-deep,—the most odious of all, for, while affecting to despise trade, it traces its origin to a successful traffic in men, women, and children, and still draws its chief revenues thence. And though, as Doctor Chamberlayne says in his *Present State of England*, "to become a Merchant, of Foreign Commerce, without serving any Apprentisage, hath been allowed no disparagement to a Gentleman born, especially to a younger Brother," yet I conceive that he would hardly have made a like exception in favour of the particular trade in question. Nor do I believe that such aristocracy as exists at the South (for I hold with Marius, *fortissimum quemque generosissimum*) will be found an element of anything like persistent strength in war,—thinking the saying of Lord Bacon (whom one quaintly called *inductionis dominus et Verulamii*) as true as it is pithy, that "the more gentlemen, ever the lower books of subsidies." It is odd enough as an historical precedent, that, while the fathers of New England were laying deep in religion, education, and freedom the basis of a polity which has substantially outlasted any then existing, the first work of the founders of Virginia, as may be seen in Wingfield's *Memorial*, was conspiracy and rebellion, —odder yet, as showing the changes which are wrought by circumstance, that the first insurrection in South Carolina was against the aristocratical scheme of the Proprietary Government. I do not find that the tuticular aristocracy of the South has added anything to the refinements of civilisation, except the carrying of bowie-knives and the chewing of tobacco, a high-toned Southern gentleman being commonly not only *quadrumanous,* but *quidruminant.*

I confess that the present letter of Mr. Sawin increases my doubts as to the sincerity of the convictions which he professes, and I am inclined to think that the triumph of the legitimate Government, sure sooner or later to take place, will find him and a large majority of his newly-adopted fellow-citizens (who hold with Dædalus, the primal sitter-on-the-fence, that *medium tenere tutissimum*) original Union men. The criticisms towards the close of his letter on certain of our failings are worthy to be seriously perpended; for he is not, as I think, without a spice of vulgar shrewdness. As to the good-nature in us which he seems to gird at, while I would not consecrate a chapel, as they have not scrupled to do in France, to *Notre Dame de la Haine* (Our Lady of Hate), yet I cannot forget that the corruption of good nature is the generation of laxity of principle. Good-nature is our national characteristic; and though it be, perhaps, nothing more than a culpable weakness or cowardice, when it leads us to put up tamely with manifold impositions and breaches of implied contracts (as too frequently in our public conveyances), it becomes a positive crime, when it leads us to look unresentfully on peculation, and to regard treason to the best Government that ever existed as something with which a gentleman may shake hands without soiling his fingers. I do not think the gallows-tree the most profitable member of our *Sylva;* but, since it continues to be planted, I would fain see a Northern limb ingrafted on it, that it may bear some other fruit than loyal Tennesseeans.

A relic has recently been discovered on the east bank of Bushy Brook, in North Jaalam, which I conceive to be an inscription in

Runic characters relating to the early expedition of the Northmen to this continent. I shall make fuller investigations, and communicate the result in due season.

Respectfully,

Your obedient servant,

HOMER WILBUR, A.M.

P.S.—I enclose a year's subscription from Deacon Tinkham.

I HED it on my min' las' time, when I to write ye started,
To tech the leadin' featurs o' my gitin' me convarted;
But, ez my letters hez to go clearn roun' by way o' Cuby,
'Twun't seem no staler now than then, by th' time it gits
    where you be.
You know up North, though secs an' things air plenty ez
    you please,
Ther' warn't nut one on 'em thet come jes' square with my
    idees;
I dessay they suit workin'-folks thet ain't noways pertic'lar,
But nut your Southun gen'leman thet keeps his perpendic'lar;
I don't blame nary man thet casts his lot along o' *his* folks,
But ef you cal'late to save *me*, 't must be with folks thet *is*
    folks;
Cov'nants o' works go 'ginst my grain, but down here I've
    found out
The true fus'-fem'ly A1 plan,—here's how it come about.
When I fus' sot up with Miss S., sez she to me, sez she,—
"Without you git religion, Sir, the thing can't never be;
Nut but wut I respeck," sez she, " your intellectle part,
But you wun't noways du for me athout a change o' heart:
Nothun religion works wal North, but it's ez soft ez
    spruce,
Compared to ourn, for keepin' sound," sez she, "upon the
    goose;

A day's experunce 'd prove to ye, ez easy 'z pull a trigger,
It takes the Southun pint o' view to raise ten bales a nigger ;
You'll fin' thet human natur, South, ain't wholesome more'n
    skin-deep,
An' once 't a darkie's took with it, he wun't be wuth his
    keep."
"How *shell* I git it, Ma'am ?" sez I.   "Attend the nex'
    camp-meetin',"
Sez she, "an' it'll come to ye ez cheap ez onbleached
    sheetin'."

Wal, so I went along an' hearn most an impressive sarmon
About besprinklin' Afriky with fourth-proof dew o' Harmon :
He did n' put no weaknin' in, but gin it tu us hot,
'Z ef he an' Satan 'd ben two bulls in one five-acre lot :
I don't purtend to foller him, but give ye jes' the heads ;
For pulpit ellerkence, you know, 'most ollers kin' o' spreads.
Ham's seed wuz gin to us in chairge, an' shouldn't we be li'ble
In Kingdom Come, ef we kep' back their priv'lege in the
    Bible ?
The cusses an' the promerses make one gret chain, an' ef
You snake one link out here, one there, how much on 't ud
    be lef' ?
All things wuz gin to man for 's use, his sarvice, an' delight ;
An' don't the Greek an' Hebrew words thet mean a Man
    mean White ?
Ain't it belittin' the Good Book in all its proudes' featurs
To think 't wuz wrote for black an' brown an' 'lasses-colored
    creaturs,
Thet could n' read it, ef they would, nor ain't by lor allowed
    to,
But ough' to take wut we think suits their naturs, an' be
    proud to ?

Warn't it more prof'table to bring your raw materil thru
Where you can work it inta grace an' inta cotton, tu,
Than sendin' missionaries out where fevers might defeat
    'em,
An' ef the butcher did n' call, their p'rishioners might eat
    'em?
An' then, agin, wut airthly use? Nor 't warn't our fault, in
    so fur
Ez Yankee skippers would keep on a-totin' on 'em over.
'T improved the whites by savin' 'em from ary need o'
    wurkin',
An' kep' the blacks from bein' lost thru idleness an' shirkin';
We took to 'em ez nat'ral ez a barn-owl doos to mice,
An' hed our hull time on our hands to keep us out o' vice;
It made us feel ez pop'lar ez a hen doos with one chicken,
An' fill our place in Natur's scale by givin' 'em a lickin';
For why should Cæsar git his dues more'n Juno, Pomp,
    an' Cuffy?
It's justifyin' Ham to spare a nigger when he's stuffy.
Where'd their soles go tu, like to know, ef we should let
    'em ketch
Freeknowledgism an' Fourierism an' Speritoolism an' sech?
When Satan sets himself to work to raise his very bes'
    muss,
He scatters roun' onscriptur'l views relatin' to Ones'mus.

You'd ough' to seen, though, how his facs an' argymunce
    an' figgers
Drawed tears o' real conviction from a lot o' pen'tent
    niggers!
It warn't like Wilbur's meetin', where you're shet up in a
    pew,
Your dickeys sorrin' off your ears, an' bilin' to be thru;

Ther' wuz a tent clost by thet hed a kag o' sunthin' in it,
Where you could go, ef you wuz dry, an' damp ye in a
    minute ;
An' ef you did dror off a spell, ther' wuzn't no occasion
To lose the thread, because, ye see, he bellered like all
    Bashan.
It's dry work follerin' argymunce, an' so, 'twix' this an' thet,
I felt conviction weighin' down somehow inside my hat ;
It growed an' growed like Jonah's gourd, a kin' o' whirlin'
    ketched me,
Ontil I fin'lly clean giv out an' owned up thet he'd fetched
    me ;
An' when nine-tenths the perrish took to tumblin' roun' an'
    hollerin',
I did n' fin' no gret in th' way o' turnin' tu an' follerin'.
Soon ez Miss S. see thet, sez she, "*Thet* 's wut I call wuth
    seein' !
Thet 's actin' like a reas'nable an' intellectle bein' ! "
An' so we fin'lly made it up, concluded to hitch hosses,
An' here I be 'n my ellermunt among creation's bosses ;
Arter I'd drawed sech heaps o' blanks, Fortin at last hez
    sent a prize,
An' choose me for a shinin' light o' missionary enterprise.

This leads me to another pint on which I've changed my
    plan
O' thinkin' so 's 't I might become a straight-out Southun
    man.
Miss S. (her maiden name wuz Higgs, o' the fus' fem'ly
    here)
On her Ma's side 's all Juggernot, on Pa's all Cavileer,
An' sence I've married into her an' stept into her shoes,
It ain't more'n nateral thet I should modderfy my views :

I've ben a-readin' in Debow ontil I've fairly gut
So 'nlightened thet I'd full ez lives ha' ben a Dook ez
    nut;
An' when we've laid ye all out stiff, an' Jeff hez gut his
    crown,
An' comes to pick his nobles out, *wun't* this child be in
    town!
We'll hev an Age o' Chivverlry surpassin' Mister Burke's,
Where every fem'ly is fus'-best an' nary white man works:
Our system's sech, the thing'll root ez easy ez a tater;
For while your lords in furrin parts ain't noways marked by
    natur',
Nor sot apart from ornery folks in featurs nor in figgers,
Ef ourn'll keep their faces washed, you'll know 'em from
    their niggers.
Ain't *sech* things wuth secedin' for, an' gettin' red o' you
Thet waller in your low idees, an' will till all is blue?
Fact is, we *air* a diff'rent race, an' I, for one, don't see,
Sech havin' ollers ben the case, how w' ever *did* agree.
It's sunthin' thet you lab'rin'-folks up North hed ough' to
    think on,
Thet Higgses can't bemean themselves to rulin' by a
    Lincoln,—
Thet men (an' guv'nors, tu) thet hez sech Normal names ez
    Pickens,
Accustomed to no kin' o' work, 'thout 't is to givin' lickins,
Can't masure votes with folks thet git their livins from their
    farms,
An' prob'ly think thet Law 's ez good ez hevin' coats o'
    arms.
Sence I've ben here, I've hired a chap to look about for
    me
To git me a transplantable an' thrifty fem'ly-tree,

An' he tells *me* the Sawins is ez much o' Normal blood
Ez Pickens an' the rest on 'em, an' older 'n Noah's flood.

Your Normal schools wun't turn ye into Normals, for it's
    clear,
Ef eddykatin' done the thing, they'd be some skurcer
    here.

Pickenses, Boggses, Pettuses, Magoffins, Letchers, Polks,—
Where can you scare up names like them among your mud-
    sill folks?

Ther' 's nothin' to compare with 'em, you'd fin', ef you
    should glance,
Among the tip-top femerlies in Englan', nor in France:

I've hearn from 'sponsible men whose word wuz full ez
    good's their note,
Men thet can run their face for drinks, an' keep a Sunday
    coat,

Thet they wuz all on 'em come down, and come down pooty
    fur,
From folks thet, 'thout their crowns wuz on, ou'doors would
    n' never stir,

Nor thet ther' warn't a Southun man but wut wuz *primy
    fashy*
O' the bes' blood in Europe, yis, an' Afriky an' Ashy:

Sech bein' the case, is 't likely we should bend like cotton-
    wickin'
Or set down under anythin' so low-lived ez a lickin'?

More'n this,—hain't we the literatoor an' science, tu, by
    gorry?
Hain't we them intellecle twins, them giants, Simms an'
    Maury,

Each with full twice the ushle brains, like nothin' thet I
    know,
'Thout 'twuz a double-headed calf I see once to a show?

For all thet, I warn't jest at fust in favor o' secedin';
I wuz for layin' low a spell to find out where 'twuz leadin',
For hevin' South-Carliny try her hand at seprit-nationin',
She takin' resks an' findin' funds, and we co-operationin',—
I mean a kin' o' hangin' roun' an' settin' on the fence,
Till Prov'dunce pinted how to jump an' save the most
    expense;
I reecollected thet 'ere mine o' lead to Shirza Centre
Thet bust up Jabez Pettibone, an' didn't want to ventur'
'Fore I wuz sartin wut come out ud pay for wut went in,
For swappin' silver off for lead ain't the sure way to win;
(An', fact, it *doos* look now ez though—but folks must live
    an' larn—
We should git lead, an' more'n we want, out o' the Old
    Consarn);
But when I see a man so wise an' honest ez Buchanan
A-lettin' us hev all the forts an' all the arms an' cannon,
Admittin' we wuz nat'lly right an' you wuz nat'lly wrong,
Coz you wuz lab'rin'-folks an' we wuz wut they call *bong-
    tong*,
An' coz there warn't no fight in ye more'n in a mashed
    potater,
While two o' *us* can't skurcely meet but wut we fight by
    natur',
An' th' ain't a bar-room here would pay for openin' on 't a
    night,
Without it giv the priverlege o' bein' shot at sight,
Which proves we're Natur's noblemen, with whom it don't
    surprise
The British aristoxy should feel boun' to sympathise,—
Seein' all this, an' seein', tu, the thing wuz strikin' roots
While Uncle Sam sot still in hopes thet some one 'd bring
    his boots,

I thought th' ole Union's hoops wuz off, and let myself be
    sucked in
To rise a peg an' jine the crowd thet went for recon-
    structin',—
Thet is, to hev the pardnership under th' ole name
    continner
Jest ez it wuz, we drorrin' pay, you findin' bone an' sinner,—
On'y to put it in the bond, an' enter 't in the journals,
Thet you're the nat'ral rank an' file, an' we the nat'ral
    kurnels.

Now this I thought a fees'ble plan, thet 'ud work smooth ez
    grease,
Suitin' the Nineteenth Century an' Upper Ten idees,
An' there I meant to stick, an' so did most o' th' leaders, tu,
Coz we all thought the chance wuz good o' puttin' on it thru;
But Jeff he hit upon a way o' helpin' on us forrard
By bein' unannermous,—a trick you aint quite up to,
    Norrard.
A baldin hain't no more 'f a chance with them new apple-
    corers
Than folks's oppersition views aginst the Ringtail Roarers;
They'll take 'em out on him 'bout east,—one canter on
    a rail
Makes a man feel unannermous ez Jonah in the whale;
Or ef he's a slow-moulded cuss thet can't seem quite 't
    agree,
He gits the noose by tellergraph upon the nighes' tree:
Their mission-work with Afrikins hez put 'em up, thet's
    sartin,
To all the mos' across-lot ways o' preachin' an' convartin';
I'll bet my hat th' ain't nary priest, nor all on 'em together,
Thet cairs conviction to the min' like Reveren' Taranfeather;

Why, he sot up with me one night, an' labored to sech
    purpose,
Thet (ez an owl by daylight 'mongst a flock o' teazin'
    chirpers
Sees clearer 'n mud the wickedness o' eatin' little birds)
I see my error an' agreed to shen it arterwurds;
An' I should say (to jedge our folks by facs in my
    possession),
Thet three's Unannermous where one's a 'Riginal Secession;
So it's a thing you fellers North may safely bet your
    chink on,
Thet we're all water-proofed agin th' usurpin' reign o'
    Lincoln.

Jeff 's *some*.   He's gut another plan thet hez pertic'lar
    merits,
In givin' things a cherfle look an' stiffnin' loose-hung sperits;
For while your million papers, wut with lyin' an' discussin',
Keep folks's tempers all on eend a-fumin' an' a-fussin',
A-wondrin' this an' guessin' thet, an' dreadin', every night,
The breechin' o' the Univarse 'll break afore it's light,
Our papers don't purtend to print on'y wut Guv'ment choose,
An' thet insures us all to git the very best o' noose:
Jeff hez it of all sorts an' kines, an' sarves it out ez wanted,
So 's 't every man gits wut he likes an' nobody ain't scanted;
Sometimes it's vict'ries (they're 'bout all ther' is that's
    cheap down here),
Sometimes it's France an' England on the jump to interfere.
Fact is, the less the people know o' wut ther' is a-doin',
The hendier 't is for Guv'ment, sence it henders trouble
    brewin';
An' noose is like a shinplaster,—it's good, ef you believe it,
Or, wut's all same, the other man thet's goin' to receive it:

Ef you've a son in th' army, wy, it's comfortin' to hear
He'll hev no gretter resk to run than seein' th' in'my's rear,
Coz, ef an F. F. looks at 'em, they ollers break an' run,
Or wilt right down ez debtors will thet stumble on a dun
(An' this, ef an'thin', proves the wuth o' proper fem'ly pride,
Fer such mean shucks ez creditors are all on Lincoln's side);
Ef I hev scrip thet wun't go off no more'n a Belgin rifle,
An' read thet it's at par on 'Change, it makes me feel
 deli'fle;
It's cheerin', tu, where every man mus' fortify his bed,
To hear thet Freedom's the one thing our darkies mos'ly
 dread,
An' thet experunce, time 'n' agin, to Dixie's Land hez shown
Ther' 's nothin' like a powder-cask f'r a stiddy corner-stone;
Ain't it ez good ez nuts, when salt is sellin' by the ounce
For its own weight in Treash'ry-bons (ef bought in small
 amounts),
When even whiskey's gittin' skurce, an' sugar can't be found,
To know thet all the ellerments o' luxury abound?
An' don't it glorify sal'-pork, to come to understand
It's wut the Richmon' editors call fatness o' the land?
Nex' thing to knowin' you're well off is *nut* to know when
 y' ain't;
An' ef Jeff says all's goin' wal, who'll ventur' t' say it ain't?

This cairn the Constitooshun roun' ez Jeff doos in his hat
Is hendier a dreffle sight, an' comes more kin' o' pat.
I tell ye wut, my jedgment is you're pooty sure to fail,
Ez long 'z the head keeps turnin' back for counsel to
 the tail:
Th' advantiges of our consarn for bein' prompt air gret,
While, 'long o' Congress, you can't strike, 'f you git an
 iron het;

They bother roun' with argooin', an' var'ous sorts o' foolin',
To make sure ef it's leg'lly het, an' all the while it's coolin',
So 's 't when you come to strike, it ain't no gret to wish ye
    j'y on,
An' hurts the hammer 'z much or more ez wut it doos the
    iron.
Jeff don't allow no jawin'-sprees for three months at a
    stretch,
Knowin' the ears long speeches suits air mostly made to
    metch;
He jes' ropes in your tonguey chaps an' reg'lar ten-inch
    bores
An' lets 'em play at Congress, ef they'll du it with closed
    doors;
So they ain't no more bothersome than ef we'd took an'
    sunk 'em,
An' yit enj'y th' exclusive right to one another's Buncombe
'Thout doin' nobody no hurt, an' 'thout its costin' nothin',
Their pay bein' jes' Confedrit funds, they findin' keep an'
    clothin';
They taste the sweets o' public life, an' plan their little jobs,
An' suck the Treash'ry (no gret harm, for it's ez dry ez
    cobs),
An' go thru all the motions jest ez safe ez in a prison,
An' hev their business to themselves, while Buregard hez
    hisn:
Ez long 'z he gives the Hessians fits, committees can't make
    bother
'Bout whether 't 's done the legle way or whether 't 's done
    the t'other.
An' *I* tell *you* you've gut to larn thet War ain't one long
    teeter
Betwixt *I wan' to* an' *'Twun't du*, debatin' like a skeetur

Afore he lights,—all is, to give the other side a millin',
An' arter thet's done, th' ain't no resk but wut the lor 'll be
    willin';
No metter wut the Guv'ment is, ez nigh ez I can hit it,
A lickin' 's constitooshunal, pervidin' *We* don't git it.
Jeff don't stan' dilly-dallyin', afore he takes a fort
(With no one in), to git the leave o' the nex' Soopreme
    Court,
Nor don't want forty-'leven weeks o' jawin' an' expoundin'
To prove a nigger hez a right to save him, ef he's drowndin';
Whereas ole Abram 'd sink afore he'd let a darkie boost
    him,
Ef Taney shouldn't come along an' hedn't interdooced him.
It ain't your twenty millions thet'll ever block Jeff's game,
But one Man thet wun't let 'em jog jest ez he's takin'
    aim:
Your numbers they may strengthen ye or weaken ye, ez 't
    heppens
They're willin' to be helpin' hands or wuss'n-nothin' cap'ns.

I've chose my side, an' 't ain't no odds ef I wuz drawed
    with magnets,
Or ef I thought it prudenter to jine the nighes' bagnets;
I've made my ch'ice, an' ciphered out, from all I see an'
    heard,
Th' ole Constitooshun never 'd git her decks for action
    cleared,
Long 'z you elect for Congressmen poor shotes thet want
    to go
Coz they can't seem to git their grub no otherways than so,
An' let your bes' men stay to home coz they wun't show ez
    talkers,
Nor can't be hired to fool ye an sof -soap ye at a caucus,—

Long 'z ye set by Rotashun more 'n ye do by folks's merits,

Ez though experunce thriv by change o' sile, like corn an'
kerrits,—

Long 'z you allow a critter's "claims" coz, spite o' shoves
an' tippins,

He's kep' his private pan jest where 't would ketch mos'
public drippins,—

Long 'z A. 'll turn tu an' grin' B.'s exe, ef B. 'll help him
grin' hisn,

(An' thet's the main idee by which your leadin' men hev
risen,)—

Long 'z you let *ary* exe be groun', 'less 't is to cut the
weasan'

O' sneaks thet dunno till they're told wut is an' wut ain't
Treason,—

Long 'z ye give out commissions to a lot o' peddlin' drones

Thet trade in whiskey with their men, an' skin 'em to their
bones,—

Long 'z ye sift out "safe" canderdates thet no one ain't
afeared on

Coz they're so thund'rin' eminent for bein' never heard
on,

An' hain't no record, ez it's called, for folks to pick a
hole in,

Ez ef it hurt a man to hev a body with a soul in,

An' it wuz ostentashun to be showin' on 't about,

When half his feller-citizens contrive to do without,—

Long 'z you suppose your votes can turn biled kebbage into
brain,

An' ary man thet's pop'lar 's fit to drive a lightnin'-train,—

Long 'z you believe democracy means *I'm ez good ez
you be*,

An' thet a feller from the ranks can't be a knave or booby,—

Long 'z Congress seems purvided, like yer street cars an'
    yer 'busses,
With ollers room for jes' one more o' your spiled-in-bakin'
    cusses,
Dough 'thout the emptins of a soul, an' yit with means
    about 'em
(Like essence-peddlers[1]) thet'll make folks long to be
    without em',
Jes' heavy 'nough to turn a scale thet's doubtfle the wrong
    way,
An' make their nat'ral arsenal o' bein' nasty pay,—
Long 'z them things last (an' *I* don't see no gret signs o'
    improvin')
I shan't up stakes, not hardly yit, nor 't wouldn't pay for
    movin' ;
For, 'fore you lick us, it'll be the long'st day ever *you* see.
Yourn (ez I 'xpec' to be nex' spring),

              B., MARKISS O' BIG BOOSY.

A MESSAGE OF JEFF. DAVIS IN SECRET SESSION.

Conjecturally Reported by H. BIGLOW.

TO THE EDITORS OF THE "ATLANTIC MONTHLY."

                    JAALAM, 10th March 1862.

GENTLEMEN,—My leisure has been so entirely occupied with the
hitherto fruitless endeavour to decipher the Runic inscription whose
fortunate discovery I mentioned in my last communication, that I have
not found time to discuss, as I had intended, the great problem of what

---

[1] A rustic euphemism for the American variety of the *Mephitis.*—
H. W.

we are to do with slavery, a topic on which the public mind in this place is at present more than ever agitated. What my wishes and hopes are I need not say, but for safe conclusions I do not conceive that we are yet in possession of facts enough on which to bottom them with certainty. Acknowledging the hand of Providence, as I do, in all events, I am sometimes inclined to think that they are wiser than we, and am willing to wait till we have made this continent once more a place where freemen can live in security and honour, before assuming any further responsibility. This is the view taken by my neighbour Habakkuk Sloansure, Esq., the president of our bank, whose opinion in the practical affairs of life has great weight with me, as I have generally found it to be justified by the event, and whose counsel, had I followed it, would have saved me from an unfortunate investment of a considerable part of the painful economies of half a century in the North-west Passage Tunnel. After a somewhat animated discussion with this gentleman, a few days since, I expanded, on the *audi alteram partem* principle, something which he happened to say by way of illustration, into the following fable:—

FESTINA LENTE.

ONCE on a time there was a pool
Fringed all about with flag-leaves cool
And spotted with cow-lilies garish,
Of frogs and pouts the ancient parish.
Alders the creaking redwings sink on,
Tussocks that house blithe Bob o' Lincoln
Hedged round the unassailed seclusion,
Where muskrats piled their cells Carthusian,
And many a moss-embroidered log,
The watering-place of summer frog,
Slept and decayed with patient skill,
As watering-places sometimes will.

Now in this Abbey of Theleme,
Which realised the fairest dream,
That ever dozing bull-frog had,
Sunned on a half-sunk lily-pad,
There rose a party with a mission
To mend the polliwogs' condition,

Who notified the sélectmen
To call a meeting there and then.
" Some kind of steps," they said, " are needed ;
They don't come on so fast as we did :
Let's dock their tails ; if that don't make 'em
Frogs by brevet, the Old One take 'em !
That boy, that came the other day
To dig some flag-root down this way,
His jack-knife left, and 'tis a sign
That Heaven approves of our design ;
'Twere wicked not to urge the step on,
When Providence has sent the weapon."

Old croakers, deacons of the mire,
That led the deep batrachian choir,
Uk! Uk! Caronk! with bass that might
Have left Lablache's out of sight,
Shook nobby heads, and said, " No go !
You'd better let 'em try to grow :
Old Doctor Time is slow, but still
He does know how to make a pill."

But vain was all their hoarsest bass,
Their old experience out of place,
And spite of croaking and entreating,
The vote was carried in marsh-meeting.

" Lord knows," protest the polliwogs,
" We're anxious to be grown-up frogs ;
But do not undertake the work
Of Nature till she prove a shirk ;
'Tis not by jumps that she advances,
But wins her way by circumstances ;
Pray wait awhile, until you know
We're so contrived as not to grow ;
Let Nature take her own direction,
And she'll absorb our imperfection ;
You mightn't like 'em to appear with,
But we must have the things to steer with."

" No," piped the party of reform,
" All great results are ta'en by storm;
Fate holds her best gifts till we show
We've strength to make her let them go:
No more reject the age's chrism,
Your cues are an anachronism;
No more the Future's promise mock,
But lay your tails upon the block,
Thankful that we the means have voted
To have you thus to frogs promoted."
The thing was done, the tails were cropped,
And home each philotadpole hopped,
In faith rewarded to exult,
And wait the beautiful result.
Too soon it came: our pool, so long
The theme of patriot bull-frogs' song,

Next day was reeking, fit to smother,
With heads and tails that missed each other,—
Here snoutless tails, there tailless snouts:
The only gainers were the pouts.

MORAL.

From lower to the higher next,
Not to the top, is Nature's text;
And embryo Good, to reach full stature,
Absorbs the Evil in its nature.

I think that nothing will ever give permanent peace and security to this continent but the extirpation of Slavery therefrom, and that the occasion is nigh; but I would do nothing hastily or vindictively, nor presume to jog the elbow of Providence. No desperate measures for me till we are sure that all others are hopeless,—*flectere si nequeo* SUPEROS, *Acheronta movebo*. To make Emancipation a reform instead of a revolution is worth a little patience, that we may have the Border States first, and then the non-slaveholders of the Cotton States with us in principle,—a consummation that seems to be nearer than many imagine. *Fiat justitia, ruat cælum,* is not to be taken in a literal sense by statesmen, whose problem is to get justice done with as little jar as

13

possible to existing order, which has at least so much of heaven in it that it is not chaos. I rejoice in the President's late Message, which at last proclaims the Government on the side of freedom, justice, and sound policy.

As I write, comes the news of our disaster at Hampton Roads. I do not understand the supineness which, after fair warning, leaves wood to an unequal conflict with iron. It is not enough merely to have the right on our side, if we stick to the old flint-lock of tradition. I have observed in my parochial experience (*haud ignarus mali*) that the Devil is prompt to adopt the latest inventions of destructive warfare, and may thus take even such a three-decker as Bishop Butler at an advantage. It is curious that, as gunpowder made armour useless on shore, so armour is having its revenge by baffling its old enemy at sea,—and that, while gunpowder robbed land-warfare of nearly all its picturesqueness to give even greater stateliness and sublimity to a sea-fight, armour bids fair to degrade the latter into a squabble between two iron-shelled turtles.

> Yours, with esteem and respect,
> HOMER WILBUR, A.M.

P.S.—I had well-nigh forgotten to say that the object of this letter is to enclose a communication from the gifted pen of Mr. Biglow.

I sent you a messige, my friens, t'other day,
To tell you I'd nothin' pertickler to say:
'Twuz the day our new nation gut kin' o' stillborn,
So 'twuz my pleasant dooty t' acknowledge the corn,
An' I see clearly then, ef I didn't before,
Thet the *augur* in inauguration means *bore*.
I needn't tell *you* thet my messige wuz written
To diffuse correc' notions in France an' Gret Britten,
An' agin to impress on the poppylar mind
The comfort an' wisdom o' goin' it blind,—
To say thet I didn't abate not a hooter
O' my faith in a happy an' glorious futur',
Ez rich in each soshle an' p'litickle blessin'
Ez them thet we now hed the joy o' possessin',

With a people united, an' longin' to die
For wut *we* call their country, without askin' why,
An' all the gret things we concluded to slope for
Ez much within reach now ez ever—to hope for.
We've all o' the ellerments, this very hour,
Thet make up a fus'-class, self-governin' power:
We've a war, an' a debt, an' a flag; an' ef this
Ain't to be inderpendunt, why, wut on airth is?
An' nothin' now henders our takin' our station
Ez the freest, enlightenedest, civerlised nation,
Built up on our bran'-new politickle thesis
Thet a Gov'ment's fust right is to tumble to pieces,—
I say nothin' henders our takin' our place
Ez the very fus'-best o' the whole human race,
A-spittin' tobacker ez proud ez you please
On Victory's bes' carpets, or loafin' at ease
In the Tool'ries front-parlor, discussin' affairs
With our heels on the backs o' Napoleon's new chairs,
An' princes a-mixin' our cocktails an' slings,—
Excep', wal, excep' jest a very few things,
Sech ez navies an' armies an' wherewith to pay,
An' gittin' our sogers to run t'other way,
An' not be too over-pertickler in tryin'
To hunt up the very las' ditches to die in.

Ther' are critters so base thet they want it explained
Jes' wut is the totle amount thet we've gained,
Ez ef we could maysure stupenjious events
By the low Yankee stan'ard o' dollars an' cents:
They seem to forgit thet, sence last year revolved,
We've succeeded in gittin' seceshed an' dissolved,
An' thet no one can't hope to git thru dissolootion
'Thout some kin' o' strain on the best Constitootion.

Who asks for a prospec' more flettrin' an' bright,
When from here clean to Texas it's all one free fight?
Hain't we rescued from Seward the gret leadin' featurs
Thet makes it wuth while to be reasonin' creaturs?
Hain't we saved Habus Coppers, improved it in fact,
By suspendin' the Unionists 'stid o' the Act?
Ain't the laws free to all? Where on airth else d'ye see
Every freeman improvin' his own rope an' tree?

It's ne'ssary to take a good confident tone
With the public; but here, jest amongst us, I own
Things looks blacker 'n thunder. Ther' 's no use denyin',
We're clean out o' money, an' 'most out o' lyin',—
Two things a young nation can't mennage without,
Ef she wants to look wal at her fust comin' out;
For the fust supplies physickle strength, while the second
Gives a morril edvantage thet's hard to be reckoned:
For this latter I'm willin' to du wut I can;
For the former you'll hev to consult on a plan,—
Though our *fust* want (an' this pint I want your best views on)
Is plausible paper to print I. O. U.s on.
Some gennlemen think it would cure all our cankers
In the way o' finance, ef we jes' hanged the bankers;
An' I own the proposle 'ud square with my views,
Ef their lives wuzn't all thet we'd left 'em to lose.
Some say thet more confidence might be inspired,
Ef we voted our cities an' towns to be fired,—
A plan thet 'ud suttenly tax our endurance,
Coz 'twould be our own bills we should git for the insurance;
But cinders, no metter how sacred we think 'em,
Mightn't strike furrin minds ez good sources of income,
Nor the people, perhaps, wouldn't like the eclaw
O' bein' all turned into paytriots by law.

Some want we should buy all the cotton an' burn it,
On a pledge, when we've gut thru the war, to return it,—
Then to take the proceeds an' hold *them* ez security
For an issue o' bonds to be met at maturity,
With an issue o' notes to be paid in hard cash
On the fus' Monday follerin' the 'tarnal Allsmash:
This hez a safe air, an', once hold o' the gold,
'Ud leave our vile plunderers out in the cold,
An' *might* temp' John Bull, ef it warn't for the dip he
Once gut from the banks o' my own Mississippi.
Some think we could make, by arrangin' the figgers,
A hendy home-currency out of our niggers;
But it wun't du to lean much on ary sech staff,
For they're gittin' tu current a'ready, by half.
One gennleman says, ef we lef' our loan out
Where Floyd could git hold on 't, *he* 'd take it, no doubt;
But 'tain't jes' the takin', though 't hez a good look,
We mus' git sunthin' out on it arter it's took,
An' we need now more 'n ever, with sorrer I own,
Thet some one another should let us a loan,
Sence a soger wun't fight, on'y jes' while he draws his
Pay down on the nail, for the best of all causes,
'Thout askin' to know wut the quarrel's about,—
An' once come to thet, why, our game is played out.
It's ez true ez though I shouldn't never hev said it
Thet a hitch hez took place in our system o' credit;
I swear it's all right in my speeches an' messiges,
But ther' 's idees afloat, ez ther' is about sessiges:
Folks wun't take a bond ez a basis to trade on,
Without nosin' round to find out wut it's made on,
An' the thought more an' more thru the public min'
    crosses
Thet our Treshry hez gut 'mos' too many dead hosses.

Wut's called credit, you see, is some like a balloon,
Thet looks while it's up 'most ez harnsome 'z a moon,
But once git a leak in 't an' wut looked so grand
Caves righ' down in a jiffy ez flat ez your hand.
Now the world is a dreffle mean place, for our sins,
Where ther' ollus is critters about with long pins
A-prickin' the globes we've blowed up with sech care,
An' provin' ther' 's nothin' inside but bad air:
They're all Stuart Millses, poor-white trash, an' sneaks,
Without no more chivverlry 'n Choctaws or Creeks,
Who think a real gennleman's promise to pay
Is meant to be took in trade's ornery way:
Them fellers an' I could n' never agree;
They're the nateral foes o' the Southun Idee;
I'd gladly take all of our other resks on me
To be red o' this low-lived politikle 'con'my!

Now a dastardly notion is gittin' about
Thet our bladder is bust an' the gas oozin' out,
An' onless we can mennage in some way to stop it,
Why, the thing's a gone coon, an' we might ez wal drop it.
Brag works wal at fust, but it ain't jes' the thing
For a stiddy inves'ment the shiners to bring,
An' votin' we're prosp'rous a hundred times over
Wun't change bein' starved into livin' on clover.
Manassas done sunthin' tow'rds drawin' the wool
O'er the green, anti-slavery eyes o' John Bull:
Oh, *warn't* it a godsend, jes' when sech tight fixes
Wuz crowdin' us mourners, to throw double-sixes!
I wuz tempted to think, an' it wuzn't no wonder,
Ther' wuz reelly a Providence,—over or under,—
When, all packed for Nashville, I fust ascertained
From the papers up North wut a victory we'd gained.

'Twuz the time for diffusin' correc' views abroad
Of our union an' strength an' relyin' on God;
An', fact, when I'd gut thru my fust big surprise,
I much ez half b'lieved in my own tallest lies,
An' conveyed the idee thet the whole Southun popperlace
Wuz Spartans all on the keen jump for Thermopperlies,
They set on the Lincolnites' bombs till they bust,
An' fight for the priv'lege o' dyin' the fust;
But Roanoke, Bufort, Millspring, an' the rest
Of our recent starn-foremost successes out West,
Hain't left us a foot for our swellin' to stand on,—
We've showed *too* much o' wut Buregard calls *abandon*,
For all our Thermopperlies (an' it's a marcy
We hain't hed no more) hev ben clean vicy-varsy,
An' wut Spartans wuz lef' when the battle wuz done
Wuz them thet wuz too unambitious to run.

Oh, ef we hed on'y jes' gut Reecognition,
Things now would ha' ben in a different position!
You'd ha' hed all you wanted: the paper blockade
Smashed up into toothpicks,—unlimited trade
In the one thing thet's needfle, till niggers, I swow,
Hed ben thicker 'n provisional shinplasters now,—
Quinine by the ton 'ginst the shakes when they seize ye,—
Nice paper to coin into C. S. A. specie;
The voice of the driver 'd be heerd in our land,
An' the univarse scringe, ef we lifted our hand:
Wouldn't *thet* be some like a fulfillin' the prophecies,
With all the fus' fem'lies in all the best offices?
'Twuz a beautiful dream, an' all sorrer is idle,—
But *ef* Lincoln *would* ha' hanged Mason an' Slidell!
They ain't no good in Európean pellices,
But think wut a help they'd ha' ben on their gallowses!

They 'd ha' felt they wuz truly fulfillin' their mission,
An', oh, how dog-cheap we'd ha' gut Reecognition!

But somehow another, wutever we've tried,
Though the the'ry's fust-rate, the facs *wun't* coincide:
Facs are contrary 'z mules, an' ez hard in the mouth,
An' they allus hev showed a mean spite to the South.
Sech bein' the case, we hed best look about
For some kin' o' way to slip *our* necks out:
Le' 's vote our las' dollar, ef one can be found,
(An', at any rate, votin' it hez a good sound,)—
Le' 's swear thet to arms all our people is flyin',
(The critters can't read, an' wun't know how we're lyin',)—
Thet Toombs is advancin' to sack Cincinnater,
With a rovin' commission to pillage an' slarter,—
Thet we've throwed to the winds all regard for wut's
    lawfle,
An' gone in for sunthin' promiscu'sly awfle.
Ye see, hitherto, it's our own knaves an' fools
Thet we've used,—those for whetstones, an' t' others ez
    tools,—
An' now our las' chance is in puttin' to test
The same kin' o' cattle up North an' out West.
I—— But, Gennlemen, here's a despatch jes' come in
Which shows thet the tide's begun turnin' agin,—
Gret Cornfedrit success! C'lumbus eevacooated!
I mus' run down an' hev the thing properly stated,
An' show wut a triumph it is, and how lucky
To fin'lly git red o' thet cussed Kentucky,—
An' how, sence Fort Donelson, winnin' the day
Consists in triumphantly gittin' away.

SPEECH OF HONOURABLE PRESERVED DOE IN SECRET CAUCUS.

TO THE EDITORS OF THE "ATLANTIC MONTHLY."

JAALAM, 12th April 1862.

GENTLEMEN,—As I cannot but hope that the ultimate, if not speedy, success of the national arms is now sufficiently ascertained, sure as I am of the righteousness of our cause and its consequent claim on the blessing of God (for I would not show a faith inferior to that of the pagan historian with his *Facile evenit quod Dîs cordi est*), it seems to me a suitable occasion to withdraw our minds a moment from the confusing din of battle to objects of peaceful and permanent interest. Let us not neglect the monuments of preterite history because what shall be history is so diligently making under our eyes. *Cras ingens iterabimus æquor;* to-morrow will be time enough for that stormy sea; to-day let me engage the attention of your readers with the Runic inscription to whose fortunate discovery I have heretofore alluded. Well may we say with the poet, *Multa renascuntur quæ jam cecidere.* And I would premise that, although I can no longer resist the evidence of my own senses from the stone before me to the ante-Columbian discovery of this continent by the Northmen, *gens inclytissima,* as they are called in a Palermitan inscription, written fortunately in a less debatable character than that which I am about to decipher, yet I would by no means be understood as wishing to vilipend the merits of the great Genoese, whose name will never be forgotten so long as the inspiring strains of "Hail, Columbia!" shall continue to be heard. Though he must be stripped also of whatever praise may belong to the experiment of the egg, which I find proverbially attributed by Castilian authors to a certain Juanito or Jack (perhaps an offshoot of our giant-killing mythus), his name will still remain one of the most illustrious of modern times. But the impartial historian owes a duty likewise to obscure merit, and my solicitude to render a tardy justice is perhaps quickened by my having known those who, had their own field of labour been less secluded, might have found a readier acceptance with the reading public. I could give an example, but I forbear: *forsitan nostris ex ossibus oritur ultor.*

Touching Runic inscriptions, I find that they may be classed under three general heads: 1°. Those which are understood by the Danish

Royal Society of Northern Antiquaries, and Professor Rafn, their Secretary; 2°. Those which are comprehensible only by Mr. Rafn; and 3°. Those which neither the Society, Mr. Rafn, nor anybody else, can be said in any definite sense to understand, and which accordingly offer peculiar temptations to enucleating sagacity. These last are naturally deemed the most valuable by intelligent antiquaries, and to this class the stone now in my possession fortunately belongs. Such give a picturesque variety to ancient events, because susceptible oftentimes of as many interpretations as there are individual archæologists; and since facts are only the pulp in which the Idea or event-seed is softly imbedded till it ripen, it is of little consequence what colour or flavour we attribute to them, provided it be agreeable. Availing myself of the obliging assistance of Mr. Arphaxad Bowers, an ingenious photographic artist, whose house-on-wheels has now stood for three years on our Meeting-House Green, with the somewhat contradictory inscription,—"*Our motto is onward*,"—I have sent accurate copies of my treasure to many learned men and societies, both native and European. I may hereafter communicate their different and (*me judice*) equally erroneous solutions. I solicit also, Messrs. Editors, your own acceptance of the copy herewith enclosed. I need only premise further, that the stone itself is a goodly block of metamorphic sandstone, and that the Runes resemble very nearly the ornithichnites or fossil bird-tracks of Dr. Hitchcock, but with less regularity or apparent design than is displayed by those remarkable geological monuments. These are rather the *non bene junctarum discordia semina rerum*. Resolved to leave no door open to cavil, I first of all attempted the elucidation of this remarkable example of lithic literature by the ordinary modes, but with no adequate return for my labour. I then considered myself amply justified in resorting to that heroic treatment the felicity of which, as applied by the great Bentley to Milton, had long ago enlisted my admiration. Indeed, I had already made up my mind that, in case good-fortune should throw any such invaluable record in my way, I would proceed with it in the following simple and satisfactory method. After a cursory examination, merely sufficing for an approximative estimate of its length, I would write down a hypothetical inscription based upon antecedent probabilities, and then proceed to extract from the characters engraven on the stone a meaning as nearly as possible conformed to this *a priori* product of my own ingenuity. The result more than justified my hopes, inasmuch as the two inscriptions were made without any great violence to tally in all essential particulars. I then proceeded, not without some anxiety, to my second test, which was to read the Runic letters diagonally, and again with the same success. With an excitement pardonable under the circumstances, yet tempered with thankful humility, I now applied my last and severest trial, my *experimentum crucis*. I turned the stone, now doubly precious in my eyes, with scrupulous exactness upside down. The physical exertion so far displaced my spectacles as to derange for a moment the focus of vision. I confess that it was with some tremulousness that I readjusted them upon my nose, and prepared my mind to bear with calmness any disappointment that might ensue. But, *O albo dies notanda lapillo!* what was my delight to find that the change of position had effected none in the sense of the writing, even by so much as a single letter! I was now, and justly, as I think, satisfied of the conscientious exactness of my interpretation. It is as follows:—

HERE
BJARNA GRIMOLFSSON
FIRST DRANK CLOUD-BROTHER
THROUGH CHILD-OF-LAND-AND-WATER:

that is, drew smoke through a reed stem. In other words, we have here a record of the first smoking of the herb *Nicotiana Tabacum* by a European on this continent. The probable results of this discovery are so vast as to baffle conjecture. If it be objected that the smoking of a pipe would hardly justify the setting up of a memorial stone, I answer that even now the Moquis Indian, ere he takes his first whiff, bows reverently toward the four quarters of the sky in succession, and that the loftiest monuments have been reared to perpetuate fame, which is the dream of the shadow of smoke. The *Saga*, it will be remembered, leaves this Bjarna to a fate something like that of Sir Humphrey Gilbert, on board a sinking ship in the " wormy sea," having generously given up his place in the boat to a certain Icelander. It is doubly pleasant, therefore, to meet with this proof that the brave old man arrived safely in Vinland, and that his declining years were cheered by the respectful attentions of the dusky denizens of our then uninvaded forests. Most of all was I gratified, however, in thus linking for ever the name of my native town with one of the most momentous occurrences of modern times. Hitherto Jaalam, though in soil, climate, and geographical position as highly qualified to be the theatre of remarkable historical incidents as any spot on the earth's surface, has been, if I may say it without seeming to question the wisdom of Providence, almost maliciously neglected, as it might appear, by occurrences of world-wide interest in want of a situation. And in matters of this nature it must be confessed that adequate events are as necessary as the *vates sacer* to record them. Jaalam stood always modestly ready, but circumstances made no fitting response to her generous intentions. Now, however, she assumes her place on the historic roll. I have hitherto been a zealous opponent of the Circean herb, but I shall now re-examine the question without bias.

I am aware that the Rev. Jonas Tutchel, in a recent communication to the Bogus Four Corners Weekly Meridian, has endeavoured to show that this is the sepulchral inscription of Thorwald Eriksson, who, as is well known, was slain in Vinland by the natives. But I think he has been misled by a preconceived theory, and cannot but feel that he has thus made an ungracious return for my allowing him to inspect the stone with the aid of my own glasses (he having by accident left his at home) and in my own study. The heathen ancients might have instructed this Christian minister in the rites of hospitality ; but much is to be pardoned to the spirit of self-love. He must indeed be ingenious who can make out the words *hèr hvílir* from any characters in the inscription in question, which, whatever else it may be, is certainly not mortuary. And even should the reverend gentleman succeed in persuading some fantastical wits of the soundness of his views, I do not see what useful end he will have gained. For if the English Courts of Law hold the testimony of grave-stones from the burial-grounds of Protestant dissenters to be questionable, even where it is essential in proving a descent, I cannot conceive that the epitaphial assertions of heathens should be esteemed of more authority by any man of orthodox sentiments.

At this moment, happening to cast my eyes upon the stone, on which a transverse light from my southern window brings out the characters with singular distinctness, another interpretation has occurred to me, promising even more interesting results. I hasten to close my letter in order to follow at once the clue thus providentially suggested.

I inclose, as usual, a contribution from Mr. Biglow, and remain,

Gentlemen, with esteem and respect,

Your Obedient Humble Servant,

HOMER WILBUR, A.M.

I THANK ye, my friens, for the warmth o' your greetin':
Ther' 's few airthly blessins but wut's vain an' fleetin';
But ef ther' is one thet hain't *no* cracks an' flaws,
An' is wuth goin' in for, it's pop'lar applause;
It sends up the sperits ez lively ez rockets,
An' I feel it—wal, down to the eend o' my pocket.
Jes' lovin' the people is Canaan in view,
But it's Canaan paid quarterly t' hev 'em love you;
It's a blessin' thet's breakin' out ollus in fresh spots;
It's a-follerin' Moses 'thout losin' the flesh-pots.
But, Gennlemen, 'scuse me, I ain't sech a raw cus
Ez to go luggin' ellerkence into a caucus,—
Thet is, into one where the call comprehens
Nut the People in person, but on'y their friens;
I'm so kin' o' used to convincin' the masses
Of th' edvantage o' bein' self-governin' asses,
I forgut thet *we*'re all o' the sort thet pull wires
An' arrange for the public their wants an' desires,
An' thet wut we hed met for wuz jes' to agree
Wut the People's opinions in futur' should be.

But to come to the nub, we've ben all disappinted,
An' our leadin' idees are a kind o' disjinted,—
Though, fur ez the nateral man could discern,
Things ough' to ha' took most an oppersite turn.
But The'ry is jes' like a train on the rail,
Thet, weather or no, puts her thru without fail,
While Fac's the ole stage thet gits sloughed in the ruts,
An' hez to allow for your darned efs an' buts,
An' so, nut intendin' no pers'nal reflections,
They don't—don't nut allus, thet is,—make connections:
Sometimes, when it really doos seem thet they'd oughter
Combine jest ez kindly ez new rum an' water,

Both 'll be jest ez sot in their ways ez a bagnet,
Ez otherwise-minded ez th' eends of a magnet,
An' folks like you 'n me, thet ain't ept to be sold,
Git somehow or 'nother left out in the cold.

I expected 'fore this, 'thout no gret of a row,
Jeff D. would ha' ben where A. Lincoln is now,
With Taney to say 'twuz all legle an' fair,
An' a jury o' Deemocrats ready to swear
Thet the ingin o' State gut throwed into the ditch
By the fault o' the North in misplacin' the switch.
Things wuz ripenin' fust-rate with Buchanan to nuss 'em ;
But the People they wouldn't be Mexicans, cuss 'em !
Ain't the safeguards o' freedom upsot, 'z you may say,
Ef the right o' rev'lution is took clean away ?
An' doosn't the right primy-fashy include
The bein' entitled to nut be subdued ?
The fact is, we'd gone for the Union so strong,
When Union meant South ollus right an' North wrong,
Thet the people gut fooled into thinkin' it might
Worry on middlin' wal with the North in the right.
We might ha' ben now jest ez prosp'rous ez France,
Where politikle enterprise hez a fair chance,
An' the people is heppy an' proud et this hour,
Long ez they hev the votes, to let Nap hev the power ;
But *our* folks they went an' believed wut we'd told 'em,
An', the flag once insulted, no mortle could hold 'em.
'Twuz pervokin' jest when we wuz cert'in to win,—
An' I, for one, wun't trust the masses agin :
For a people thet knows much ain't fit to be free
In the self-cockin', back-action style o' J. D.

I can't believe now but wut half on't is lies ;
For who'd thought the North wuz a-goin' to rise,

Or take the pervokin'est kin' of a stump,
'Thout 'twuz sunthin' ez pressin' ez Gabr'el's las' trump?
Or who'd ha' supposed, arter *sech* swell an' bluster
'Bout the lick-ary-ten-on-ye fighters they'd muster,
Raised by hand on briled lightnin', ez op'lent 'z you please
In a primitive furrest o' femmily-trees,
Who'd ha' thought thet them Southuners ever 'ud show
Starns with pedigrees to 'em like theirn to the foe,
Or, when the vamosin' come, ever to find
Nat'ral masters in front an' mean white folks behind?
By ginger, ef I'd ha' known half I know now,
When I wuz to Congress, I wouldn't, I swow,
Hev let 'em cair on so high-minded an' sarsy,
'Thout *some* show o' wut you may call vicy-varsy.
To be sure, we wuz under a contrac' jes' then
To be dreffle forbearin' towards Southun men;
We hed to go sheers in preservin' the bellance:
An' ez they seemed to feel they wuz wastin' their tellents
'Thout some un to kick, 't warn't more 'n proper, you
    know,
Each should funnish his part; an' sence they found the
    toe,
An' we wuzn't cherubs—wal, we found the buffer,
For fear thet the Compromise System should suffer.

I wun't say the plan hedn't onpleasant featurs,—
For men are perverse an' onreasonin' creaturs,
An' forgit thet in this life 't ain't likely to heppen
Their own privit fancy should ollus be cappen,—
But it worked jest ez smooth ez the key of a safe,
An' the gret Union bearins played free from all chafe.
They warn't hard to suit, ef they hed their own way;
An' we (thet is, some on us) made the thing pay:

'Twuz a fair give-an'-take out of Uncle Sam's heap;
Ef they took wut warn't theirn, wut we give come ez cheap;
The elect gut the offices down to tidewaiter,
The people took skinnin' ez mild ez a tater,
Seemed to choose who they wanted tu, footed the bills,
An' felt kind o' 'z though they wuz havin' their wills,
Which kep' 'em ez harmless an' cherfle as crickets,
While all we invested wuz names on the tickets:
Wal, ther' 's nothin' for folks fond o' lib'ral consumption,
Free o' charge, like democ'acy tempered with gumption!

Now warn't thet a system wuth pains in presarvin',
Where the people found jints an' their friens done the
          carvin', —
Where the many done all o' their thinkin' by proxy,
An' were proud on 't ez long ez 'twuz christened De-
          moc'cy, —
Where the few let us sap all o' Freedom's foundations,
Ef you called it reformin' with prudence an' patience,
An' were willin' Jeff's snake-egg should hetch with the rest,
Ef you writ "Constitootional" over the nest?
But it's all out o' kilter ('twuz too good to last),
An' all jes' by J. D.'s perceedin' too fast;
Ef he'd on'y hung on for a month or two more,
We'd ha' gut things fixed nicer 'n they hed ben before:
Afore he drawed off an' lef' all in confusion,
We wuz safely intrenched in the ole Constitootion,
With an outlyin', heavy-gun, casemated fort
To rake all assailants, — I mean th' S. J. Court.
Now I never 'll acknowledge (nut ef you should skin me)
'Twuz wise to abandon sech works to the in'my,
An' let him fin' out thet wut scared him so long,
Our whole line of argyments, lookin' so strong,

All our Scriptur' an' law, every the'ry an' fac',
Wuz Quaker-guns daubed with Pro-slavery black.
Why, ef the Republicans ever should git
Andy Johnson or some one to lend 'em the wit
An' the spunk jes' to mount Constitootion an' Court
With Columbiad guns, your real ekle-rights sort,
Or drill out the spike from the ole Declaration
Thet can kerry a solid shot clearn roun' creation,
We'd better take maysures for shettin' up shop,
An' put off our stock by a vendoo or swop.

But they wun't never dare tu; you'll see 'em in Edom
'Fore they ventur' to go where their doctrines 'ud lead 'em :
They've ben takin' our princerples up ez we dropt 'em,
An' thought it wuz terrible 'cute to adopt 'em ;
But they'll fin' out 'fore long thet their hop's ben deceivin' 'em,
An' thet princerples ain't o' no good, ef you b'lieve in 'em ;
It makes 'em tu stiff for a party to use,
Where they'd ough' to be easy 'z an ole pair o' shoes.
If *we* say 'n our pletform thet all men are brothers,
We don't mean thet some folks ain't more so 'n some
    others ;
An' it's wal understood thet we make a selection,
An' thet brotherhood kin' o' subsides arter 'lection.
The fust thing for sound politicians to larn is,
Thet Truth, to dror kindly in all sorts o' harness,
Mus' be kep' in the abstract,—for, come to apply it,
You're ept to hurt some folks's interists by it.
Wal, these 'ere Republicans (some on 'em) acs
Ez though gineral mexims 'ud suit speshle facs ;
An' there's where we'll nick 'em, there's where they'll be
    lost :
For applyin' your princerple 's wut makes it cost,

14

An' folks don't want Fourth o' July t' interfere
With the business-consarns o' the rest o' the year,
No more 'n they want Sunday to pry an' to peek
Into wut they are doin' the rest o' the week.

A ginooine statesman should be on his guard,
Ef he *must* hev beliefs, nut to b'lieve 'em tu hard;
For, ez sure ez he does, he'll be blartin' 'em out
'Thout regardin' the natur' o' man more 'n a spout,
Nor it don't ask much gumption to pick out a flaw
In a party whose leaders are loose in the jaw:
An' so in our own case I ventur' to hint
Thet we'd better nut air our perceedins in print,
Nor pass resserlootions ez long ez your arm
Thet may, ez things heppen to turn, do us harm;
For when you've done all your real meanin' to smother,
The darned things 'll up an' mean sunthin' or 'nother.
Jeff'son prob'ly meant wal with his " born free an' ekle,"
But it's turned out a real crooked stick in the sekle;
It's taken full eighty-odd year—don't you see?—
For the pop'lar belief to root out thet idee,
An', arter all, sprouts on't keep on buddin' forth
In the nat'lly onprincipled mind o' the North.
No, never say nothin' without you're compelled tu,
An' then don't say nothin' thet you can be held tu,
Nor don't leave no friction-idees layin' loose
For the ign'ant to put to incend'ary use.

You know I'm a feller thet keeps a skinned eye
On the leetle events thet go skurryin' by,
Coz it's of'ner by them than by gret ones you'll see
Wut the p'litickle weather is likely to be.

Now I don't think the South's more 'n begun to be licked,
But I *du* think, ez Jeff says, the wind-bag's gut pricked;
It'll blow for a spell an' keep puffin' an' wheezin',
The tighter our army an' navy keep squeezin',—
For they can't help spread-eaglein' long 'z ther' 's a mouth
To blow Enfield's Speaker thru lef' at the South.
But it's high time for us to be settin' our faces
Towards reconstructin' the national basis,
With an eye to beginnin' agin on the jolly ticks
We used to chalk up 'hind the back-door o' politics;
An' the fus' thing's to save wut of Slav'ry ther' 's lef'
Arter this (I mus' call it) imprudence o' Jeff
For a real good Abuse, with its roots fur an' wide,
Is the kin' o' thing *I* like to hev on my side;
A Scriptur' name makes it ez sweet ez a rose,
An' it's tougher the older an' uglier it grows—
(I ain't speakin' now o' the righteousness of it,
But the p'litickle purchase it gives, an' the profit).
Things look pooty squally, it must be allowed,
An' I don't see much signs of a bow in the cloud:
Ther' 's too many Deemocrats—leaders, wut's wuss—
Thet go for the Union 'thout carin' a cuss
Ef it helps ary party thet ever wuz heard on,
So our eagle ain't made a split Austrian bird on.
But ther' 's still some conservative signs to be found
Thet shows the gret heart o' the People is sound:
(Excuse me for usin' a stump-phrase agin,
But, once in the way on 't, they *will* stick like sin :)
There's Phillips, for instance, hez jes' ketched a Tartar
In the Law-'n'-Order Party of ole Cincinnater;
An' the Compromise System ain't gone out o' reach,
Long 'z you keep the right limits on freedom o' speech
'Twarn't none too late, neither, to put on the gag,

For he's dangerous now he goes in for the flag:
Nut thet I altogether approve o' bad eggs,
They're mos' gin'lly argymunt on its las' legs,—
An' their logic is ept to be tu indiscriminate,
Nor don't ollus wait the right objecs to 'liminate;
But there is a variety on 'em, you'll find,
Jest ez usefle an' more, besides bein' refined,—
I mean o' the sort thet are laid by the dictionary,
Sech ez sophisms an' cant thet'll kerry conviction ary
Way thet you want to the right class o' men,
An' are staler than all 't ever come from a hen:
" Disunion " done wal till our resh Southun friends
Took the savor all out on 't for national ends;
But I guess " Abolition " 'll work a spell yit,
When the war's done, an' so will " Forgive-an'-forgit."
Times mus' be pooty thoroughly out o' all jint,
Ef we can't make a good constitootional pint;
An' the good time 'll come to be grindin' our exes,
When the war goes to seed in the nettle o' texes:
Ef Jon'than don't squirm, with sech helps to assist him,
I give up my faith in the free-suffrage system;
Democ'cy wun't be nut a mite interestin',
Nor p'litikle capital much wuth investin';
An' my notion is, to keep dark an' lay low
Till we see the right minute to put in our blow.—
But I've talked longer now 'n I hed any idee,
An' ther' 's others you want to hear more 'n you du me;
So I'll set down an' give thet 'ere bottle a skrimmage,
For I've spoke till I'm dry ez a real graven image.

SUNTHIN' IN THE PASTORAL LINE.

To the Editors of the "Atlantic Monthly."

JAALAM, 17th May 1862.

GENTLEMEN,—At the special request of Mr. Biglow, I intended to enclose, together with his own contribution (into which, at my suggestion, he has thrown a little more of pastoral sentiment than usual), some passages from my sermon on the day of the National Fast, from the text, "Remember them that are in bonds, as bound with them," Heb. xiii. 3. But I have not leisure sufficient at present for the copying of them, even were I altogether satisfied with the production as it stands. I should prefer, I confess, to contribute the entire discourse to the pages of your respectable miscellany, if it should be found acceptable upon perusal, especially as I find the difficulty of selection of greater magnitude than I had anticipated. What passes without challenge in the fervour of oral delivery cannot always stand the colder criticism of the closet. I am not so great an enemy of Eloquence as my friend Mr. Biglow would appear to be from some passages in his contribution for the current month. I would not, indeed, hastily suspect him of covertly glancing at myself in his somewhat caustic animadversions, albeit some of the phrases he girds at are not entire strangers to my lips. I am a more hearty admirer of the Puritans than seems now to be the fashion, and believe that, if they Hebraized a little too much in their speech, they showed remarkable practical sagacity as statesmen and founders. But such phenomena as Puritanism are the results rather of great religious than merely social convulsions, and do not long survive them. So soon as an earnest conviction has cooled into a phrase, its work is over, and the best that can be done with it is to bury it. *Ite, missa est.* I am inclined to agree with Mr. Biglow that we cannot settle the great political questions which are now presenting themselves to the nation by the opinions of Jeremiah or Ezekiel as to the wants and duties of the Jews in their time, nor do I believe that an entire community with their feelings and views would be practicable or even agreeable at the present day. At the same time I could wish that their habit of subordinating the actual to the moral, the flesh to the spirit, and this world to the other, were more common. They had found out, at least, the great military secret that soul weighs more than body.—But I am suddenly called to a sick-bed in the household of a valued parishioner.

With esteem and respect,

Your obedient servant,

HOMER WILBUR.

ONCE git a smell o' musk into a draw
An' it clings hold like precerdents in law :
Your gran'ma'am put it there, — when, goodness
    knows—
To jes' this-worldify her Sunday-clo'es ;
But the old chist wun't sarve her gran'son's wife,
(For, 'thout new funnitoor, wut good in life ?)
An' so ole clawfoot, from the precinks dread
O' the spare chamber, slinks into the shed,
Where, dim with dust, it fust or last subsides
To holdin' seeds an' fifty things besides ;
But better days stick fast in heart an' husk,
An' all you keep in 't gits a scent o' musk.

Jes' so with poets : wut they've airly read
Gits kind o' worked into their heart an' head,
So 's 't they can't seem to write but jest on sheers
With furrin countries or played-out ideers,
Nor hev a feelin', ef it doosn't smack
O' wut some critter chose to feel 'way back :
This makes 'em talk o' daisies, larks, an' things,
Ez though we'd nothin' here that blows an' sings,—
(Why, I'd give more for one live bobolink
Than a square mile o' larks in printer's ink,)—
This makes 'em think our fust o' May is May,
Which 't ain't, for all the almanicks can say.

O little city-gals, don't never go it
Blind on the word o' noospaper or poet!
They're apt to puff, an' May-day seldom looks
Up in the country ez it doos in books ;
They're no more like than hornets'-nests an' hives,
Or printed sarmons be to holy lives.
I, with my trouses perched on cow-hide boots,
Tuggin' my foundered feet out by the roots,
Hev seen ye come to fling on April's hearse
Your muslin nosegays from the milliner's,
Puzzlin' to find dry ground your queen to choose,
An' dance your throats sore in morocker shoes :
I've seen ye an' felt proud, thet, come wut would,
Our Pilgrim stock wuz pithed with hardihood.
Pleasure doos make us Yankees kind o' winch,
Ez though 'twuz sunthin' paid for by the inch ;
But yit we du contrive to worry thru,
Ef Dooty tells us thet the thing 's to du,
An' kerry a hollerday, ef we set out,
Ez stiddily ez though 'twuz a redoubt.

I, country-born an' bred, know where to find
Some blooms thet make the season suit the mind,
An' seem to metch the doubtin' bluebird's notes,—
Half-vent'rin' liverworts in furry coats,
Bloodroots, whose rolled-up leaves ef you oncurl,
Each on 'em 's cradle to a baby-pearl,—
But these are jes' Spring's pickets ; sure ez sin,
The rebble frosts 'll try to drive 'em in ;
For half our May 's so awfully like May n't,
'Twould rile a Shaker or an evrige saint ;
Though I own up I like our back'ard springs
Thet kind o' haggle with their greens an' things,

An' when you 'most give up, without more words
Toss the fields full o' blossoms, leaves, an' birds :
Thet's Northun natur', slow an' apt to doubt,
But when it *doos* git stirred, ther' 's no gin-out !

Fust come the blackbirds clatt'rin' in tall trees,
An' settlin' things in windy Congresses,—
Queer politicians, though, for I'll be skinned,
Ef all on 'em don't head aginst the wind.
'Fore long the trees begin to show belief,—
The maple crimsons to a coral-reef,
Then saffern swarms swing off from all the willers
So plump they look like yaller caterpillars,
Then grey hossches'nuts leetle hands unfold
Softer 'n a baby's be at three days old :
This is the robin's almanick ; he knows
Thet arter this ther' 's only blossom-snows ;
So, choosin' out a handy crotch an' spouse,
He goes to past'rin' his adobe house.

Then seems to come a hitch,—things lag behind,
Till some fine mornin' Spring makes up her mind,
An' ez, when snow-swelled rivers cresh their dams
Heaped-up with ice thet dovetails in an' jams,
A leak comes spirtin' thru some pin-hole cleft,
Grows stronger, fercer, tears out right an' left,
Then all the waters bow themselves an' come,
Suddin, in one gret slope o' shedderin' foam,
Jes' so our Spring gits everythin' in tune
An' gives one leap from April into June :
Then all comes crowdin' in ; afore you think,
The oak-buds mist the side-hill woods with pink,

The catbird in the laylock-bush is loud,
The orchards turn to heaps o' rosy cloud,
In ellum-shrouds the flashin' hangbird clings
An' for the summer vy'ge his hammock slings,
All down the loose-walled lanes in archin' bowers
The barb'ry droops its strings o' golden flowers,
Whose shrinkin' hearts the school-gals love to try
With pins,—they'll worry yourn so, boys, bimeby !
But I don't love your cat'logue style,—do you ?—
Ez ef to sell all Natur' by vendoo ;
One word with blood in 't 's twice ez good ez two
'Nuff sed, June's bridesman, poet o' the year,
Gladness on wings, the bobolink, is here ;
Half-hid in tip-top apple-blooms he swings,
Or climbs aginst the breeze with quiverin' wings,
Or, givin' way to 't in a mock despair,
Runs down, a brook o' laughter, thru the air.

I ollus feel the sap start in my veins
In Spring, with curus heats an' prickly pains,
Thet drive me, when I git a chance, to walk
Off by myself to hev a privit talk
With a queer critter thet can't seem to 'gree
Along o' me like most folks,—Mister Me.
Ther' 's times when I'm unsoshle ez a stone,
An' sort o' suffocate to be alone,—
I'm crowded jes' to think thet folks are nigh,
An' can't bear nothin' closer than the sky ;
Now the wind's full ez shifty in the mind
Ez wut it is ou'-doors, ef I ain't blind,
An' sometimes, in the fairest sou'west weather,
My innard vane pints east for weeks together,

My natur' gits all goose-flesh, an' my sins
Come drizzlin' on my conscience sharp ez pins :
Wal, et sech times I jes' slip out o' sight
An' take it out in a fair stan'-up fight
With the one cuss I can't lay on the shelf,
The crook'dest stick in all the heap,—Myself.

'Twuz so las' Sabbath arter meetin'-time :
Findin' my feelins wouldn't noways rhyme
With nobody's, but off the hendle flew
An' took things from an east-wind pint o' view,
I started off to lose me in the hills
Where the pines be, up back o' 'Siah's Mills :
Pines, ef you're blue, are the best friends I know,
They mope an' sigh an' sheer your feelins so,—
They hesh the ground beneath so, tu, I swan,
You half-forgit you've gut a body on.

Ther' 's a small school'us' there where four roads meet,
The door-steps hollered out by little feet,
An' side-posts carved with names whose owners grew
To gret men, some on 'em, an' deacons, tu ;
'T ain't used no longer, coz the town hez gut
A high-school, where they teach the Lord knows wut ;
Three-story larnin' 's pop'lar now ; I guess
We thriv' ez wal on jes' two stories less,
For it strikes me ther' 's sech a thing ez sinnin'
By overloadin' children's underpinnin' :
Wal, here it wuz I larned my A B C,
An' it's a kind o' favorite spot with me.

We're curus critters : Now ain't jes' the minute
Thet ever fits us easy while we're in it ;

Long ez 'twuz futur', 'twould be perfect bliss,—
Soon ez it's past, *thet* time's wuth ten o' this;
An' yit there ain't a man thet need be told
Thet Now's the only bird lays eggs o' gold.
A knee-high lad, I used to plot an' plan
An' think 'twuz life's cap-sheaf to be a man;
Now, gittin' grey, ther's nothin' I enjoy
Like dreamin' back along into a boy:
So the ole school'us' is a place I choose
Afore all others, ef I want to muse;
I set down where I used to set, an' git
My boyhood back, an' better things with it,—
Faith, Hope, an' sunthin', ef it isn't Cherrity,
It's want o' guile, an' thet's ez gret a rerrity.

Now, 'fore I knowed, thet Sabbath arternoon
Thet I sot out to tramp myself in tune,
I found me in the school'us' on my seat,
Drummin' the march to No-wheres with my feet.
Thinkin' o' nothin', I've heerd ole folks say,
Is a 'hard kind o' dooty in its way:
It's thinkin' everythin' you ever knew,
Or ever hearn, to make your feelins blue.
I sot there tryin' thet on for a spell:
I thought o' the Rebellion, then o' Hell,
Which some folks tell you now is just a metterfor
(A the'ry, p'raps, it wun't *feel* none the better for);
I thought o' Reconstruction, wut we'd win
Patchin' our patent self-blow-up agin:
I thought ef this 'ere milkin' o' the wits,
So much a month, warn't givin' Natur' fits,—
Ef folks warn't druv, findin' their own milk fail,
To work the cow thet hez an iron tail,

An' ef idees 'thout ripenin' in the pan
Would send up cream to humor ary man :
From this to thet I let my worryin' creep,
Till finally I must ha' fell asleep.

Our lives in sleep are some like streams thet glide
'Twixt flesh an' sperrit boundin' on each side,
Where both shores' shadders kind o' mix an' mingle
In sunthin' thet ain't jes' like either single ;
An' when you cast off moorins from To-day,
An' down towards To-morrer drift away,
The imiges thet tengle on the stream
Make a new upside-down'ard world o' dream :
Sometimes they seem like sunrise-streaks an' warnins
O' wut 'll be in Heaven on Sabbath-mornins,
An', mixed right in ez ef jest out o' spite,
Sunthin' thet says your supper ain't gone right.
I'm gret on dreams, an' often, when I wake,.
I've lived so much it makes my mem'ry ache,
An' can't skurce take a cat-nap in my cheer
'Thout hevin' em, some good, some bad, all queer.

Now I wuz settin' where I'd ben, it seemed,
An' ain't sure yit whether I r'ally dreamed,
Nor, ef I did, how long I might ha' slep',
When I hearn some un stompin' up the step,
An' lookin' round, ef two and two make four,
I see a Pilgrim Father in the door.
He wore a steeple-hat, tall boots, an' spurs
With rowels to 'em big ez ches'nut-burrs,
An' his gret sword behind him sloped away
Long 'z a man's speech thet dunno wut to say.—

"Ef your name's Biglow, an' your given-name
Hosee," sez he, "it's arter you I came;
I'm your gret-gran'ther multiplied by three."—
"My *wut?*" sez I.—"Your gret-gret-gret," says he:
"You wouldn't ha' never ben here but for me.
Two hunderd an' three year ago this May
The ship I come in sailed up Boston Bay;
I'd ben a cunnle in our Civil War,—
But wut on airth hev *you* gut up one for?
I'm told you write in public prints: ef true,
It's nateral you should know a thing or two."—
"Thet air's an argymunt I can't endorse,—
'Twould prove, coz you wear spurs, you kep' a horse:
For brains," sez I, "wutever you may think,
Ain't boun' to cash the drafs o' pen-an'-ink,—
Though mos' folks write ez ef they hoped jes' quickenin
The churn would argoo skim-milk into thickenin';
But skim-milk ain't a thing to change its view
O' usefleness, no more 'n a smoky flue.
But do pray tell me, 'fore we furder go,
How in all Natur' did you come to know
'Bout our affairs," sez I, "in Kingdom-Come?"—
"Wal, I worked round at sperrit-rappin' some,
In hopes o' larnin' wut wuz goin' on,"
Sez he, "but mejums lie so like all-split
Thet I concluded it wuz best to quit.
But, come now, ef you wun't confess to knowin',
You've some conjecturs how the thing's a-goin'."—
"Gran'ther," sez I, "a vane warn't never known
Nor asked to hev a jedgment of its own;
An' yit, ef 't ain't gut rusty in the jints,
It's safe to trust its say on certin pints:
It knows the wind's opinions to a T,

An' the wind settles wut the weather 'll be."—
"I never thought a scion of our stock
Could grow the wood to make a weathercock;
When I wuz younger 'n you, skurce more 'n a shaver,
No airthly wind," sez he, "could make me waver!"
(Ez he said this, he clinched his jaw an' forehead,
Hitchin' his belt to bring his sword-hilt forrard.)—
"Jes' so it wuz with me," sez I, "I swow,
When *I* wuz younger 'n wut you see me now,—
Nothin', from Adam's fall to Huldy's bonnet,
Thet I warn't full-cocked with my jedgment on it;
But now I'm gittin' on in life, I find
It's a sight harder to make up my mind,—
Nor I don't often try tu, when events
Will du it for me free of all expense.
The moral question's ollus plain enough,—
It's jes' the human-natur' side thet's tough;
Wut's best to think mayn't puzzle me nor you,—
The pinch comes in decidin' wut to *du;*
Ef you *read* History, all runs smooth ez grease,
Coz there the men ain't nothin' more 'n idees,—
But come to *make* it, ez we must to-day,
Th' idees hev arms an' legs an' stop the way:
It's easy fixin' things in facts an' figgers,—
They can't resist, nor warn't brought up with niggers;
But come to try your the'ry on,—why, then
Your facts an' figgers change to ign'ant men
Actin' ez ugly "———"Smite 'em hip an' high!"
Sez gran'ther, "and let every man-child die!
Oh for three weeks o' Crommle an' the Lord!
O Israel, to your tents an' grind the sword!"—
"Thet kind o' thing worked wal in ole Judee,
But you forgit how long it's ben A.D.;

You think thet's ellerkence,—I call it shoddy,
A thing," sez I, "wun't cover soul nor body;
I like the plain all-wool o' common sense,
Thet warms ye now, an' will a twelvemonth hence.
  You took to follerin' where the Prophets beckoned,
An', fust you knowed on, back come Charles the
      Second;
Now wut I want 's to hev all *we* gain stick,
An' not to start Millennium too quick;
We hain't to punish only, but to keep,
An' the cure's gut to go a cent'ry deep."—
  "Wal, milk-an'-water ain't a good cement,"
Sez he, "an' so you'll find it in th' event;
Ef reshness venters sunthin', shilly-shally
Loses ez often wut's ten times the vally.
Thet exe of ourn, when Charles's neck gut split,
Opened a gap thet ain't bridged over yit:
Slav'ry's your Charles, the Lord hez gin the exe,"—
  "Our Charles," sez I, "hez gut eight million necks.
The hardest question ain't the black man's right,—
The trouble is to 'mancipate the white;
One's chained in body an' can be sot free,—
The other's chained in soul to an idee:
It's a long job, but we shall worry thru it;
Ef bag'nets fail, the spellin'-book must do it."—
  "Hosee," sez he, "I think you're goin' to fail:
The rettlesnake ain't dangerous in the tail;
This 'ere rebellion's nothin' but the rettle,—
You'll stomp on thet an' think you've won the bettle;
It's Slavery thet's the fangs and thinkin' head,
An' ef you want selvation, cresh it dead,—
An' cresh it suddin, or you'll larn by waitin'
Thet Chance wun't stop to listen to debatin'!"—

" God's truth ! " sez I,—"an' ef *I* held the club,
An' knowed jes' where to strike,—but there's the rub !"—
" Strike soon," sez he, " or you'll be deadly ailin',—
Folks thet's afeared to fail are sure o' failin' ;
God hates your sneakin' creturs thet believe
He'll settle things they run away an' leave ! "
He brought his foot down fercely, ez he spoke,
An' give me sech a startle thet I woke.

LATEST VIEWS OF MR. BIGLOW.

PRELIMINARY NOTE.

It is with feelings of the liveliest pain that we inform our readers of the death of the Reverend Homer Wilbur, A.M., which took place suddenly, by an apoplectic stroke, on the afternoon of Christmas Day, 1862. Our venerable friend (for so we may venture to call him, though we never enjoyed the high privilege of his personal acquaintance) was in his eighty-fourth year, having been born June 12, 1779, at Pigsgusset Precinct (now West Jerusha) in the then District of Maine. Graduated with distinction at Hubville College in 1805, he pursued his theological studies with the late Reverend Preserved Thacker, D.D., and was called to the charge of the First Society in Jaalam in 1809, where he remained till his death.

" As an antiquary he has probably left no superior, if, indeed, an equal," writes his friend and colleague, the Reverend Jeduthun Hitchcock, to whom we are indebted for the above facts ; " in proof of which I need only allude to his *History of Jaalam, Genealogical, Topographical, and Ecclesiastical*, 1849, which has won him an eminent and enduring place in our more solid and useful literature. It is only to be regretted that his intense application to historical studies should have so entirely withdrawn him from the pursuit of poetical composition, for which he was endowed by Nature with a remarkable aptitude. His well-known hymn, beginning ' With clouds of care encompassed round,' has been attributed in some collections to the late President Dwight, and it is hardly presumptuous to affirm that the simile of the rainbow in the eighth stanza would do no discredit to that polished pen."

We regret that we have not room at present for the whole of Mr. Hitchcock's exceedingly valuable communication. We hope to lay more liberal extracts from it before our readers at an early day. A summary of its contents will give some notion of its importance and interest. It contains: 1st, A biographical sketch of Mr. Wilbur, with notices of his predecessors in the pastoral office, and of eminent clerical contemporaries; 2nd, An obituary of deceased, from the *Punkin-Falls Weekly Parallel;* 3rd, A list of his printed and manuscript productions and of projected works; 4th, Personal anecdotes and recollections, with specimens of table-talk; 5th, A tribute to his relict, Mrs. Dorcas (Pilcox) Wilbur; 6th, A list of graduates fitted for different colleges by Mr. Wilbur, with biographical memoranda touching the more distinguished; 7th, Concerning learned, charitable, and other societies, of which Mr. Wilbur was a member, and of those with which, had his life been prolonged, he would doubtless have been associated, with a complete catalogue of such Americans as have been Fellows of the Royal Society; 8th, A brief summary of Mr. Wilbur's latest conclusions concerning the Tenth Horn of the Beast in its special application to recent events, for which the public, as Mr. Hitchcock assures us, have been waiting with feelings of lively anticipation; 9th, Mr. Hitchcock's own views on the same topic; and 10th, a brief essay on the importance of local histories. It will be apparent that the duty of preparing Mr. Wilbur's biography could not have fallen into more sympathetic hands.

In a private letter, with which the reverend gentleman has since favoured us, he expresses the opinion that Mr. Wilbur's life was shortened by our unhappy civil war. It disturbed his studies, dislocated all his habitual associations and trains of thought, and unsettled the foundations of a faith, rather the result of habit than conviction, in the capacity of man for self-government. "Such has been the felicity of my life," he said to Mr. Hitchcock, on the very morning of the day he died, "that, through the divine mercy, I could always say, *Summum nec metuo diem, nec opto.* It has been my habit, as you know, on every recurrence of this blessed anniversary, to read Milton's 'Hymn of the Nativity,' till its sublime harmonies so dilated my soul and quickened its spiritual sense that I seemed to hear that other song which gave assurance to the shepherds that there was One who would lead them also in green pastures and beside the still waters. But to-day I have been unable to think of anything but that mournful text, 'I came not to send peace, but a sword,' and, did it not smack of pagan presumptuousness, could almost wish I had never lived to see this day."

Mr. Hitchcock also informs us that his friend " lies buried in the Jaalam graveyard, under a large red-cedar which he specially admired. A neat and substantial monument is to be erected over his remains, with a Latin epitaph written by himself; for he was accustomed to say pleasantly that there was at least one occasion in a scholar's life when he might show the advantages of a classical training."

The following fragment of a letter addressed to us, and apparently intended to accompany Mr. Biglow's contribution to the present number, was found upon his table after his decease.—EDITORS " ATLANTIC MONTHLY."

To the Editors of the " ATLANTIC MONTHLY."

JAALAM, 24th, 1862.

RESPECTED SIRS,—The infirm state of my bodily health would be a sufficient apology for not taking up the pen at this time, wholesome as I deem it for the mind to apricate in the shelter of epistolary confidence, were it not that a considerable, I might even say a large, number of individuals in this parish expect from their pastor some public expression of sentiment at this crisis. Moreover, *Qui tacitus ardet magis uritur.* In trying times like these, the besetting sin of undisciplined minds is to seek refuge from inexplicable realities in the dangerous stimulant of angry partisanship, or the indolent narcotic of vague and hopeful vaticination: *fortunamque suo temperat arbitrio.* Both by reason of my age and my natural temperament, I am unfitted for either. Unable to penetrate the inscrutable judgments of God, I am more than ever thankful that my life has been prolonged till I could in some small measure comprehend His mercy. As there is no man who does not at some time render himself amenable to the one,—*quum vix justus sit securus,*—so there is none that does not feel himself in daily need of the other.

I confess I cannot feel, as some do, a personal consolation for the manifest evils of this war in any remote or contingent advantages that may spring from it. I am old and weak, I can bear little, and can scarce hope to see better days; nor is it any adequate compensation to know that Nature is old and strong and can bear much. Old men philosophise over the past, but the present is only a burthen and a weariness. The one lies before them like a placid evening landscape; the other is full of the vexations and anxieties of housekeeping. It may be true enough that *miscet hæc illis, prohibetque Clotho fortunam stare*, but he who said it was fain at last to call in Atropos with her shears before her time; and I cannot help selfishly mourning that the fortune of our Republic could not at least stand till my days were numbered.

Tibullus would find the origin of wars in the great exaggeration of riches, and does not stick to say that in the days of the beechen trencher there was peace. But averse as I am by nature from all wars, the more as they have been especially fatal to libraries, I would have this one go on till we are reduced to wooden platters again, rather than surrender the principle to defend which it was undertaken. Though I believe Slavery to have been the cause of it, by so thoroughly demoralising Northern politics for its own purposes as to give opportunity and hope to treason, yet I would not have our thought and purpose diverted from their true object,—the maintenance of the idea of Government. We are not merely suppressing an enormous riot, but contending for the possibility of permanent order co-existing with democratical fickleness; and while I would not superstitiously venerate form to the sacrifice of substance, neither would I forget that an adherence to precedent and prescription can alone give that continuity and coherence under a democratical constitution which are inherent in the person of a despotic monarch and the selfishness of an aristocratical class. *Stet pro ratione voluntas* is as dangerous in a majority as in a tyrant.

I cannot allow the present production of my young friend to go out without a protest from me against a certain extremeness in his views, more pardonable in the poet than the philosopher. While I agree with him that the only cure for rebellion is suppression by force, yet I must animadvert upon certain phrases where I seem to see a coincidence with a popular fallacy on the subject of compromise. On the one hand, there are those who do not see that the vital principle of Government and the seminal principle of Law cannot properly be made a subject of compromise at all; and on the other, those who are equally blind to the truth that without a compromise of individual opinions, interests, and even rights, no society would be possible. *In medio tutissimus.* For my own part, I would gladly—

> EF I a song or two could make,
>   Like rockets druv by their own burnin',
> All leap an' light, to leave a wake
>   Men's hearts an' faces skyward turnin'!—

But, it strikes me, 'tain't jest the time
  Fer stringin' words with settisfaction:
Wut's wanted now 's the silent rhyme
  'Twixt upright Will an' downright Action.

Words, ef you keep 'em, pay their keep,
  But gabble 's the short cut to ruin;
It's gratis (gals half-price), but cheap
  At no rate, ef it henders doin';
Ther' 's nothin' wuss, 'less 'tis to set
  A martyr-prem'um upon jawrin':
Teapots git dangerous, ef you shet
  Their lids down on 'em with Fort Warren.

'Bout long enough it's ben discussed
  Who sot the magazine afire,
An' whether, ef Bob Wickliffe bust,
  'Twould scare us more or blow us higher.
D'ye s'pose the Gret Foreseer's plan
  Wuz settled fer him in town-meetin'?
Or thet ther' 'd ben no Fall o' Man,
  Ef Adam 'd on'y bit a sweetin'?

Oh, Jon'than, ef you want to be
  A rugged chap agin an' hearty,
Go fer wutever 'll hurt Jeff D.,
  Nut wut 'll boost up ary party.
Here's hell broke loose, an' we lay flat
  With half the univarse a-singein',
Till Sen'tor This an' Gov'nor Thet
  Stop squabblin' fer the garding-ingin'.

It's war we're in, not politics ;
   It's systems wrastlin' now, not parties ;
An' victory in the eend 'll fix
   Where longest will an' truest heart is.
An' wut's the Guv'ment folks about ?
   Tryin' to hope ther' 's nothin' doin',
An' look ez though they didn't doubt
   Sunthin' pertickler wuz a-brewin'.

Ther' 's critters yit thet talk an' act
   Fer wut they call Conciliation ;
They 'd hand a buff'lo-drove a tract
   When they wuz madder than all Bashan.
Conciliate ? it jest means *be kicked*,
   No metter how they phrase an' tone it ;
It means thet we're to set down licked,
   Thet we're poor shotes an' glad to own it !

A war on tick 's ez dear 'z the deuce,
   But it wun't leave no lastin' traces,
Ez 'twould to make a sneakin' truce
   Without no moral specie-basis :
Ef green-backs ain't nut jest the cheese,
   I guess ther' 's evils thet's extremer,—
Fer instance,—shinplaster idees
   Like them put out by Gov'nor Seymour.

Last year, the Nation, at a word,
   When tremblin' Freedom cried to shield her,
Flamed weldin' into one keen sword
   Waitin' an' longin' fer a wielder :

A splendid flash !—an' how 'd the grasp
   With sech a chance ez thet wuz tally?
Ther' warn't no meanin' in our clasp,—
   Half this, half thet, all shilly-shally.

More men? More Man! It's there we fail ;
   Weak plans grow weaker yit by lengthenin' :
Wut use in addin' to the tail,
   When it's the head 's in need o' strengthenin'?
We wanted one thet felt all Chief
   From roots o' hair to sole o' stockin',
Square-sot with thousan'-ton belief
   In him an' us, ef earth went rockin' !

Ole Hick'ry wouldn't ha' stood see-saw
   'Bout doin' things till they wuz done with,—
He'd smashed the tables o' the Law
   In time o' need to load his gun with ;
He couldn't see but jest one side,—
   Ef his, 'twuz God's, an' thet wuz plenty ;
An' so his "*Forrards !*" multiplied
   An army's fightin' weight by twenty.

But this 'ere histin', creak, creak, creak,
   Your cappen's heart up with a derrick,
This tryin' to coax a lightnin'-streak
   Out of a half-discouraged hay-rick,
This hangin' on mont' arter mont'
   Fer one sharp purpose 'mongst the twitter,—
I tell ye, it doos kind o' stunt
   The peth an' sperit of a critter.

In six months where'll the People be,
    Ef leaders look on revolution
Ez though it wuz a cup o' tea,—
    Jest social el'ments in solution?
This weighin' things doos wal enough
    When war cools down, an' comes to writin';
But while it's makin', the true stuff
    Is pison-mad, pig-headed fightin'.

Democ'acy gives every man
    A right to be his own oppressor;
But a loose Gov'ment ain't the plan,
    Helpless ez spilled beans on a dresser:
I tell ye one thing we might larn
    From them smart critters, the Seceders,—
Ef bein' right 's the fust consarn,
    The 'fore-the-fust 's cast-iron leaders.

But 'pears to me I see some signs
    Thet we're a-goin' to use our senses:
Jeff druv us into these hard lines,
    An' ough' to bear his half th' expenses;
Slavery 's Secession's heart an' will,
    South, North, East, West, where'er you find it,
An' ef it drors in the War's mill,
    D'ye say them thunder-stones shan't grind it?

D'ye s'pose, ef Jeff give *him* a lick,
    Ole Hick'ry 'd tried his head to sof'n
So 's 'twouldn't hurt thet ebony stick
    Thet's made our side see stars so of'n?

"No!" he'd ha' thundered, "on your knees,
  An' own one flag, one road to glory!
Soft-heartedness, in times like these,
  Shows sof'ness in the upper story!"

An' why should we kick up a muss
  About the Pres'dunt's proclamation?
It ain't a-goin' to lib'rate us,
  Ef we don't like emancipation:
The right to be a cussed fool
  Is safe from all devices human,
It's common (ez a gin'l rule)
  To every critter born o' woman.

So *we* 're all right, an' I, fer one,
  Don't think our cause 'll lose in vally
By rammin' Scriptur' in our gun,
  An' gittin' Natur' fer an ally:
Thank God, say I, fer even a plan
  To lift one human bein's level,
Give one more chance to make a man,
  Or, anyhow, to spile a devil!

Not thet I'm one thet much expec'
  Millennium by express to morrer;
They *will* miscarry,—I rec'lec'
  Tu many on 'em, to my sorrer:
Men ain't made angels in a day,
  No matter how you mould an' labor 'em,—
Nor 'riginal ones, I guess, don't stay
  With Abe so of'n ez with Abraham.

The'ry thinks Fact a pooty thing,
    An' wants the banns read right ensuin';
But Fact wun't noways wear the ring
    'Thout years o' settin' up an' wooin';
But, arter all, Time's dial-plate
    Marks cent'ries with the minute-finger,
An' Good can't never come tu late,
    Though it doos seem to try an' linger.

An' come wut will, I think it's grand
    Abe's gut his will et last bloom-furnaced
In trial-flames till it 'll stand
    The strain o' bein' in deadly earnest:
Thet's wut we want,—we want to know
    The folks on our side hez the bravery
To b'lieve ez hard, come weal, come woe,
    In Freedom ez Jeff doos in Slavery.

Set the two forces foot to foot,
    An' every man knows who'll be winner,
Whose faith in God hez ary root
    Thet goes down deeper than his dinner:
Then 'twill be felt from pole to pole,
    Without no need o' proclamation,
Earth's Biggest Country 's gut her soul
    An' risen up Earth's Greatest Nation!

KETELOPOTOMACHIA.

PRELIMINARY NOTE.

In the month of February 1866 the editors of the *Atlantic Monthly* received from the Rev. Mr. Hitchcock of Jaalam a letter enclosing the macaronic verses which follow, and promising to send more, if more should be communicated. " They were rapped out on the evening of Thursday last past," he says, " by what claimed to be the spirit of my late predecessor in the ministry here, the Rev. Dr. Wilbur, through the medium of a young man at present domiciled in my family. As to the possibility of such spiritual manifestations, or whether they be properly so entitled, I express no opinion, as there is a division of sentiment on that subject in the parish, and many persons of the highest respectability in social standing entertain opposing views. The young man who was improved as a medium submitted himself to the experiment with manifest reluctance, and is still unprepared to believe in the authenticity of the manifestations. During his residence with me his deportment has always been exemplary; he has been constant in his attendance upon our family devotions and the public ministrations of the Word, and has more than once privately stated to me that the latter had often brought him under deep concern of mind. The table is an ordinary quadrupedal one, weighing about thirty pounds, three feet seven inches and a half in height, four feet square on the top, and of beech or maple, I am not definitely prepared to say which. It had once belonged to my respected predecessor, and had been, so far as I can learn upon careful inquiry, of perfectly regular and correct habits up to the evening in question. On that occasion the young man previously alluded to had been sitting with his hands resting carelessly upon it, while I read over to him at his request certain portions of my last Sabbath's discourse. On a sudden the rappings, as they are called, commenced to render themselves audible, at first faintly, but in process of time more distinctly and with violent agitation of the table. The young man expressed himself both surprised and pained by the wholly unexpected, and, so far as he was concerned, unprecedented occurrence. At the earnest solicitation, however, of several who happened to be present, he consented to go on with the experiment, and with the assistance of the alphabet commonly employed in similar emergencies, the following communication was obtained and written down immediately by myself. Whether any, and if so, how much weight should be attached to it, I venture no decision. That Dr. Wilbur had sometimes employed his leisure in Latin versification I have ascertained to be the case, though all that has been discovered of that nature among his papers consists of some fragmentary passages of a version into hexameters of portions of the Song of Solomon. These I had communicated about a week or ten days previous [ly] to the young gentleman who officiated as medium in the communication afterwards received. I have thus, I believe, stated all the material facts that have any elucidative bearing upon this mysterious occurrence."

So far Mr. Hitchcock, who seems perfectly master of Webster's unabridged quarto, and whose flowing style leads him into certain further expatiations for which we have not room. We have since learned that the young man he speaks of was a sophomore, put under his care during a sentence of rustication from —— College, where he had distinguished himself rather by physical experiments on the comparative power of resistance in window-glass to various solid substances, than in the more regular studies of the place. In answer to a letter of inquiry, the professor of Latin says, "There was no harm in the boy that I know of beyond his loving mischief more than Latin, nor can I think of any spirits likely to possess him except those commonly called animal. He was certainly not remarkable for his Latinity, but I see nothing in verses you enclose that would lead me to think them beyond his capacity, or the result of any special inspiration, whether of beech or maple. Had that of *birch* been tried upon him earlier and more faithfully, the verses would perhaps have been better in quality and certainly in quantity." This exact and thorough scholar then goes on to point out many false quantities and barbarisms. It is but fair to say, however, that the author, whoever he was, seems not to have been unaware of some of them himself, as is shown by a great many notes appended to the verses as we received them, and purporting to be by Scaliger, Bentley, and others,—among them the *Esprit de Voltaire!* These we have omitted as clearly meant to be humorous and altogether failing therein.

Though entirely satisfied that the verses are altogether unworthy of Mr. Wilbur, who seems to have been a tolerable Latin scholar after the fashion of his day, yet we have determined to print them here partly as belonging to the *res gestæ* of this collection, and partly as a warning to their putative author which may keep him from such indecorous pranks for the future.

KETELOPOTOMACHIA.

P. Ovidii Nasonis carmen heroicum macaronicum perplexametrum, inter Getas getico more compostum, denuo per medium ardentispiritualem, adjuvante mensa diabolice obsessa, recuperatum, curaque Jo. Conradi Schwarzii umbræ, aliis necnon plurimis adjuvantibus, restitutum.

LIBER I.

PUNCTORUM garretos colens et cellara Quinque,
Gutteribus quæ et gaudes sundayam abstingere frontem,
Plerumque insidos solita fluitare liquore
Tanglepedem quem homines appellant Di quoque rotgut,
Pimpliidis, rubicundaque, Musa, O, bourbonolenseque,   5
Fenianas rixas procul, alma, brogipotentis
Patricii cyathos iterantis et horrida bella,
Backos dum virides viridis Brigitta remittit,
Linquens, eximios celebrem, da, Virginienses
Rowdes, præcipue et TE, heros alte, Polarde!   10
Insignes juvenesque, illo certamine lictos,
Colemane, Tylere, nec vos oblivione relinquam.

Ampla aquilæ invictæ fausto est sub tegmine terra,
Backyfer, ooiskeo pollens, ebenoque bipede,
Socors præsidum et altrix (denique quidruminantium),   15
Duplefveorum uberrima; illis et integre cordi est
Deplere assidue et sine proprio incommodo fiscum;
Nunc etiam placidum hoc opus invictique secuti,
Goosam aureos ni eggos voluissent immo necare
Quæ peperit, saltem ac de illis meliora merentem.   20
      Condidit hanc Smithius Dux, Captinus inclytus ille
Regis Ulyssæ instar, docti arcum intendere longum;
Condidit illi Johnsmith, Virginiamque vocavit,
Settledit autem Jacobus rex, nomine primus,

Rascalis implens ruptis, blagardisque deboshtis,   25
Militibusque ex Falstaffi legione fugatis
Wenchisque illi quas poterant seducere nuptas;
Virgineum, ah, littus matronis talibus impar!
Progeniem stirpe ex hoc non sine stigmate ducunt
Multi sese qui jactant regum esse nepotes: 30
Haud omnes, Mater, genitos quæ nuper habebas
Bello fortes, consilio cautos, virtute decoros,
Jamque et habes, sparso si patrio in sanguine virtus,
Mostrabisque iterum, antiquis sub astris reducta!
De illis qui upkikitant, dicebam, rumpora tanta,   35
Letcheris et Floydis magnisque Extra ordine Billis:
Est his prisca fides jurare et breakere wordum;
Poppere fellerum a tergo, aut stickere clam bowiknifo,
Haud sane facinus, dignum sed victrice lauro;
Larrupere et nigerum, factum præstantius ullo: 40
Ast chlamydem piciplumatam, Icariam, flito et ineptam,
Yanko gratis induere, illum et valido railo
Insuper acri equitare docere est hospitio uti.

Nescio an ille Polardus duplefveoribus ortus,
Sed reputo potius de radice poorwitemanorum;   45
Fortuiti proles, ni fallor, Tylerus erat
Præsidis, omnibus ab Whiggis nominatus a poor cuss;
Et nobilem tertium evincit venerabile nomen.
Ast animosi omnes bellique ad tympana ha! ha!
Vociferant læti, procul et si proelia, sive   50
Hostem incautum atsito possunt shootere salvi;
Imperiique capaces, esset si stylus agmen,
Pro dulci spoliabant et sine dangere fito.
Præ ceterisque Polardus: si Secessia licta,
Se nunquam licturum jurat, res et unheardof,   55
Verbo hæsit, similisque audaci roosteri invicto,
Dunghilli solitus rex pullos whoppere molles,

Grantum, hirelingos stripes quique et splendida tollunt
Sidera, et Yankos, territum et omnem sarsuit orbem.

Usque dabant operam isti omnes, noctesque diesque,   60
Samuelem demulgere avunculum, id vero siccum ;
Uberibus sed ejus, et horum est culpa, remotis,
Parvam domi vaccam, nec mora minima, quærunt,
Lacticarentem autem et droppam vix in die dantem ;
Reddite avunculi, et exclamabant, reddite pappam !   65
Polko ut consule, gemens, Billy immurmurat Extra ;
Echo respondit, thesauro ex vacuo, pappam !
Frustra explorant pocketa, ruber nare repertum ;
Officia expulsi aspiciunt rapta, et Paradisum
Occlusum, viridesque haud illis nascere backos ;   70
Stupent tunc oculis madidis spittantque silenter.
Adhibere usu ast longo vires prorsus inepti,
Si non ut qui grindeat axve trabemve revolvat,
Virginiam excruciant totis nunc mightibu' matrem ;
Non melius, puta, nono panis dimidiumne est ?   75

Readere ibi non posse est casus commoner ullo ;
Tanto intentius imprimere est opus ergo statuta ;
Nemo propterea pejor, melior, sine doubto,
Obtineat qui contractum, si et postea rhino ;
Ergo Polardus, si quis, inexsuperabilis heros,   80
Colemanus impavidus nondum, atque in purpure natus
Tylerus Iohanides celerisque in flito Nathaniel,
Quisque optans digitos in tantum stickere pium,
Adstant accincti imprimere aut perrumpere leges :
Quales os miserum rabidi tres ægre molossi,   85
Quales aut dubium textum atra in veste ministri,
Tales circumstabant nunc nostri inopes hoc job.

Hisque Polardus voce canoro talia fatus :
Primum autem, veluti est mos, præceps quisque liquorat,
Quisque et Nicotianum ingens quid inserit atrum,   90

Heroûm nitidum decus et solamen avitum,
Masticat ac simul altisonans, spittatque profuse ;
Quis de Virginia meruit præstantius unquam ?
Quis se pro patria curavit impigre tutum ?
Speechisque articulisque hominum quis fortior ullus,   95
Ingeminans pennæ lickos et vulnera vocis ?
Quisnam putidius (hic) sarsuit Yankinimicos,
Sæpius aut dedit ultro datam et broke his parolam ?
Mente inquassatus solidaque, tyranno minante,
Horrisonis (hic) bombis mœnia et alta quatente,   100
Sese promptum (hic) jactans Yankos lickere centum,
Atque ad lastum invictus non surrendidit unquam ?
Ergo haud meddlite, posco, mique relinquite (hic) hoc job,
Si non——knifumque enormem mostrat spittatque tre-
      mendus.

  Dixerat ; ast alii reliquorant et sine pauso   105
Pluggos incumbunt maxillis, uterque vicissim
Certamine innocuo valde madidam inquinit assem :
Tylerus autem, dumque liquorat aridus hostis,
Mirum aspicit duplumque bibententem, astante Lyæo ;
Ardens impavidusque edidit tamen impia verba ;   110
Duplum quamvis te aspicio, esses atque virginti,
Mendacem dicerem totumque (hic) thrasherem acervum ;
Nempe et thrasham, doggonatus (hic) sim nisi faxem ;
Lambastabo omnes catawompositer-(hic)-que chawam !
Dixit et impulsus Ryeo ruitur bene titus,   115
Illi nam gravidum caput et laterem habet in hatto.

  Hunc inhiat titubansque Polardus, optat et illum
Stickere inermem, protegit autem rite Lyæus,
Et pronos geminos, oculis dubitantibus, heros
Cernit et irritus hostes, dumque excogitat utrum   120
Primum inpitchere, corruit, inter utrosque recumbit,
Magno asino similis nimio sub pondere quassus :

Colemanus hos mœstus, triste ruminansque solamen,
Inspicit hiccans, circumspittat terque cubantes;
Funereisque his ritibus humidis inde solutis,   125
Sternitur, invalidusque illis superincidit infans:
Hos sepelit somnus et snorunt cornisonantes,
Watchmanus inscios ast calybooso deinde reponit.

[The Editors of the *Atlantic* have received so many letters of inquiry
concerning the literary remains of the late Mr. Wilbur, mentioned by
his colleague and successor, Rev. Jeduthan Hitchcock, in a communication from which we made some extracts in our number for February
1863, and have been so repeatedly urged to print some part of them for
the gratification of the public, that they felt it their duty at least to
make some effort to satisfy so urgent a demand.   They have accordingly carefully examined the papers intrusted to them, but find most of
the productions of Mr. Wilbur's pen so fragmentary, and even chaotic,
written as they are on the backs of letters in an exceedingly cramped
chirography,—here a memorandum for a sermon; there an observation
of the weather; now the measurement of an extraordinary head of
cabbage, and then of the cerebral capacity of some reverend brother
deceased; a calm inquiry into the state of modern literature, ending in
a method of detecting if milk be impoverished with water, and the
amount thereof; one leaf beginning with a genealogy, to be interrupted
half-way down with an entry that the brindle cow had calved,—that
any attempts at selection seemed desperate.   His only complete work,
An Enquiry concerning the Tenth Horn of the Beast, even in the
abstract of it given by Mr. Hitchcock, would, by a rough computation
of the printers, fill five entire numbers of our journal, and as he attempts,
by a new application of decimal fractions, to identify it with the Emperor
Julian, seems hardly of immediate concern to the general reader.   Even
the Table-Talk, though doubtless originally highly interesting in the
domestic circle, is so largely made up of theological discussion and
matters of local or preterite interest, that we have found it hard to
extract anything that would at all satisfy expectation.   But, in order to
silence further inquiry, we subjoin a few passages as illustrations of its
general character.]

I think I could go near to be a perfect Christian if I were always a
visitor, as I have sometimes been, at the house of some hospitable

friend. I can show a great deal of self-denial where the best of every-thing is urged upon me with kindly importunity. It is not so very hard to turn the other cheek for a kiss. And when I meditate upon the pains taken for our entertainment in this life, on the endless variety of seasons, of human character and fortune, on the costliness of the hangings and furniture of our dwelling here, I sometimes feel a singular joy in looking upon myself as God's guest, and cannot but believe that we should all be wiser and happier, because more grateful, if we were always mindful of our privilege in this regard. And should we not rate more cheaply any honour that men could pay us, if we remembered that every day we sat at the table of the Great King? Yet must we not forget that we are in strictest bonds His servants also; for there is no impiety so abject as that which expects to be *dead-headed* (*ut ita dicam*) through life, and which, calling itself trust in Providence, is in reality asking Providence to trust us and taking up all our goods on false pretences. It is a wise rule to take the world as we find it, not always to leave it so.

It has often set me thinking when I find that I can always pick up plenty of empty nuts under my shagbark-tree. The squirrels know them by their lightness, and I have seldom seen one with the marks of their teeth in it. What a school-house is the world, if our wits would only not play truant! For I observe that men set most store by forms and symbols in proportion as they are mere shells. It is the outside they want and not the kernel. What stores of such do not many, who in material things are as shrewd as the squirrels, lay up for the spiritual winter-supply of themselves and their children! I have seen churches that seemed to me garners of these withered nuts, for it is wonderful how prosaic is the apprehension of symbols by the minds of most men. It is not one sect nor another, but all, who, like the dog of the fable, have let drop the spiritual substance of symbols for their material shadow. If one attribute miraculous virtues to mere holy water, that beautiful emblem of inward purification at the door of God's house, another cannot comprehend the significance of baptism without being ducked over head and ears in the liquid vehicle thereof.

Perhaps a word of historical comment may be permitted here. My late revered predecessor was, I would humbly affirm, as free from prejudice as falls to the lot of the most highly favoured individuals of our species. To be sure, I have heard him say that, "what were called strong prejudices were in fact only the repulsion of sensitive organisation from that moral and even physical effluvium through which some natures by providential appointment, like certain unsavoury quadrupeds, gave warning of their neighbourhood. Better ten mistaken suspicions of this kind than one close encounter." This he said somewhat in heat, on being questioned as to his motives for always refusing his pulpit to those itinerant professors of vicarious benevolence who end their discourses by taking up a collection. But at another time I remember his saying, "that there was one large thing which small minds always found room for, and that was great prejudices." This, however, by the way. The statement which I purposed to make was simply this. Down to A.D. 1830, Jaalam had consisted of a single parish, with one house set apart for religious services. In that year the foundations of a Baptist Society were laid by the labours of Elder Joash Q. Balcom, 2d. As the members of the new body were drawn from the First Parish, Mr. Wilbur was for a time considerably exercised in mind. He even went so far as on one occasion to follow the reprehensible practice of the earlier Puritan divines in choosing a punning text, and preached from Hebrews xiii. 9: "Be not carried about with *divers* and strange doctrines." He afterwards, in accordance with one of his own maxims,—"to get a dead injury out of the mind as soon as is decent, bury it, and then ventilate,"—in accordance with this maxim, I say, he lived on very friendly terms with Rev. Shearjashub Scrimgour, present pastor of the Baptist Society in Jaalam. Yet I think it was never unpleasing to him that the church edifice of that society (though otherwise a creditable specimen of architecture) remained without a bell, as indeed it does to this day. So much seemed necessary to do away with any appearance of acerbity toward a respectable community of professing Christians, which might be suspected in the conclusion of the above paragraph.—J. H.]

In lighter moods he was not averse from an innocent play upon words. Looking up from his newspaper one morning as I entered his study he said, "When I read a debate in Congress, I feel as if I were sitting at the feet of Zeno in the shadow of the Portico." On my expressing a natural surprise, he added, smiling, "Why, at such times the only view which honourable members give me of what goes on in the world is through their intercalumniations." I smiled at this after a moment's reflection, and he added gravely, "The most punctilious refinement of manners is the only salt that will keep a democracy from stinking; and what are we to expect from the people, if their representatives set them such lessons? Mr. Everett's whole life has been a sermon from this text. There was, at least, this advantage in duelling, that it set a certain limit on the tongue." In this connection I may be permitted to recall a playful remark of his upon another occasion. The painful divisions in the First Parish, A.D. 1844, occasioned by the wild notions in respect to the rights of (what Mr. Wilbur, so far as concerned the reasoning faculty, always called) the unfairer part of creation, put forth by Miss Parthenia Almira Fitz, are too well known to need more than a passing allusion. It was during these heats, long since happily allayed, that Mr. Wilbur remarked that "The Church had more trouble in dealing with one *she*resiarch than with twenty *he*resiarchs," and that the men's *conscia recti*, or certainty of being right, was nothing to the women's.

When I once asked his opinion of a poetical composition on which I had expended no little pains, he read it attentively, and then remarked, "Unless one's thought pack more neatly in verse than in prose, it is wiser to refrain. Commonplace gains nothing by being translated into rhyme, for it is something which no hocus-pocus can transubstantiate with the real presence of living thought. You entitle your piece, 'My Mother's Grave,' and expend four pages of useful paper in detailing your emotions there. But, my dear sir, watering does not improve the quality of ink, even though you should do it with tears. To publish a sorrow to Tom, Dick, and Harry is in some sort to advertise its unreality, for I have observed in my intercourse with the afflicted that the deepest grief instinctively hides its face with its hands and is silent. If your piece were printed, I have no doubt it would be popular, for people like to fancy that they feel much better than the trouble of feeling. I would put all poets on oath whether they have striven to say everything they possibly could think of, or to leave out all they could not help saying. In your own case, my worthy young friend, what you have written is merely a deliberate exercise, the gymnastic of sentiment. For your excellent maternal relative is still alive, and is to take tea with me this evening, *D. V.* Beware of simulated feeling; it is hypocrisy's first cousin; it is especially dangerous to a preacher; for he who says one day, 'Go to, let me seem to be pathetic,' may be nearer than he thinks to saying, 'Go to, let me seem to be virtuous, or earnest, or under sorrow for sin.' Depend upon it, Sappho loved her verses more sincerely than she did Phaon, and Petrarch his sonnets better than Laura, who was indeed but his poetical stalking-horse. After you shall have once heard that muffled rattle of the clods on the coffin-lid of an irreparable loss, you will grow acquainted with a pathos that will make all elegies hateful. When I was of your age, I also for a time mistook my desire to write verses for an authentic call of my nature in that direction. But one day as I was going forth for a walk, with my head full of an 'Elegy on the Death of Flirtilla,' and vainly groping after a rhyme for *lily* that should not be *silly* or *chilly*, I saw my eldest boy Homer busy over the rain-water hogshead, in that childish experiment at parthenogenesis, the changing a horse-hair into a water-snake. An immersion of six weeks showed no change in the obstinate filament. Here was a stroke of unintended sarcasm. Had I not been doing in my study precisely what my boy was doing out of doors? Had my thoughts any more chance of coming to life by being submerged in rhyme than his hair by soaking in water? I burned my elegy and took a course of Edwards on the Will. People do not make poetry; it is made out of *them* by a process for which I do not find myself fitted. Nevertheless, the writing of verses is a good rhetorical exercitation, as teaching us what to shun most carefully in prose. For prose bewitched is like window-glass with bubbles in it, distorting what it should show with pellucid veracity."

It is unwise to insist on doctrinal points as vital to religion. The Bread of Life is wholesome and sufficing in itself, but gulped down with these kick-shaws cooked up by theologians, it is apt to produce an indigestion, nay, even at last, an incurable dyspepsia of scepticism.

One of the most inexcusable weaknesses of Americans is in signing their names to what are called credentials. But for my interposition, a person who shall be nameless would have taken from this town a recommendation for an office of trust subscribed by the select men and all the voters of both parties, ascribing to him as many good qualities as if it had been his tombstone. The excuse was that it would be well for the town to be rid of him, as it would ere long be obliged to maintain him. I would not refuse my name to modest merit, but I would be as cautious as in signing a bond. [I trust I shall be subjected to no imputation of unbecoming vanity, if I mention the fact that Mr. W. indorsed my own qualifications as teacher of the high school at Pequash Junction.—J. H.] When I see a certificate of character with everybody's name to it, I regard it as a letter of introduction from the Devil. Never give a man your name unless you are willing to trust him with your reputation.

There seem nowadays to be two sources of literary inspiration,—fulness of mind and emptiness of pocket.

I am often struck, especially in reading Montaigne, with the obviousness and familiarity of a great writer's thoughts, and the freshness they gain because said by him. The truth is, we mix their greatness with all they say and give it our best attention. Johannes Faber sic cogitavit would be no enticing preface to a book, but an accredited name gives credit like the signature of a note of hand. It is the advantage of fame that it is always privileged to take the world by the button, and a thing is weightier for Shakespeare's uttering it by the whole amount of his personality.

It is singular how impatient men are with overpraise of others, how patient with overpraise of themselves; and yet the one does them no injury, while the other may be their ruin.

People are apt to confound mere alertness of mind with attention. The one is but the flying abroad of all the faculties to the open doors and windows at every passing rumour; the other is the concentration of every one of them in a single focus, as in the alchemist over his alembic at the moment of expected projection. Attention is the stuff that memory is made of, and memory is accumulated genius.

Do not look for the Millennium as imminent. One generation is apt to get all the wear it can out of the cast clothes of the last, and is always sure to use up every paling of the old fence that will hold a nail in building the new.

You suspect a kind of vanity in my genealogical enthusiasm. Perhaps you are right; but it is a universal foible. Where it does not show itself in a personal and private way, it becomes public and gregarious. We flatter ourselves in the Pilgrim Fathers, and the Virginian offshoot of a transported convict swells with the fancy of a cavalier ancestry. Pride of birth, I have noticed, takes two forms. One complacently traces himself up to a coronet; another, defiantly, to a lap-stone. The sentiment is precisely the same in both cases, only that one is the positive and the other the negative pole of it.

Seeing a goat the other day kneeling in order to graze with less trouble, it seemed to me a type of the common notion of prayer. Most people are ready enough to go down on their knees for material blessings, but how few for those spiritual gifts which alone are an answer to our orisons, if we but knew it!

Some people, nowadays, seem to have hit upon a new moralisation of the moth and the candle. They would lock up the light of Truth, lest poor Psyche should put it out in her effort to draw nigh to it.

MR. HOSEA BIGLOW TO THE EDITOR OF THE "ATLANTIC MONTHLY."

DEAR SIR,—Your letter come to han',
    Requestin' me to please be funny;
But I ain't made upon a plan
    Thet knows wut's comin', gall or honey:
Ther' 's times the world does look so queer,
    Odd fancies come afore I call 'em;
An' then again, for half a year,
    No preacher 'thout a call 's more solemn.

You're 'n want o' sunthin' light an' cute,
    Rattlin' an' shrewd an' kin' o' jingleish,
An' wish, pervidin' it 'ould suit,
    I'd take an' citify my English.
I *ken* write long-tailed, ef I please,—
    But when I'm jokin', no, I thankee;
Then, 'fore I know it, my idees
    Run helter-skelter into Yankee.

Sence I begun to scribble rhyme,
    I tell ye wut, I hain't ben foolin';
The parson's books, life, death, an' time
    Hev took some trouble with my schoolin';

Nor th' airth don't git put out with me,
    Thet love her 'z though she wuz a woman;
Why, th' ain't a bird upon the tree
    But half forgives my bein' human.

An' yit I love th' unhighschooled way
    Ol' farmers hed when I wuz younger;
Their talk wuz meatier, an' 'ould stay,
    While book-froth seems to whet your hunger;
For puttin' in a downright lick
    'Twixt Humbug's eyes, ther' 's few can metch it,
An' then it helves my thoughts ez slick
    Ez stret-grained hickory doos a hetchet.

But when I can't, I can't, thet's all,
    For Natur' won't put up with gullin';
Idees you hev to shove an' haul
    Like a druv pig ain't wuth a mullein:
Live thoughts ain't sent for; thru all rifts
    O' sense they pour an' resh ye onwards,
Like rivers when south-lyin' drifts
    Feel thet th' old airth 's a-wheelin' sunwards.

Time wuz, the rhymes come crowdin' thick
    Ez office-seekers arter 'lection,
An' into ary place 'ould stick
    Without no bother nor objection;
But sence the war my thoughts hang back
    Ez though I wanted to enlist 'em,
An' subs'tutes,—*they* don't never lack,
    But them they'll slope afore you've mist 'em.

Nothin' don't seem like wut it wuz;
 I can't see wut there is to hender,
An' yit my brains jes' go buzz, buzz,
 Like bumblebees agin a winder;
'Fore these times come, in all airth's row,
 Ther' wuz one quiet place, my head in,
Where I could hide an' think,—but now
 It's all one teeter, hopin', dreadin'.

Where's Peace? I start, some clear-blown night,
 When gaunt stone walls grow numb an' number,
An', creakin' 'cross the snow-crus' white,
 Walk the col' starlight into summer;
Up grows the moon, an' swell by swell
 Thru the pale pasturs silvers dimmer
Than the last smile thet strives to tell
 O' love gone heavenward in its shimmer.

I hev ben gladder o' sech things
 Than cocks o' spring or bees o' clover,
They filled my heart with livin' springs,
 But now they seem to freeze 'em over;
Sights innercent ez babes on knee,
 Peaceful ez eyes o' pastur'd cattle,
Jes' coz they be so, seem to me
 To rile me more with thought o' battle.

In-doors an' out by spells I try;
 Ma'am Natur' keeps her spin-wheel goin',
But leaves my natur' stiff and dry
 Ez fiel's o' clover arter mowin';

An' her jes' keepin' on the same,
   Calmer 'n a clock, an' never carin',
An' findin' nary thing to blame,
   Is wus than ef she took to swearin'.

Snow-flakes come whisperin' on the pane
   The charm makes blazin' logs so pleasant,
But I can't hark to wut they're say'n',
   With Grant or Sherman ollers present ;
The chimbleys shudder in the gale,
   Thet lulls, then suddin takes to flappin'
Like a shot hawk, but all's ez stale
   To me ez so much sperit-rappin'.

Under the yaller-pines I house,
   When sunshine makes 'em all sweet-scented,
An' hear among their furry boughs
   The baskin' west-wind purr contented,
While 'way o'erhead, ez sweet an' low
   Ez distant bells thet ring for meetin,
The wedged wil' geese their bugles blow,
   Further an' further South retreatin'.

Or up the slippery knob I strain
   An' see a hundred hills like islan's
Lift their blue woods in broken chain
   Out o' the sea o' snowy silence ;
The farm-smokes, sweetes' sight on airth,
   Slow thru the winter air a-shrinkin'
Seem kin' o' sad, an' roun' the hearth
   Of empty places set me thinkin'.

Beaver roars hoarse with meltin' snows,
 An' rattles di'mon's from his granite;
Time wuz, he snatched away my prose,
 An' into psalms or satires ran it;
But he, nor all the rest thet once
 Started my blood to country-dances,
Can't set me goin' more 'n a dunce
 Thet hain't no use for dreams an' fancies.

Rat-tat-tat-tattle thru the street
 I hear the drummers makin' riot,
An' I set thinkin' o' the feet
 Thet follered once an' now are quiet,—
White feet ez snowdrops innercent,
 Thet never knowed the paths o' Satan,
Whose comin' step ther' 's ears thet won't,
 No, not lifelong, leave off awaitin'.

Why, hain't I held 'em on my knee?
 Didn't I love to see 'em growin',
Three likely lads ez wal could be,
 Hahnsome an' brave an' not tu knowin'?
I set an' look into the blaze
 Whose natur', jes' like theirn, keeps climbin'
Ez long 'z it lives, in shinin' ways,
 An' half despise myself for rhymin'.

Wut's words to them whose faith an' truth
 On War's red techstone rang true metal,
Who ventered life an' love an' youth
 For the gret prize o' death in battle?

To him who, deadly hurt, agen
    Flashed on afore the charge's thunder,
Tippin' with fire the bolt of men
    Thet rived the Rebel line asunder?

'Tain't right to hev the young go fust,
    All throbbin' full o' gifts an' graces,
Leavin' life's paupers dry ez dust
    To try an' make b'lieve fill their places:
Nothin' but tells us wut we miss,
    Ther' 's gaps our lives can't never fay in,
An' *thet* world seems so fur from this
    Lef' for us loafers to grow grey in!

My eyes cloud up for rain; my mouth
    Will take to twitchin' roun' the corners;
I pity mothers, tu, down South,
    For all they sot among the scorners;
I'd sooner take my chance to stan'
    At Jedgment where your meanest slave is,
Than at God's bar hol' up a han'
    Ez drippin' red ez yourn, Jeff Davis!

Come, Peace! not like a mourner bowed
    For honour lost an' dear ones wasted,
But proud, to meet a people proud,
    With eyes thet tell o' triumph tasted!
Come, with han' grippin' on the hilt,
    An' step thet proves ye Victory's daughter!
Longin' for you, our sperits wilt
    Like shipwrecked men's on raf's for water.

Come, while our country feels the lift
    Of a gret instinct shoutin' forwards,
An' knows thet freedom ain't a gift
    Thet tarries long in han's o' cowards!
Come, sech ez mothers prayed for, when
    They kissed their cross with lips thet quivered,
An' bring fair wages for brave men,
    A nation saved, a race delivered!

MR. HOSEA BIGLOW'S SPEECH IN MARCH MEETING.

To the Editor of the "Atlantic Monthly."

JAALAM, April 5, 1866.

MY DEAR SIR,—

(an' noticin' by your kiver thet you're some dearer than wut you wuz, I enclose the deffrence) I dunno ez I know jest how to interdroce this las' perduction of my mews, ez Parson Willber allus called 'em, which is goin' to *be* the last an' *stay* the last onless sunthin' pertikler sh'd interfear which I don't expec' ner I wun't yield tu ef it wuz ez pressin' ez a deppity Shiriff. Sence Mr. Wilbur's disease I hevn't hed no one thet could dror out my talons. He ust to kind o' wine me up an' set the penderlum agoin' an' then somehow I seemed to go on tick as it wear tell I run down, but the noo minister ain't of the same brewin' nor I can't seem to git ahold of no kine of huming nater in him but sort of slide rite off as you du on the eedge of a mow. Minnysteeril natur is wal enough an' a site better 'n most other kines I know on, but the other sort sech as Welbor hed wuz of the Lord's makin' an' naterally more wonderfle an' sweet tastin' leastways to me so fur as heerd from. He used to interdooce 'em smooth ez ile athout sayin' nothin' in pertickler an' I misdoubt he didn't set so much by the sec'nd Ceres as wut he done by the Fust, fact, he let on onct thet his mine misgive him of a sort of fallin' off in spots. He wuz as outspoken as a norwester *he* wuz, but I tole him I hoped the fall wuz from so high up thet a feller could ketch a good many times fust afore comin' bunt onto the ground as I see Jethro C. Swett from the meetin' house steeple up to th' old perrish, an' took up for dead but he's alive now an' spry as wut you be. Turnin' of it over I recclected how they ust to put wut they called Argymunce onto the frunts of poymns, like poorches afore housen whare you could rest ye a spell whilst you wuz concludin' whether you'd go in or nut espeshully ware tha wuz darters, though I most allus found it the best plen to go in fust an' think afterwards an' the gals likes it best tu. I dno as speechis ever hez any argimunts to 'em, I never see none thet hed an' I guess they never du but tha must allus be a B'ginnin' to every-thin' athout it is Etarnity so I'll begin rite away an' anybody may put it afore any of his speeches ef it soots an' welcome. I don't claim no paytent.

THE ARGYMUNT.

Interducshin, wich may be skipt. Begins by talkin' about himself: thet's jest natur an' most gin'ally allus pleasin', I b'leeve I've notist, to *one* of the cumpany, an' thet's more than wut you can say of most speshes of talkin'. Nex' comes the gittin' the goodwill of the orjunce by lettin' 'em gether from wut you kind of ex'dentally let drop thet they air about East, A one, an' no mistaik, skare 'em up an' take 'em as they rise. Spring interdooced with a fiew approput flours. Speach finally begins witch nobuddy needn't feel obolygated to read as I never read 'em an' never shell this one ag'in. Subjick staited ; expanded ; delayted ; extended. Pump lively. Subjick staited ag'in so's to avide all mistaiks. Ginnle remarks ; continooed ; kerried on ; pushed surder ; kind o' gin out. Subjick *re*staited ; dielooted ; stirred up permiscoous. Pump ag'in. Gits back to where he sot out. Can't seem to stay thair. Ketches into Mr. Seaward's hair. Breaks loose ag'in an' staits his subjick ; stretches it ; turns it ; folds it ; onfolds it ; folds it ag'in so's 't no one can't find it. Argoos with an imedginary bean thet ain't aloud to say nothin' in repleye. Gives him a real good dressin' an' is settysfide he's rite. Gits into Johnson's hair. No use tryin' to git into his head. Gives it up. Hez to stait his subjick ag'in ; doos it back'ards, side-ways, eendways, criss-cross, bevellin', noways. Gits finally red on it. Concloods. Concloods more. Reads some xtrax. Sees his subjick a-nosin' round arter him ag'in. Tries to avide it. Wun't du. *Mis-*states it. Can't conjectur' no other plawsable way of stayin' on it. Tries pump. No fx. Finely concloods to conclood. Yeels the flore.

You kin spall an' punctooate thet as you please. I allus do, it kind of puts a noo soot of close onto a word, thisere funattick spellin' doos an' takes 'em out of the prissen dress they wair in the Dixonary. Ef I squeeze the cents out of 'em it's the main thing, an' wut they wuz made for; wut's left 's jest pummis.

Mistur Wilbur sez he to me onct, sez he, "Hosee," sez he, "in litterytoor the only good thing is Natur. It's amazin' hard to come at," sez he, "but onct git it an' you've gut everythin',. Wut's the sweetest small on airth?" sez he. "Noomone hay," sez I, pooty bresk, for he wuz allus hankerin' round in hayin'. "Nawthin' of the kine," sez he. "My leetle Huldy's breath," sez I ag'in. "You're a good lad," sez he, his eyes sort of ripplin' like, for he lost a babe onct nigh about her age,—"You're a good lad; but 'tain't thet nuther," sez he. "Ef you want to know," sez he, "open your winder of a mornin' et ary season, and you'll larn thet the best of perfooms is jest fresh air, *fresh air*," sez he, emphysizin', "athout no mixtur. Thet's wut *I* call natur in writin', and it bathes my lungs and washes 'em sweet whenever I git a whiff on 't," sez he. I offen think o' thet when I set down to write, but the winders air *so* ept to git stuck, an' breakin' a pane costs sunthin'.

Yourn for the last time,

Nut to be continooed,

Hosea Biglow.

I don't much s'pose, hows'ever I should plen it,
I could git boosted into th' House or Sennit,—
Nut while the two-legged gab-machine's so plenty,
'Nablin' one man to du the talk o' twenty;
I'm one o' them thet finds it ruther hard
To mannyfactur' wisdom by the yard,
An' maysure off, accordin' to demand,
The piece-goods el'kence that I keep on hand,
The same ole pattern runnin' thru an' thru,
An' nothin' but the customer thet's new.
I sometimes think, the furder on I go,
Thet it gits harder to feel sure I know,
An' when I've settled my idees, I find
'Twarn't I sheered most in makin' up my mind;

'Twuz this an' thet an' t'other thing thet done it,
Sunthin' in th' air, I could n' seek nor shun it.
Mos' folks go off so quick now in discussion,
All th' ole flint locks seems altered to percussion,
Whilst I in agin' sometimes git a hint
Thet I'm percussion changin' back to flint;
Wal, ef it's so, I ain't agoin' to werrit,
For th' ole Queen's-arm hez this pertickler merit,—
It gives the mind a hahnsome wedth o' margin
To kin' o' make its will afore dischargin';
I can't make out but jest one ginnle rule,—
No man need go an' *make* himself a fool,
Nor jedgment ain't like mutton, thet can't bear
Cookin' tu long, nor be took up tu rare.

Ez I wuz say'n', I hain't no chance to speak
So 's 't all the country dreads me onct a week,
But I've consid'ble o' thet sort o' head
Thet sets to home an' thinks wut *might* be said,
The sense thet grows an' werrits underneath,
Comin' belated like your wisdom-teeth,
An' git so el'kent, sometimes, to my gardin
Thet I don' vally public life a fardin'.
Our Parson Wilbur (blessin's on his head!)
'Mongst other stories of ole times he hed,
Talked of a feller that rehearsed his spreads
Beforehan' to his rows o' kebbigeheads,
(Ef 't warn't Demossenes, I guess 'twuz Sisro,)
Appealin' fust to thet an' then to this row,
Accordin' ez he thought thet his idees
Their diff'runt ev'riges o' brains 'ould please;
"An'," sez the Parson, "to hit right, you must
Git used to maysurin' your hearers fust;

For, take my word for 't, when all 's come an' past,
The kebbige-heads 'll cair the day et last ;
Th' ain't ben a meetin' sence the worl' begun
But they made (raw or biled ones) ten to one."

I've allus foun' 'em, I allow, sence then
About ez good for talkin' to ez men ;
They 'll take edvice, like other folks, to keep
(To use it 'ould be holdin' on 't tu cheap),
They listen wal, don' kick up when you scold 'em,
An' ef they've tongues, hev sense enough to hold 'em ;
Though th' ain't no denger we shall lose the breed,
I gin'lly keep a score or so for seed,
An' when my sappiness gits spry in spring,
So 's 't my tongue itches to run on full swing,
I fin' 'em ready-planted in March-meetin',
Warm ez a lyceum-audience in their greetin',
An' pleased to hear my spoutin' frum the fence,—
Comin', ez 't doos, entirely free 'f expense.
This year I made the follerin' observations
Extrump'ry, like most other tri'ls o' patience,
An', no reporters bein' sent express
To work their abstrac's up into a mess
Ez like th' oridg'nal ez a woodcut pictur'
Thet chokes the life out like a boy-constrictor,
I've writ 'em out, an' so avide all jeal'sies
'Twixt nonsense o' my own an' some one's else's.

(N.B.—Reporters gin'lly git a hint
To make dull orjunces seem 'live in print,
An', ez I hev t' report myself, I vum,
I'll put th' applauses where they'd *ough'* to come !)

MY FELLER KEBBIGE-HEADS, who look so green,
I vow to gracious thet ef I could dreen
The world of all its hearers but jest you,
'Twould leave 'bout all tha' is wuth talkin' to,
An' you, my ven'able ol' frien's, thet show
Upon your crowns a sprinklin' o' March snow,
Ez ef mild Time had christened every sense
For wisdom's church o' second innocence,
Nut Age's winter, no, no sech a thing,
But jest a kin' o' slippin'-back o' spring,—

[Sev'ril noses blowed.]

We've gathered here, ez ushle, to decide
Which is the Lord's an' which is Satan's side,
Coz all the good or evil thet can heppen
Is 'long o' which on 'em you choose for Cappen.

[Cries o' "Thet's so!"]

Aprul's come back; the swellin' buds of oak
Dim the fur hillsides with a purplish smoke;
The brooks are loose an', singing to be seen
(Like gals), make all the hollers soft an' green;
The birds are here, for all the season's late;
They take the sun's height an' don' never wait;
Soon 'z he officially declares it's spring
Their light hearts lift 'em on a north'ard wing,
An' th' ain't an acre, fur ez you can hear,
Can't by the music tell the time o' year;
But thet white dove Carliny scared away,
Five year ago, jes' sech an Aprul day;
Peace, that we hoped 'ould come an' build last year
An' coo by every housedoor, isn't here,—
No, nor wun't never be, for all our jaw,
Till we're ez brave in pol'tics ez in war!

O Lord, ef folks wuz made so 's 't they could see
The begnet-pint there is to an idee!

[Sensation.

Ten times the danger in 'em th' is in steel;
They run your soul thru an' you never feel,
But crawl about an' seem to think you're livin',
Poor shells o' men, nut wuth the Lord's forgivin',
Till you come bunt ag'in a real live fect,
An' go to pieces when you'd ough' to ect!
Thet kin' o' begnet 's wut we're crossin' now,
An' no man, fit to nevvigate a scow,
'Ould stan' expectin' help from Kingdom Come,
While t'other side druv their cold iron home.

My frien's, you never gethered from my mouth,
No, nut one word ag'in the South ez South,
Nor th' ain't a livin' man, white, brown, nor black,
Gladder 'n wut I should be to take 'em back;
But all I ask of Uncle Sam is fust
To write up on his door, "No goods on trust;"

[Cries of "Thet's the ticket!"]

Give us cash down in ekle laws for all,
An' they'll be snug inside afore nex' fall.
Give wut they ask, an' we shall hev Jamaker,
Wuth minus some consid'able an acre;
Give wut they need, an' we shell get 'fore long
A nation all one piece, rich, peacefle, strong;
Make 'em Amerikin, an' they'll begin
To love their country ez they loved their sin;
Let 'em stay Southun, an' you've kep' a sore
Ready to fester ez it done afore.
No mortle man can boast of perfic vision,
But the one moleblin' thing is Indecision,

An' th' ain't no futur' for the man nor state
Thet out of j-u-s-t can't spell great.
Some foiks 'ould call thet reddikle; do you?
'Twas common-sense afore the war wuz thru;
Thet loaded all our guns an' made 'em speak
So's 't Europe heared 'em clearn acrost the creek;
"They're drivin' o' their spiles down now," sez she,
"To the hard grennit o' God's fust idee;
Ef they reach thet, Democ'cy needn't fear
The tallest airthquakes *we* can git up here."
Some call't insultin' to ask *ary* pledge,
An' say 'twill only set their teeth on edge,
But folks you've jest licked, fur 'z I ever see,
Are 'bout ez mad 'z they wal know how to be;
It's better than the Rebs themselves expected
'Fore they see Uncle Sam wilt down henpected;
Be kind 'z you please, but fustly make things fast,
For plain Truth 's all the kindness thet 'll last;
Ef treason is a crime, ez *some* folks say,
How could we punish it a milder way
Than sayin' to 'em, "Brethren, lookee here,
We'll jes' divide things with ye, sheer an' sheer,
An' sence both come o' pooty strongbacked daddies,
You take the Darkies, ez we've took the Paddies;
Ign'ant an' poor we took 'em by the hand,
An' they're the bones an' sinners o' the land."
I ain't o' them thet fancy there's a loss on
Every inves'ment thet don't start from Bos'on;
But I know this: our money 's safest trusted
In sunthin', come wut will, thet *can't* be busted,
An' thet's the old Amerikin idee,
To make a man a Man an' let him be.

[Gret applause.]

Ez for their l'yalty, don't take a goad to't,
But I do want to block their only road to't
By lettin' 'em believe thet they can git
Mor'n wut they lost, out of our little wit;
I tell ye wut, I'm 'fraid we'll drif' to leeward
'Thout we can put more stiffenin' into Seward;
He seems to think Columby 'd better ect
Like a scared widder with a boy stiff-necked
Thet stomps an' swears he wun't come in to supper;
She mus' set up for him, ez weak ez Tupper,
Keepin' the Constitootion on to warm,
Tell he'll eccept her 'pologies in form;
The neighbours tell her he's a cross-grained cuss
Thet needs a hidin' 'fore he comes to wus;
"No," sez Ma Seward, "he's ez good 'z the best,
All he wants now is sugar-plums an' rest;"
" He's sarsed my Pa," sez one; " He stoned my son,"
Another edds.　" Oh, wal, 'twuz jest his fun."
" He tried to shoot our Uncle Samwell dead."
"'Twuz only tryin' a noo gun he hed."
" Wal, all we ask 's to hev it understood
You'll take his gun away from him for good;
We don't, wal, nut exac'ly, like his play,
Seein' he allus kin' o' shoots our way.
You kill your fatted calves to no good eend,
'Thout his fust sayin', ' Mother, I hev sinned!'"
["Amen!" frum Deac'n Greenleaf.]

The Pres'dunt *he* thinks thet the slickest plan
'Ould be t' allow thet he's our on'y man,
An' thet we fit thru all thet dreffle war
Jes' for his private glory an' eclor;
"Nobody ain't a Union man," sez he,
"'Thout he agrees, thru thick an' thin, with me;

Warn't Andrew Jackson's 'nitials jes' like mine?
An' ain't thet sunthin' like a right divine
To cut up ez kentenkerous ez I please,
An' treat your Congress like a nest o' fleas?"
Wal, I expec' the People wouldn't care, if
The question now wuz techin' bank or tariff,
But I conclude they've 'bout made up their mind
This ain't the fittest time to go it blind,
Nor these ain't metters thet with pol'tics swings,
But goes 'way down amongst the roots o' things;
Coz Sumner talked o' whitewashin' one day
They wun't let four years' war be throwed away.
"Let the South hev her rights?"   They say, "Thet's you!
But nut greb hold of other folks's tu."
Who owns this country, is it they or Andy?
Leastways it ough' to be the People *and* he;
Let him be senior pardner, ef he's so,
But let them kin' o' smuggle in ez Co;   [Laughter.]
Did he diskiver it?   Consid'ble numbers
Think thet the job wuz taken by Columbus.
Did he set tu an' make it wut it is?
Ef so, I guess the One-Man-power *hez* riz.
Did he put thru the rebbles, clear the docket,
An' pay th' expenses out of his own pocket?
Ef thet's the case, then everythin' I exes
Is t' hev him come an' pay my ennooal texes.

[Profound sensation.]

Was't he thet shou'dered all them million guns?
Did he lose all the fathers, brothers, sons?
Is this ere pop'lar gov'ment thet we run
A kin o' sulky, made to kerry one?
An' is the country goin' to knuckle down
To hev Smith sort their letters 'stid o' Brown?

Who wuz the 'Nited States 'fore Richmon' fell?
Wuz the South needfle their full name to spell?
An' can't we spell it in that short-han' way
Till th' underpinnin' 's settled so's to stay?
Who cares for the Resolves of '61,
Thet tried to coax an airthquake with a bun?
Hez act'ly nothin' taken place sence then
To larn folks they must hendle fects like men?
Ain't *this* the true p'int? Did the Rebs accep' 'em?
Ef nut, whose fault is't thet we hevn't kep' 'em?
Warn't there *two* sides? an' don't it stend to reason
Thet this week's 'Nited States ain't las' week's treason?
When all these sums is done, with nothin' missed,
An' nut afore, this school 'll be dismissed.

I knowed ez wal ez though I'd seen't with eyes
Thet when the war wuz over copper 'd rise,
An' thet we'd hev a rile-up in our kettle
'Twould need Leviathan's whole skin to settle;
I thought 'twould take about a generation
'Fore we could wal begin to be a nation,
But I allow I never did imegine
'Twould be our Pres'dunt thet 'ould drive a wedge in
To keep the split from closin' ef it could,
An' healin' over with new wholesome wood;
For th' ain't no chance o' healin' while they think
Thet law an' gov'ment's only printer's ink;
I mus' confess I thank him for discoverin'
The curus way in which the States are sovereign;
They ain't nut *quite* enough so to rebel,
But, when they fin' it's costly to raise h——,
                                        [A groan from Deac'n G.]
Why, then, for jes' the same superl'tive reason,

They're 'most too much so to be tetched for treason;
They *can't* go out, but ef they somehow *du*,
Their sovereignty don't noways go out tu;
The State goes out, the sovereignty don't stir,
But stays to keep the door ajar for her.
He thinks secession never took 'em out,
An' mebby he's correc', but I misdoubt;
Ef they warn't out, then why, 'n the name o' sin,
Make all this row 'bout lettin' of 'em in?
In law, p'r'aps nut; but there's a diffurence, ruther,
Betwixt your mother-'n-law an' real mother,

[Derisive cheers.

An' I, for one, shall wish they'd all been *som'eres*,
Long 'z U. S. Texes are sech reg'lar comers.
But, O my patience! must we wriggle back
Into th' ole crooked, pettyfoggin' track,
When our artil'ry-wheels a road hev cut
Stret to our purpose ef we keep the rut?
War's jes' dead waste excep' to wipe the slate
Clean for the ciph'rin of some nobler fate.

[Applause.

Ez for dependin' on their oaths an' thet,
'Twun't bind em' mor'n the ribbin roun' my het;
I heard a fable once from Othniel Starns,
That pints it slick ez weathercocks do barns:
Onct on a time the wolves hed certing rights
Inside the fold: they used to sleep their nights,
An', bein' cousins o' the dogs, they took
Their turns et watchin', reg'lar ez a book;
But somehow, when the dogs hed gut asleep,
Their love o' mutton beat their love o' sheep,
Till gradilly the shepherds come to see
Things warn't agoin' ez they'd ough' to be;

So they sent off a deacon to remonstrate
Along 'th the wolves an' urge 'em to go on straight;
They didn' seem to set much by the deacon,
Nor preachin' didn' cow 'em, nut to speak on;
Fin'ly they swore thet they'd go out an' stay,
An' hev their fill o' mutton every day;
Then dogs an' shepherds, after much hard dammin',

[Groan from Deac'n G.]

Turned tu an gave 'em a tormented lammin',
An' sez, "Ye shan't go out, the murrain rot ye,
To keep us wastin' half our time to watch ye!"
But then the question come, How live together
'Thout losin' sheep, nor nary yew nor wether?
Now there wuz some dogs (noways wuth their keep)
Thet sheered their cousins' tastes an' sheered the sheep;
They sez, "Be gin'rous, let 'em swear right in,
An', ef they backslide, let 'em swear ag'in;
Jes' let 'em put on sheep-skins whilst they're swearin':
To ask for more 'ould be beyond all bearin'."
"Be gin'rous for yourselves, where *you*'re to pay,
Thet's the best prectice," sez a shepherd gray;
"Ez for their oaths they wun't be wuth a button,
Long 'z you don't cure 'em o' their taste for mutton;
Th' ain't but one solid way, howe'er you puzzle:
Tell they're converted, let 'em wear a muzzle."

[Cries of "Bully for you!"]

I've noticed thet each half-baked scheme's abetters
Are in the hebbit o' producin' letters
Writ by all sorts o' never-heared-on fellers,
'Bout ez oridge'nal ez the wind in bellers;
I've noticed, tu, it's the quack med'cines gits
(An' needs) the grettest heaps o' stiffykits;

[Two apothekeries goes out.]

Now, sence I lef' off creepin' on all fours,
I hain't ast no man to endorse my course;
It's full ez cheap to be your own endorser,
An' ef I've made a cup, I'll fin' the saucer;
But I've some letters here from t'other side,
An' them's the sort thet helps me to decide;
Tell me for wut the copper-comp'nies hanker,
An' I'll tell you jest where it's safe to anchor.

[Faint hiss.]

Fus'ly the Hon'ble B. O. Sawin writes
Thet for a spell he could'n sleep o' nights,
Puzzlin' which side wuz preudentest to pin to,
Which wuz th' ole homestead, which the temp'ry lean to;
Et fust he jedged 'twould right-side-up his pan
To come out ez a 'ridge'nal Union man,
"But now," he sez, "I ain't nut quite so fresh;
The winnin' horse is goin' to be Secesh;
You might, las' spring, hev eas'ly walked the course,
'Fore we contrived to doctor th' Union horse;
Now *we*'re the ones to walk aroun' the nex' track:
Jest you take hold an' read the follerin' extrac',
Out of a letter I received last week
From an ole frien' thet never sprung a leak,
A Nothun Dem'crat o' th' ole Jarsey blue,
Born copper-sheathed an' copper-fastened tu."

"These four years past it hez been tough
To say which side a feller went for;
Guideposts all gone, roads muddy 'n' rough,
An' nothin' doin' wut 'twuz meant for;
Pickets a-firin' left an' right,
Both sides a lettin' rip et sight,—
Life warn't wuth hardly payin' rent for.

"Columby gut her back up so,
It warn't no use a-tryin' to stop her,—
War's emptin's riled her very dough
An' made it rise an' act improper;
'Twuz full ez much ez I could du
To jes' lay low an' worry thru,
'Thout hevin' to sell out my copper.

"Afore the war your mod'rit men
Could set an' sun 'em on the fences,
Ciph'rin' the chances up, an' then
Jump off which way bes' paid expenses;
Sence, 'twus so resky ary way,
I didn't hardly darst to say
I 'greed with Paley's Evidences.
                [Groan from Deac'n G.]

"Ask Mac ef tryin' to set the fence
Warn't like bein' rid upon a rail on't,
Headin' your party with a sense
O' bein' tipjint in the tail on't,
And tryin' to think thet, on the whole,
You kin' o' quasi your own soul
When Belmont's gut a bill o' sale on't?
                [Three cheers for Grant and Sherman.]

"Come peace, I sposed thet folks 'ould like
Their pol'tics done ag'in by proxy,
Give their noo loves the bag an' strike
A fresh trade with their reg'lar doxy;
But the drag's broke, now slavery's gone,
An' there's gret resk they'll blunder on,
Ef they ain't stopped, to real Democ'cy.

"We've gut an awful row to hoe
In this 'ere job o' reconstructin';
Folks dunno skurce which way to go,
Where th' ain't some boghole to be ducked in;
But one thing's clear; there *is* a crack,
Ef we pry hard, 'twixt white and black,
Where the old makebate can be tucked in.

"No white man sets in airth's broad aisle
Thet I ain't willin' t' own ez brother,
An' ef he's heppened to strike ile,
I dunno, fin'ly, but I'd ruther;
An' Paddies, long 'z they vote all right,
Though they ain't jest a nat'ral white,
I hold one on 'em good 'z another.

[Applause.]

"Wut *is* there lef' I'd like to know,
Ef 'tain't the difference o' colour,
To keep up self-respec' an' show
The human natur' of a fullah?
Wut good in bein' white, onless
It's fixed by law, nut lef' to guess,
That we are smarter an' they duller?

"Ef we're to hev our ekle rights,
'T wun't du to 'low no competition;
Th' ole debt doo us for bein' whites
Ain't safe onless we stop th' emission
O' these noo notes, whose specie base
Is human natur', 'thout no trace
O' shape, nor colour, nor condition.

[Continood applause.]

"So fur I'd writ an' could n' jedge
Aboard wut boat I'd best take pessige,
My brains all mincemeat, 'thout no edge
Upon 'em more than tu a sessige,
But now it seems ez though I see
Sunthin' resemblin' an idee,
Sence Johnson's speech an' veto message.

"I like the speech best, I confess,
The logic, preudence, an' good taste on 't,
An' it's so mad, I ruther guess
There's some dependence to be placed on 't;
                                        [Laughter.]
It's narrer, but 'twixt you an' me,
Out o' the allies o' J. D.
A temp'ry party can be based on 't.

"Jes' to hold on till Johnson 's thru
An' dug his Presidential grave is,
An' *then!*—who knows but we could slew
The country roun' to put in——?
Wun't some folks rare up when we pull
Out o' their eyes our Union wool
An' larn 'em wut a p'lit'cle shave is!

"O, did it seem 'z ef Providence
Could ever send a second Tyler?
To see the South all back to once,
Reapin' the spiles o' the Freesiler,
Is cute ez though an ingineer
Should claim th' old iron for his sheer
Coz 'twas himself that bust the biler!"
                                        [Gret laughter.]

Thet tells the story! Thet's wut we shall git
By tryin' squirtguns on the burnin' Pit;
For the day never comes when it'll du
To kick off Dooty like a worn-out shoe.
I seem to hear a whisperin' in the air,
A sighin' like, of unconsoled despair,
Thet comes from nowhere an' from everywhere,
An' seems to say, "Why died we? warn't it, then,
To settle, once for all, thet men wuz men?
O, airth's sweet cup snetched from us barely tasted,
The grave's real chill is feelin' life wuz wasted!
O, you we lef', long-lingerin' et the door,
Lovin' you best, coz we loved Her the more,
Thet Death, not we, had conquered, we should feel
Ef she upon our memory turned her heel,
An' unregretful throwed us all away
To flaunt it in a Blind Man's Holiday!"

My frien's, I've talked nigh on to long enough.
I hain't no call to bore ye coz ye're tough;
My lungs are sound, an' our own v'ice delights
Our ears, but even kebbige-heads hez rights.
It's the las' time thet I shell e'er address ye,
But you'll soon fin' some new tormentor: bless ye!

[Tumult'ous applause and cries of "Go on!' "Don't stop!"]

THE WALTER SCOTT PRESS, NEWCASTLE-ON-TYNE.

The Contemporary Science Series.

EDITED BY HAVELOCK ELLIS.

Crown 8vo, Cloth, 3s. 6d. per vol.; Half Morocco, 6s. 6d.

I. THE EVOLUTION OF SEX. By Professor PATRICK GEDDES and J. ARTHUR THOMSON. With 90 Illustrations. Second Edition.

"The authors have brought to the task—as indeed their names guarantee—a wealth of knowledge, a lucid and attractive method of treatment, and a rich vein of picturesque language."—*Nature*.

II. ELECTRICITY IN MODERN LIFE. By G. W. DE TUNZELMANN. With 88 Illustrations.

"A clearly-written and connected sketch of what is known about electricity and magnetism, the more prominent modern applications, and the principles on which they are based."—*Saturday Review*.

III. THE ORIGIN OF THE ARYANS. By Dr. ISAAC TAYLOR. Illustrated. Second Edition.

"Canon Taylor is probably the most encyclopædic all-round scholar now living. His new volume on the Origin of the Aryans is a first-rate example of the excellent account to which he can turn his exceptionally wide and varied information. . . . Masterly and exhaustive."—*Pall Mall Gazette*.

IV. PHYSIOGNOMY AND EXPRESSION. By P. MANTEGAZZA. Illustrated.

"Professor Mantegazza is a writer full of life and spirit, and the natural attractiveness of his subject is not destroyed by his scientific handling of it."—*Literary World* (Boston).

V. EVOLUTION AND DISEASE. By J. B. SUTTON, F.R.C.S. With 135 Illustrations.

"The book is as interesting as a novel, without sacrifice of accuracy or system, and is calculated to give an appreciation of the fundamentals of pathology to the lay reader, while forming a useful collection of illustrations of disease for medical reference."—*Journal of Mental Science*.

VI. THE VILLAGE COMMUNITY. By G. L. GOMME. Illustrated.

"The fruit of some years of investigation on a subject which has of late attracted much attention, and is of much importance, inasmuch as it lies at the basis of our society."—*Antiquary*.

VII. THE CRIMINAL. By HAVELOCK ELLIS. Illustrated.

"An ably written, an instructive, and a most entertaining book."—*Law Quarterly Review*.

London: WALTER SCOTT, LIMITED, 24 Warwick Lane.

The Contemporary Science Series—continued.

VIII. SANITY AND INSANITY. By Dr. CHARLES MERCIER. Illustrated.

"Taken as a whole, it is the brightest book on the physical side of mental science published in our time."—*Pall Mall Gazette.*

IX. HYPNOTISM. By Dr. ALBERT MOLL. Second Edition.

"Marks a step of some importance in the study of some difficult physiological and psychological problems which have not yet received much attention in the scientific world of England."—*Nature.*

X. MANUAL TRAINING. By Dr. C. M. WOODWARD, Director of the Manual Training School, St. Louis. Illustrated.

"There is no greater authority on the subject than Professor Woodward."—*Manchester Guardian.*

XI. THE SCIENCE OF FAIRY TALES. By E. SIDNEY HARTLAND.

"Mr. Hartland's book will win the sympathy of all earnest students, both by the knowledge it displays, and by a thorough love and appreciation of his subject, which is evident throughout."—*Spectator.*

XII. PRIMITIVE FOLK. By ELIE RECLUS.

"For an introduction to the study of the questions of property, marriage, government, religion,—in a word, to the evolution of society,—this little volume will be found most convenient."—*Scottish Leader.*

XIII. THE EVOLUTION OF MARRIAGE. By Professor LETOURNEAU.

"Among the distinguished French students of sociology, Professor Letourneau has long stood in the first rank. He approaches the great study of man free from bias and shy of generalisations. To collect, scrutinise, and appraise facts is his chief business."—*Science.*

XIV. BACTERIA AND THEIR PRODUCTS. By Dr. G. SIMS WOODHEAD. Illustrated.

"An excellent summary of the present state of knowledge of the subject."—*Lancet.*

XV. EDUCATION AND HEREDITY. By J. M. GUYAU.

"It is a sign of the value of this book that the natural impulse on arriving at its last page is to turn again to the first, and try to gather up and co-ordinate some of the many admirable truths it presents."—*Anti-Jacobin.*

XVI. THE MAN OF GENIUS. By Professor LOMBROSO. Illustrated.

"By far the most comprehensive and fascinating collection of facts and generalisations concerning genius which has yet been brought together."—*Journal of Mental Science.*

XVII. THE GRAMMAR OF SCIENCE. By KARL PEARSON, M.A., Gresham Professor of Geometry. Illustrated.

"The problems discussed with great ability and lucidity, and often in a most suggestive manner, by Prof. Pearson, are such as should interest *all* students of natural science."—*Natural Science.*

XVIII. PROPERTY : ITS ORIGIN AND DEVELOPMENT. By Professor LETOURNEAU.

"M. Letourneau has read a great deal, and he seems to us to have selected and interpreted his facts with considerable judgment and learning."—*Westminster Review.*

London : WALTER SCOTT, LIMITED, 24 Warwick Lane.

XIX. VOLCANOES: PAST AND PRESENT. By EDWARD HULL, M.A., LL.D., F.R.S. With 45 Illustrations.

"A very readable account of the phenomena of volcanoes and earthquakes."—*Nature*.

XX. PUBLIC HEALTH. By Dr. J. F. J. SYKES. With numerous Illustrations. *(In Preparation.)*

The increased knowledge of the internal and external influences upon health obtained within recent years, and the practical applications of which it is capable in the prevention of disease, gives rise to many interesting problems, some of which are being solved, some are only partially touched, and others remain unelucidated. In this volume an attempt will be made to summarise and bring to a focus the essential points in evolution, environment, parasitism, prophylaxis, and sanitation bearing upon the preservation of the public health.

The following Writers are preparing Volumes for this Series:—

Prof. E. D. Cope, Prof. G. F. Fitzgerald, Prof. J. Geikie, Prof. A. C. Haddon, Prof. C. H. Herford, Prof. J. Jastrow (Wisconsin), Dr. J. B. Longstaff, Prof. James Mavor, Prof. Aug. Weismann, etc.

London: WALTER SCOTT, LIMITED, 24 Warwick Lane.

PEER GYNT: A Dramatic Poem.
By HENRIK IBSEN.

TRANSLATED BY

WILLIAM AND CHARLES ARCHER.

This Translation, though unrhymed, preserves throughout the various rhythms of the original.

"In *Brand* the hero is an embodied protest against the poverty of spirit and half-heartedness that Ibsen rebelled against in his country-men. In *Peer Gynt* the hero is himself the embodiment of that spirit. In *Brand* the fundamental antithesis, upon which, as its central theme, the drama is constructed, is the contrast between the spirit of com-promise on the one hand, and the motto 'everything or nothing' on the other. And *Peer Gynt* is the very incarnation of a compromising dread of decisive committal to any one course. In *Brand* the problem of self-realisation and the relation of the individual to his surroundings is obscurely struggling for recognition, and in *Peer Gynt* it becomes the formal theme upon which all the fantastic variations of the drama are built up. In both plays alike the problems of heredity and the influence of early surroundings are more than touched upon; and both alike culminate in the doctrine that the only redeeming power on earth or in heaven is the power of love."—Mr. P. H. WICKSTEED.

London : WALTER SCOTT, LIMITED, 24 Warwick Lane.

Foolscap 8vo, Cloth, Price 3s. 6d.

THE INSPECTOR-GENERAL

(Or "REVIZÓR,")

A RUSSIAN COMEDY.

By NIKOLAI VASILIYEVICH GOGOL.

Translated from the original Russian, with Introduction and Notes, by A. A. SYKES, B.A., Trinity College, Cambridge.

Though one of the most brilliant and characteristic of Gogol's works, and well-known on the Continent, the present is the first translation of his *Revizór*, or Inspector-General, which has appeared in English. A satire on Russian administrative functionaries, the *Revizór* is a comedy marked by continuous gaiety and invention, full of "situation," each development of the story accentuating the satire and emphasising the characterisation, the whole play being instinct with life and interest. Every here and there occurs the note of caprice, of naïveté, of unexpected fancy, characteristically Russian. The present translation will be found to be admirably fluent, idiomatic, and effective.

London: WALTER SCOTT, LIMITED, 24 Warwick Lane.

Demy 8vo, Cloth, 420 *Pages, Price* 7s. 6d.

A SHORT HISTORY

OF

ANGLO-SAXON FREEDOM.

THE POLITY OF THE ENGLISH-SPEAKING RACE.

By JAMES K. HOSMER, Professor in Washington University; Author of
" *A Life of Young Sir Harry Vane,*" etc.

In this book an effort is made to compress a sketch of
constitutional history for a period of nearly two thousand
years, from the time of the Teutons of Cæsar and Tacitus
to the British Empire and United States of 1890. Anglo
Saxon polity, in its long history, has shown adaptation to
the needs of ever vaster multitudes and higher civilisations,
manifold development and elaboration, one spirit, however,
surviving throughout it all, apparent in the deliberations of
the ancient folk-moots as in those of a modern Parliament.
It is this unity which is traced in this highly interesting and
brilliantly-written book.

"A volume in which Professor Hosmer ably pro-
pounds and justifies his well-known views. . . . The
work might very properly be used in schools, but is
also interesting to grown people, and may be strongly
recommended to mechanics' institutes, workmen's
clubs, and public libraries."—*Athenæum.*

London : WALTER SCOTT, 24 Warwick Lane, Paternoster Row.

THE SCOTT LIBRARY.

Cloth, Uncut Edges, Gilt Top.   Price 1s. 6d. per Volume.

VOLUMES ALREADY ISSUED—

London : WALTER SCOTT, LIMITED, Paternoster Square.

THE SCOTT LIBRARY—continued.

London: WALTER SCOTT, LIMITED, Paternoster Square.

THE SCOTT LIBRARY—continued.

31 VOLSUNGA SAGA. WILLIAM MORRIS. WITH INTRO-
duction by H. H. Sparling.

32 SARTOR RESARTUS. BY THOMAS CARLYLE. WITH
Introduction by Ernest Rhys.

33 SELECT WRITINGS OF EMERSON. WITH INTRO-
duction by Percival Chubb.

34 AUTOBIOGRAPHY OF LORD HERBERT. EDITED,
with an Introduction, by Will H. Dircks.

35 ENGLISH PROSE, FROM MAUNDEVILLE TO
Thackeray. Chosen and Edited by Arthur Galton.

36 THE PILLARS OF SOCIETY, AND OTHER PLAYS. BY
Henrik Ibsen. Edited, with an Introduction, by Havelock Ellis.

37 IRISH FAIRY AND FOLK TALES. EDITED AND
Selected by W. B. Yeats.

38 ESSAYS OF DR. JOHNSON, WITH BIOGRAPHICAL
Introduction and Notes by Stuart J. Reid.

39 ESSAYS OF WILLIAM HAZLITT. SELECTED AND
Edited, with Introduction and Notes, by Frank Carr.

40 LANDOR'S PENTAMERON, AND OTHER IMAGINARY
Conversations. Edited, with a Preface, by H. Ellis.

41 POE'S TALES AND ESSAYS. EDITED, WITH INTRO-
duction, by Ernest Rhys.

42 VICAR OF WAKEFIELD. BY OLIVER GOLDSMITH.
Edited, with Preface, by Ernest Rhys.

43 POLITICAL ORATIONS, FROM WENTWORTH TO
Macaulay. Edited, with Introduction, by William Clarke.

44 THE AUTOCRAT OF THE BREAKFAST-TABLE. BY
Oliver Wendell Holmes.

45 THE POET AT THE BREAKFAST-TABLE. BY OLIVER
Wendell Holmes.

46 THE PROFESSOR AT THE BREAKFAST-TABLE. BY
Oliver Wendell Holmes.

47 LORD CHESTERFIELD'S LETTERS TO HIS SON.
Selected, with Introduction, by Charles Sayle.

London : WALTER SCOTT, LIMITED, Paternoster Square.

THE SCOTT LIBRARY—continued.

London: WALTER SCOTT, LIMITED, Paternoster Square.

THE SCOTT LIBRARY—continued.

London: WALTER SCOTT, LIMITED, Paternoster Square.

London: WALTER SCOTT, LIMITED, Paternoster Square.

Great Writers.

A NEW SERIES OF CRITICAL BIOGRAPHIES.

Edited by E. ROBERTSON and F. T. MARZIALS.

Cloth, Uncut Edges, Gilt Top.   Price 1/6.

A Complete Bibliography to each Volume, by
J. P. ANDERSON, British Museum, London.

Library Edition of "Great Writers," Demy 8vo, 2/6.

London: WALTER SCOTT, LIMITED.

LIBRARY OF HUMOUR

Cloth Elegant, Large Crown 8vo, Price 3/6 per vol.

VOLUMES ALREADY ISSUED.

THE HUMOUR OF FRANCE. Translated, with an Introduction and Notes, by Elizabeth Lee. With numerous Illustrations by Paul Frénzeny.

THE HUMOUR OF GERMANY. Translated, with an Introduction and Notes, by Hans Müller-Casenov. With numerous Illustrations by C. E. Brock.

THE HUMOUR OF ITALY. Translated, with an Introduction and Notes, by A. Werner. With 50 Illustrations and a Frontispiece by Arturo Faldi.

THE HUMOUR OF AMERICA. Selected with a copious Biographical Index of American Humorists, by James Barr.

THE HUMOUR OF HOLLAND. Translated, with an Introduction and Notes, by A. Werner. With numerous Illustrations by Dudley Hardy.

THE HUMOUR OF IRELAND. Selected by D. J. O'Donoghue. With numerous Illustrations by Oliver Paque.

THE HUMOUR OF SPAIN. Translated, with an Introduction and Notes, by S. Taylor. With numerous Illustrations by H. R. Millar.

THE HUMOUR OF RUSSIA. Translated, with Notes, by E. L. Boole, and an Introduction by Stepniak. With 50 Illustrations by Paul Frénzeny.

THE HUMOUR OF JAPAN. Translated, with an Introduction, by A. M. With Illustrations by George Bigot (from Drawings made in Japan). [*In preparation.*

London : WALTER SCOTT, LIMITED, Paternoster Square.

COMPACT AND PRACTICAL.

In Limp Cloth; for the Pocket.   Price One Shilling.

THE EUROPEAN
CONVERSATION BOOKS.

FRENCH   ITALIAN
SPANISH   GERMAN
NORWEGIAN

CONTENTS.

Hints to Travellers—Everyday Expressions—Arriving at and Leaving a Railway Station—Custom House Enquiries—In a Train—At a Buffet and Restaurant—At an Hotel—Paying an Hotel Bill—Enquiries in a Town—On Board Ship—Embarking and Disembarking—Excursion by Carriage—Enquiries as to Diligences—Enquiries as to Boats—Engaging Apartments—Washing List and Days of Week—Restaurant Vocabulary—Telegrams and Letters, etc., etc.

The contents of these little handbooks are so arranged as to permit direct and immediate reference.   All dialogues or enquiries not considered absolutely essential have been purposely excluded, nothing being introduced which might confuse the traveller rather than assist him.   A few hints are given in the introduction which will be found valuable to those unaccustomed to foreign travel.

London : WALTER SCOTT, LIMITED, Paternoster Square.

NEW ENGLAND LIBRARY.

GRAVURE EDITION.

PRINTED ON ANTIQUE PAPER. 2s. 6d. PER VOL.

Each Volume with a Frontispiece in Photogravure.

By NATHANIEL HAWTHORNE.

THE SCARLET LETTER.
THE HOUSE OF THE SEVEN GABLES.
THE BLITHEDALE ROMANCE.
TANGLEWOOD TALES.
TWICE-TOLD TALES.
A WONDER-BOOK FOR GIRLS AND BOYS.
OUR OLD HOME.
MOSSES FROM AN OLD MANSE.
THE SNOW IMAGE.
TRUE STORIES FROM HISTORY AND BIOGRAPHY.
THE NEW ADAM AND EVE.
LEGENDS OF THE PROVINCE HOUSE.

By OLIVER WENDELL HOLMES.

THE AUTOCRAT OF THE BREAKFAST-TABLE.
THE PROFESSOR AT THE BREAKFAST-TABLE.
THE POET AT THE BREAKFAST-TABLE.
ELSIE VENNER.

By HENRY THOREAU.

ESSAYS AND OTHER WRITINGS.
WALDEN; OR, LIFE IN THE WOODS.
A WEEK ON THE CONCORD.

London : WALTER SCOTT, LIMITED, Paternoster Square.

Crown 8vo, Cloth, 3s. 6d. each; Half Morocco, 6s. 6d.

THE

Contemporary Science Series.

EDITED BY HAVELOCK ELLIS.

Illustrated Volumes containing between 300 and 400 pp.

EVOLUTION OF SEX. By Prof. GEDDES and THOMSON.
ELECTRICITY IN MODERN LIFE. By G. W. DE TUNZELMANN.
THE ORIGIN OF THE ARYANS. By Dr. TAYLOR.
PHYSIOGNOMY AND EXPRESSION. P. MANTEGAZZA.
EVOLUTION AND DISEASE. By J. B. SUTTON.
THE VILLAGE COMMUNITY. By G. L. GOMME.
THE CRIMINAL. By HAVELOCK ELLIS.
SANITY AND INSANITY. By Dr. C. MERCIER.
HYPNOTISM. By Dr. ALBERT MOLL (Berlin).
MANUAL TRAINING. By Dr. WOODWARD (St. Louis).
SCIENCE OF FAIRY TALES. By E. S. HARTLAND.
PRIMITIVE FOLK. By ELIE RECLUS.
EVOLUTION OF MARRIAGE. By LETOURNEAU.
BACTERIA AND THEIR PRODUCTS. Dr. WOODHEAD.
EDUCATION AND HEREDITY. By J. M. GUYAU.
THE MAN OF GENIUS. By Prof. LOMBROSO.
THE GRAMMAR OF SCIENCE. By Prof. PEARSON.
PROPERTY: ITS ORIGIN. By CH. LETOURNEAU.
VOLCANOES, PAST AND PRESENT. By Prof. HULL.
PUBLIC HEALTH PROBLEMS. By Dr. J. F. SYKES.
MODERN METEOROLOGY. By FRANK WALDO, Ph.D.
THE GERM-PLASM. By Professor WEISMANN. 6s.
THE INDUSTRIES OF ANIMALS. By F. HOUSSAY.
MAN AND WOMAN. By HAVELOCK ELLIS. 6s.
THE EVOLUTION OF MODERN CAPITALISM.
MODERN CAPITALISM. By JOHN A. HOBSON, M.A.
THOUGHT-TRANSFERENCE. By F. PODMORE, M.A.
COMPARATIVE PSYCHOLOGY. Prof. C. L. MORGAN. 6s.
THE ORIGINS OF INVENTION. By O. T. MASON.

London: WALTER SCOTT, LIMITED, Paternoster Square.

SPECIAL EDITION OF THE

CANTERBURY POETS.

Square 8vo, Cloth, Gilt Top Elegant, Price 2s.

Each Volume with a Frontispiece in Photogravure.

33 PARADISE REGAINED. With Portrait of Milton.
34 CAVALIER POETS. With Portrait of Suckling.
35 HUMOROUS POEMS. With Portrait of Hood.
36 HERBERT. With Portrait of Herbert.
37 POE. With Portrait of Poe.
38 OWEN MEREDITH. With Portrait of late Lord Lytton.
39 LOVE LYRICS. With Portrait of Raleigh.
40 GERMAN BALLADS. With Portrait of Schiller.
41 CAMBELL. With Portrait of Campbell.
42 CANADIAN POEMS. With View of Mount Stephen.
43 EARLY ENGLISH POETRY. With Portrait of Earl of Surrey.
44 ALLAN RAMSAY. With Portrait of Ramsay.
45 SPENSER. With Portrait of Spenser.
46 CHATTERTON. With Engraving, "The Death of Chatterton."
47 COWPER. With Portrait of Cowper.
48 CHAUCER. With Portrait of Chaucer.
49 COLERIDGE. With Portrait of Coleridge.
50 POPE. With Portrait of Pope.
51 BYRON. Miscellaneous ⎫ With Portraits of Byron.
52 BYRON. Don Juan ⎭
53 JACOBITE SONGS. With Portrait of Prince Charlie.
54 BORDER BALLADS. With View of Neidpath Castle.
55 AUSTRALIAN BALLADS. With Portrait of A. L. Gordon.
56 HOGG. With Portrait of Hogg.
57 GOLDSMITH. With Portrait of Goldsmith.
58 MOORE. With Portrait of Moore.
59 DORA GREENWELL. With Portrait of Dora Greenwell.
60 BLAKE. With Portrait of Blake.
61 POEMS OF NATURE. With Portrait of Andrew Lang.
62 PRAED. With Portrait.
63 SOUTHEY. With Portrait.
64 HUGO. With Portrait.
65 GOETHE. With Portrait.
66 BERANGER. With Portrait.
67 HEINE. With Portrait.
68 SEA MUSIC. With View of Corbière Rocks, Jersey.
69 SONG-TIDE. With Portrait of Philip Bourke Marston.
70 LADY OF LYONS. With Portrait of Bulwer Lytton.
71 SHAKESPEARE: Songs and Sonnets. With Portrait.
72 CRABBE. With Portrait.
73 BEN JONSON. With Portrait.
74 CRADLE SONGS. With Drawing by T. Eyre Macklin